WHATEVER HAPPENED TO FRANKIE KING

WHATEVER HAPPENED TO FRANKIE KING

STORY BY JAY NEUGEBOREN
ART BY ELI NEUGEBOREN

GRAPHIC MUNDI

Library of Congress Cataloging-in-Publication Data

Names: Neugeboren, Jay, author.
Title: Whatever happened to Frankie King / story by Jay
    Neugeboren ; art by Eli Neugeboren.
Description: University Park, Pennsylvania : Graphic Mundi,
    [2024]
Summary: "Follows the life, in graphic novel format, of New
    York City basketball legend Frankie King from his early
    promising sports career to his later work authoring cozy
    cat mysteries under a female pseudonym"—Provided by
    publisher.
Identifiers: LCCN 2024028008 | ISBN 9781637790779
    (paperback)
Subjects: LCSH: King, Frank, 1936–2015—Comic books,
    strips, etc. | Novelists, American—Biography—Comic
    books, strips, etc. | Basketball players—United States—
    Biography—Comic books, strips, etc. | Recluses—United
    States—Biography—Comic books, strips, etc. | Brooklyn
    (New York, N.Y.)—Biography—Comic books, strips, etc.
Classification: LCC PS3561.I4755 Z+
LC record available at https://lccn.loc.gov/2024028008

Published by The Pennsylvania State University Press,
University Park, PA 16802–1003

10 9 8 7 6 5 4 3 2 1

Graphic Mundi is an imprint of The Pennsylvania State
University Press.

The Pennsylvania State University Press is a member of the
Association of University Presses.

It is the policy of The Pennsylvania State University Press to
use acid-free paper. Publications on uncoated stock satisfy
the minimum requirements of American National Standard
for Information Sciences—Permanence of Paper for Printed
Library Material, ANSI Z39.48–1992.

FOR JEN, ZACK, AND LEO

IN 1951, AT THE AGE OF FIFTEEN, FRANKIE KING BECAME THE YOUNGEST NEW YORK CITY HIGH SCHOOL PLAYER EVER TO MAKE FIRST TEAM ALL-CITY. SPORTSWRITERS WERE COMPARING HIM TO THE GREATEST COLLEGE AND PRO PLAYERS OF ALL TIME. HE WAS RECRUITED BY THE UNIVERSITY OF NORTH CAROLINA TO BE A STARTING GUARD ON A TEAM THAT WOULD EVENTUALLY DEFEAT THE UNIVERSITY OF KANSAS JAYHAWKS, AND WILT CHAMBERLAIN, FOR THE NATIONAL CHAMPIONSHIP, BUT KING DROPPED OUT OF NORTH CAROLINA BEFORE HE EVER PLAYED A GAME. AND FOR THE NEXT SIXTY YEARS HE DISAPPEARED FROM THE LIVES OF EVERYONE WHO HAD KNOWN HIM.

FRIENDS WHO'D GROWN UP WITH HIM DID, HOWEVER, HEAR THAT A DECADE AFTER HE LEFT THE UNIVERSITY OF NORTH CAROLINA HE'D PLAYED KAREEM ABDUL-JABBAR IN A NIGHTTIME GAME OF ONE-ON-ONE IN A HARLEM SCHOOLYARD...

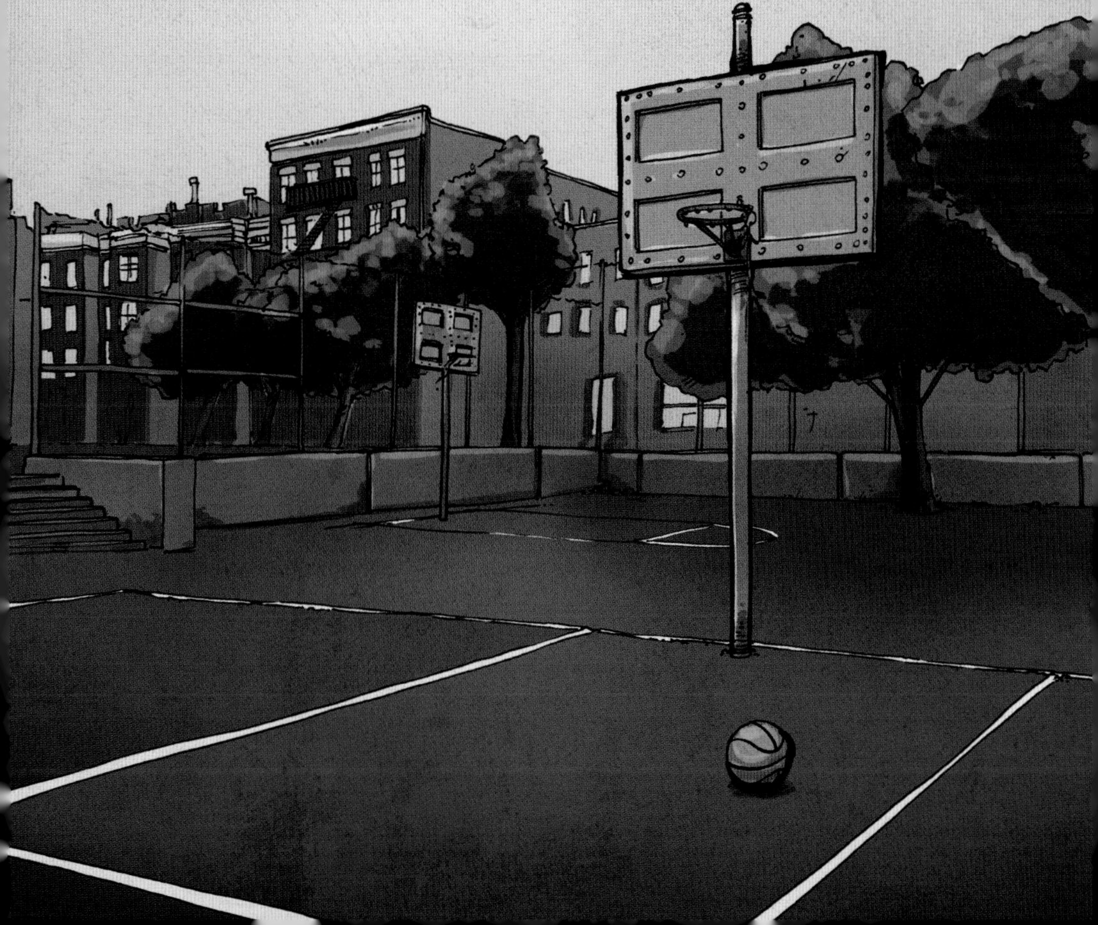

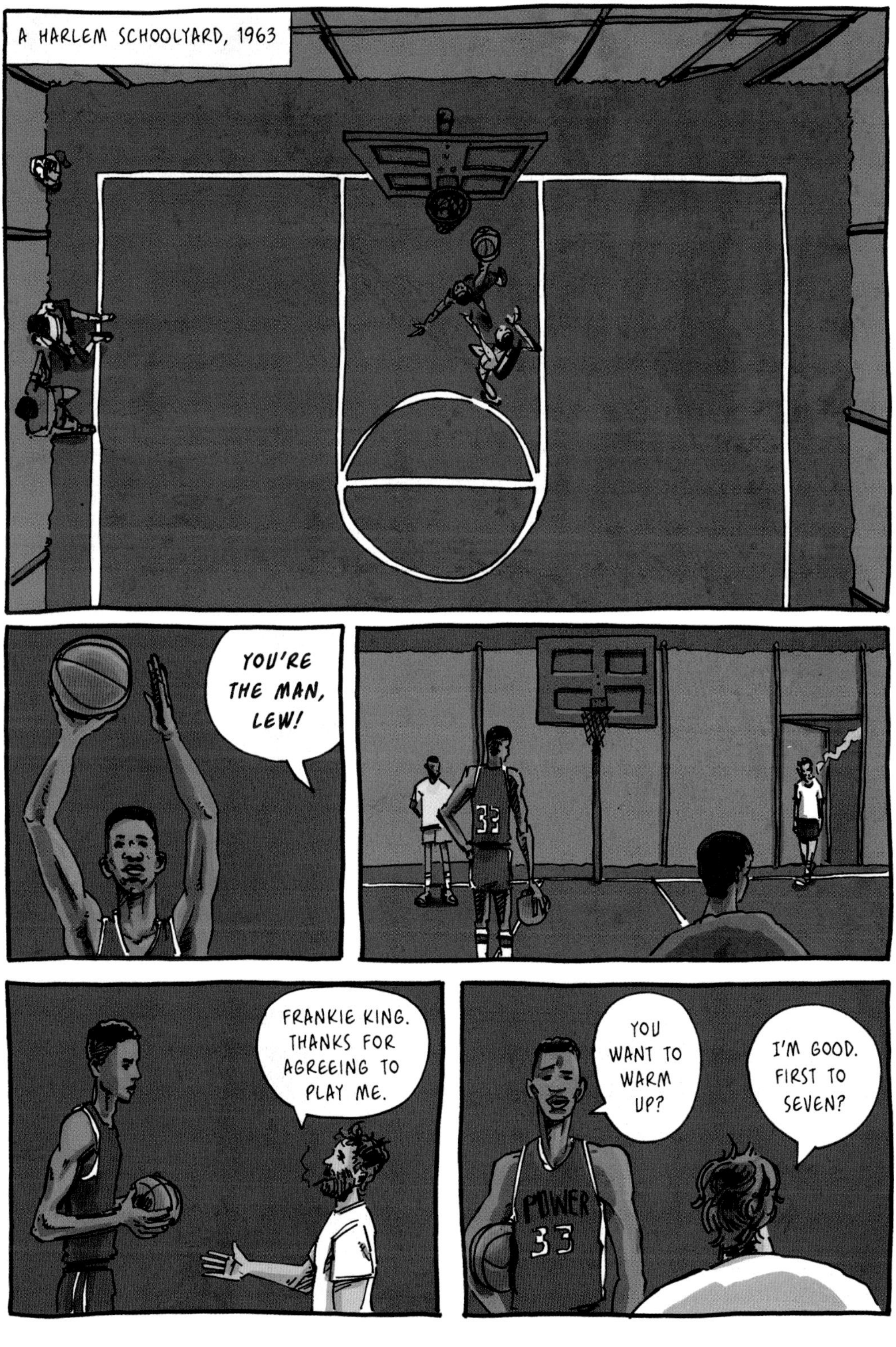
A HARLEM SCHOOLYARD, 1963
YOU'RE THE MAN, LEW!
FRANKIE KING. THANKS FOR AGREEING TO PLAY ME.
YOU WANT TO WARM UP?
I'M GOOD. FIRST TO SEVEN?
POWER 33

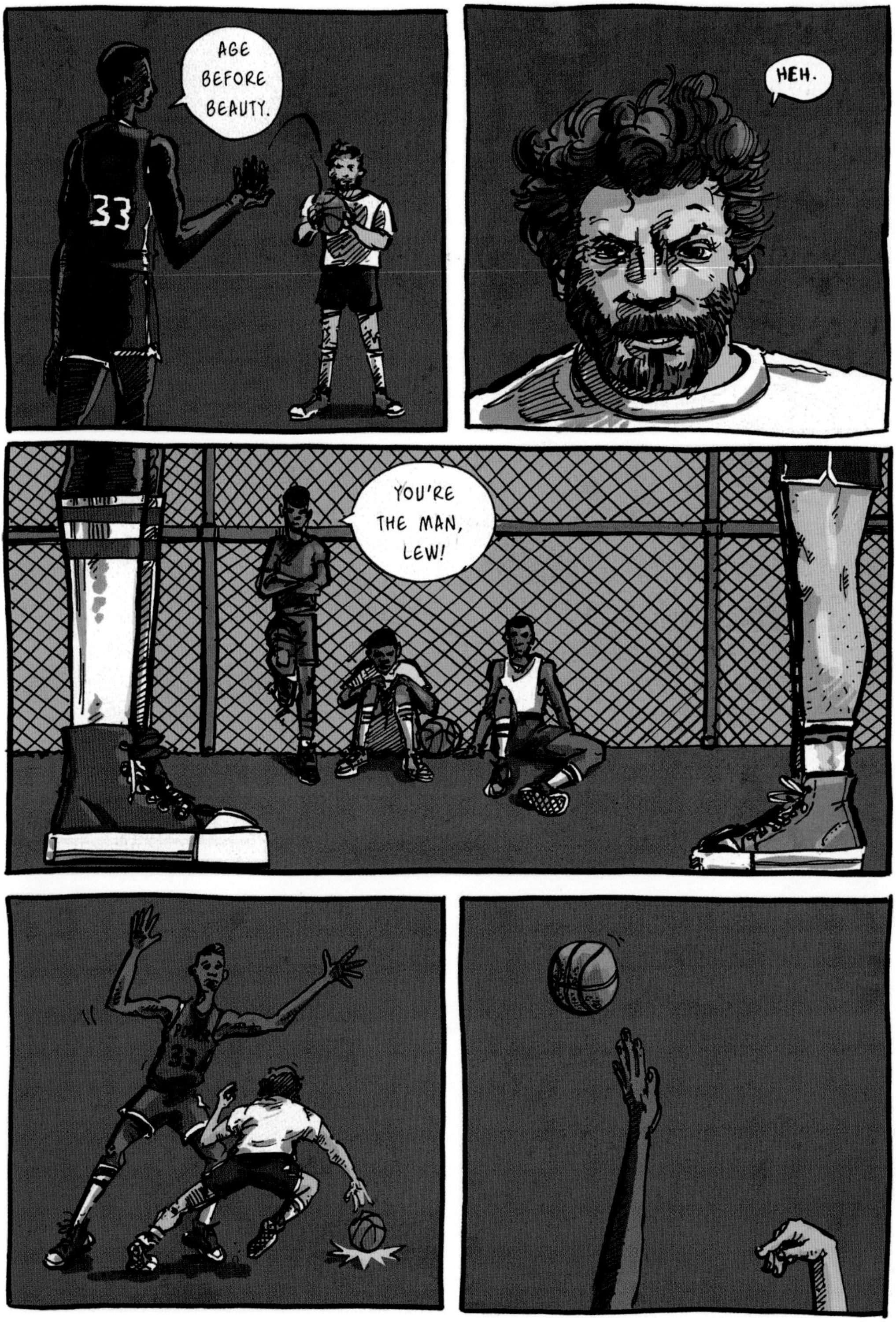
AGE BEFORE BEAUTY.
HEH.
YOU'RE THE MAN, LEW!

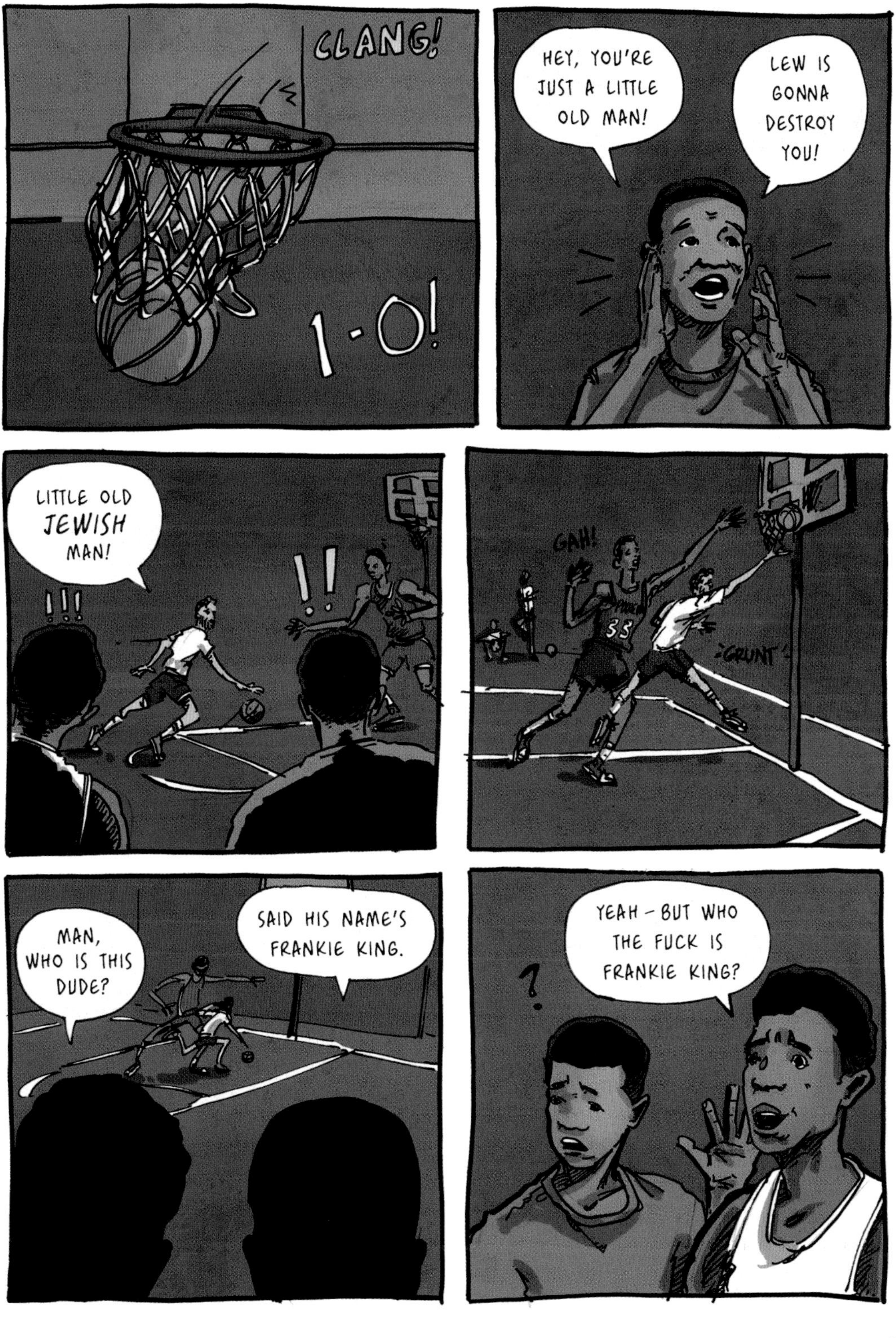
CLANG!
1-0!
HEY, YOU'RE JUST A LITTLE OLD MAN!
LEW IS GONNA DESTROY YOU!
LITTLE OLD JEWISH MAN!
!!!
!!
GAH!
GRUNT
MAN, WHO IS THIS DUDE?
SAID HIS NAME'S FRANKIE KING.
?
YEAH - BUT WHO THE FUCK IS FRANKIE KING?

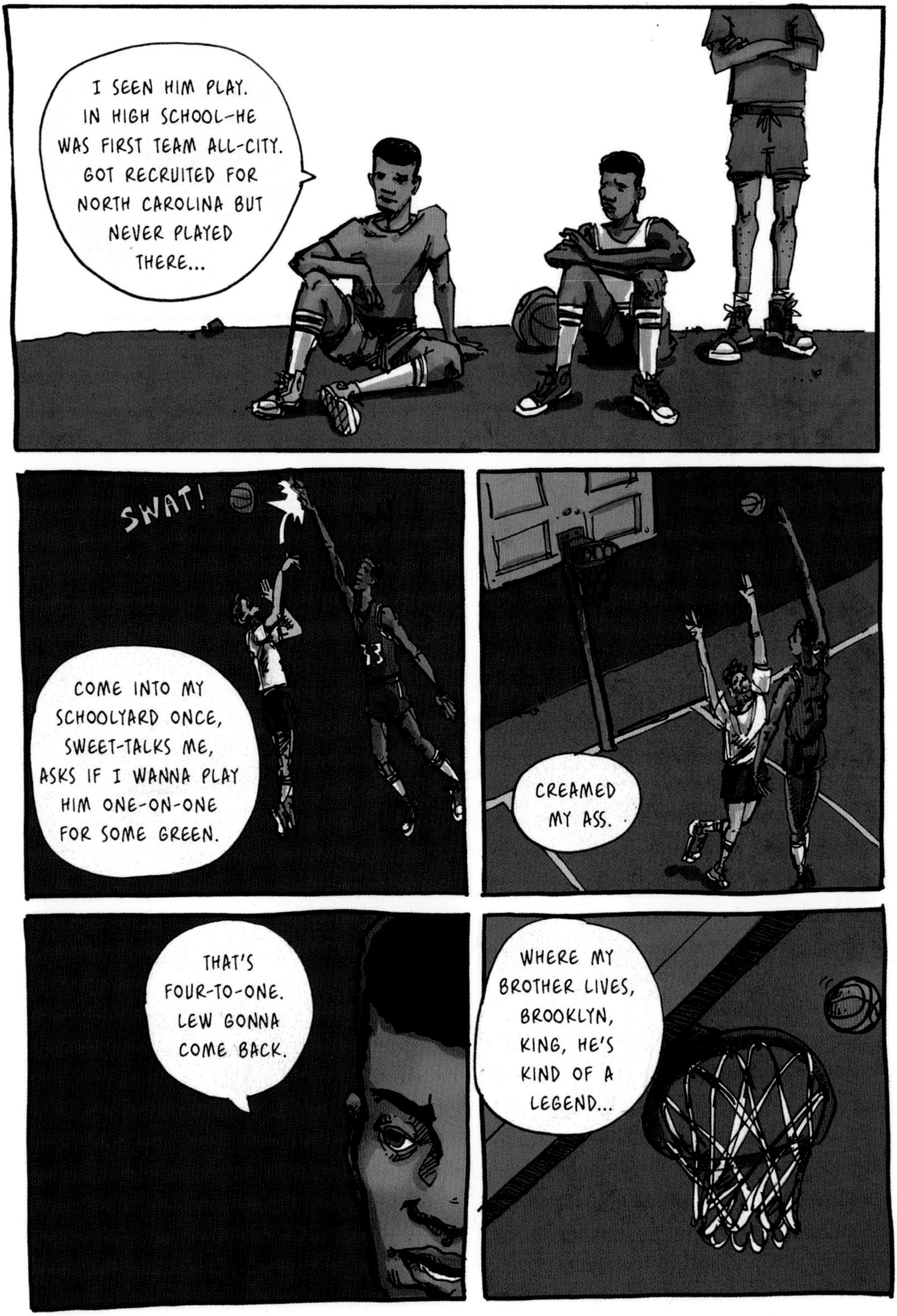
I SEEN HIM PLAY. IN HIGH SCHOOL—HE WAS FIRST TEAM ALL-CITY. GOT RECRUITED FOR NORTH CAROLINA BUT NEVER PLAYED THERE...
SWAT!
COME INTO MY SCHOOLYARD ONCE, SWEET-TALKS ME, ASKS IF I WANNA PLAY HIM ONE-ON-ONE FOR SOME GREEN.
CREAMED MY ASS.
THAT'S FOUR-TO-ONE. LEW GONNA COME BACK.
WHERE MY BROTHER LIVES, BROOKLYN, KING, HE'S KIND OF A LEGEND...

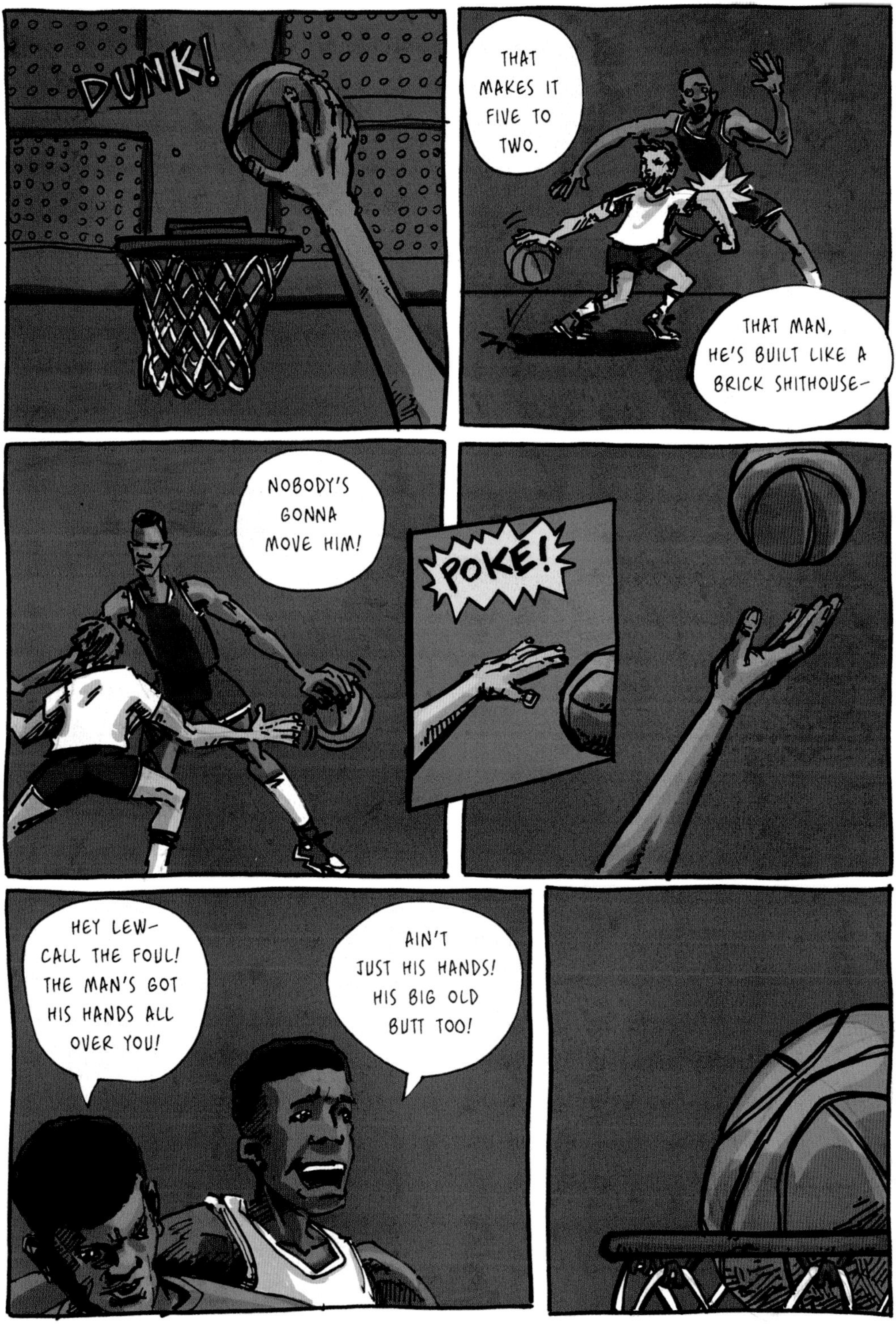
DUNK!
THAT MAKES IT FIVE TO TWO.
THAT MAN, HE'S BUILT LIKE A BRICK SHITHOUSE-
NOBODY'S GONNA MOVE HIM!
POKE!
HEY LEW- CALL THE FOUL! THE MAN'S GOT HIS HANDS ALL OVER YOU!
AIN'T JUST HIS HANDS! HIS BIG OLD BUTT TOO!

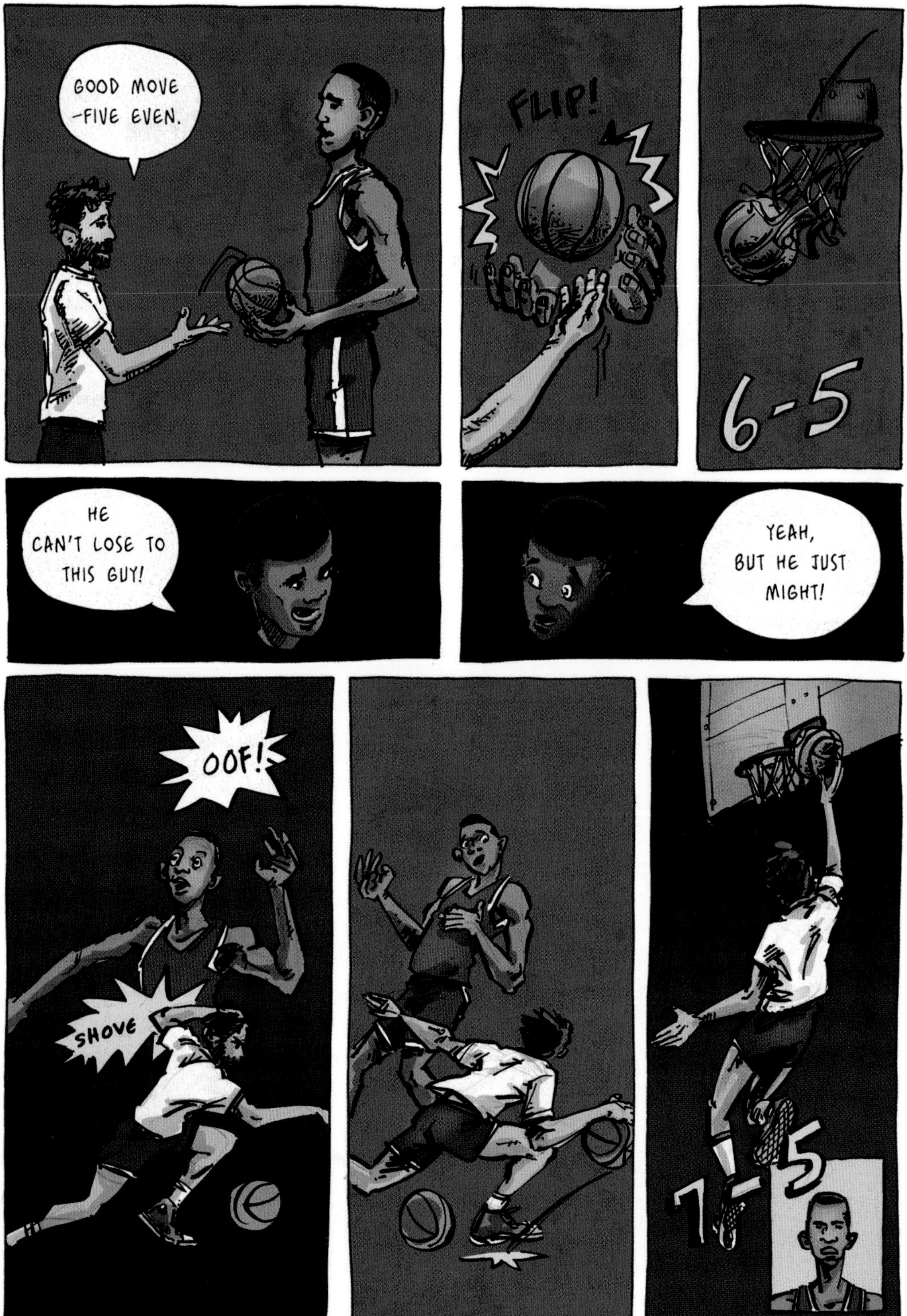
GOOD MOVE
-FIVE EVEN.
FLIP!
6-5
HE CAN'T LOSE TO THIS GUY!
YEAH, BUT HE JUST MIGHT!
OOF!
SHOVE
7-5

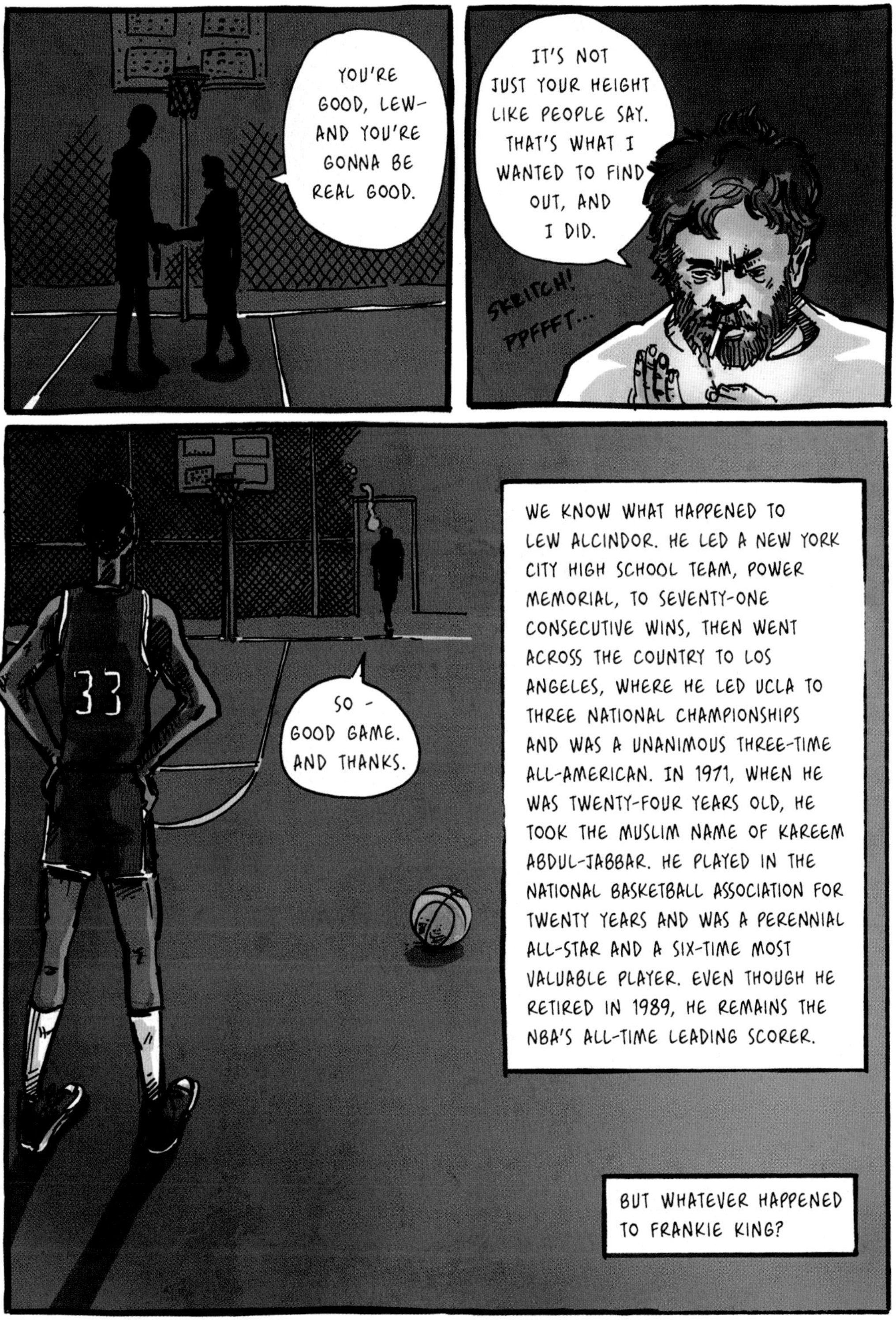
YOU'RE GOOD, LEW- AND YOU'RE GONNA BE REAL GOOD.
IT'S NOT JUST YOUR HEIGHT LIKE PEOPLE SAY. THAT'S WHAT I WANTED TO FIND OUT, AND I DID.
SKRITCH!
PPFFFT...
SO - GOOD GAME. AND THANKS.
WE KNOW WHAT HAPPENED TO LEW ALCINDOR. HE LED A NEW YORK CITY HIGH SCHOOL TEAM, POWER MEMORIAL, TO SEVENTY-ONE CONSECUTIVE WINS, THEN WENT ACROSS THE COUNTRY TO LOS ANGELES, WHERE HE LED UCLA TO THREE NATIONAL CHAMPIONSHIPS AND WAS A UNANIMOUS THREE-TIME ALL-AMERICAN. IN 1971, WHEN HE WAS TWENTY-FOUR YEARS OLD, HE TOOK THE MUSLIM NAME OF KAREEM ABDUL-JABBAR. HE PLAYED IN THE NATIONAL BASKETBALL ASSOCIATION FOR TWENTY YEARS AND WAS A PERENNIAL ALL-STAR AND A SIX-TIME MOST VALUABLE PLAYER. EVEN THOUGH HE RETIRED IN 1989, HE REMAINS THE NBA'S ALL-TIME LEADING SCORER.
BUT WHATEVER HAPPENED TO FRANKIE KING?

> "His quick set shot has been compared with that of Max Zaslofsky—a short step back and then a quick flip...King's accuracy is on a par with Zaslofsky and... he may top Zaslofsky in a couple of years. In addition, he has a fine running hook shot in the style of Sid Tanenbaum, who set an all-time scoring record at NYU..."
>
> —*Brooklyn Eagle* 4/5/53

See Bright Hoop Reign For King of Madison

By FRANK BLAUSCHILD

If you build a better mousetrap the world will beat a path to your door and if you're a better high school basketball player college coaches will do the same thing. In two years our prediction is that these gentlemen will be staging a rush act to land James Madison's Frankie King.

King is currently the star of Madison's undefeated basketeers. What makes this 5-11, 155-lb. Brooklynite news is the fact that he is only 15½ years old and a fourth termer. Only once before has a sophmore made Madison's varsity starting five and this was LIU's Lou Lipman.

Right now, according to such collegiate coaches as St. John's Frank McGuire and Brooklyn College's Tubby Raskin, among others, he is at least ready for college jayvee ball so you can imagine what two more years of secondary school experience will do.

Last week, King broke open Madison's game with then unbeaten Erasmus for the Group II lead. It was close while he was on the bench because of fouls but once he came back he took ... was the game. ... pair of hands and ... on the style of ... former college ... who is recognized ... greatest dribblers ... holds the ball low ... ach, Jammy Mos... ed, "It's almost ... one man to play ... some coaches and ... that he will be one ... dribblers ever produced in the East.

King, a lefthander, developed his game at Kelley Park, Avenue S and E. 14th St., Brooklyn. Even now he continues his playground activities, working out against a number of current and ex-collegiate stars, all of whom extol his ability. This also prompted Moscowitz to say,

"That's the tipoff on the kid. He's always played with the older boys and if they accept him he got to be good."

His quick set shot has been compared with that of the Knick' Max Zaslofsky—a short step back and then a quick flip. It has been said that Zaslofsky ...

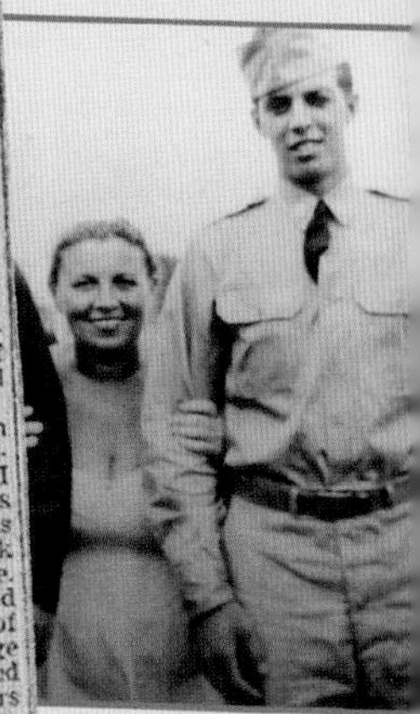

Frankie King, an All-Star!

By Dick Kossoff '53

Frankie King '53, who died in May 2015, was one of Madison's greatest hoopsters, powering the Highwaymen to two divisional championships. Playing during the early '50s under legendary coach Jammy Moskowitz, this 5'11" southpaw could score from anywhere on the court with a dazzling array of shots. Many opponents called him "unstoppable." At 15, Frankie was selected to play on the PSAL all-city team, an honor repeated in his senior year. He graduated from CCNY and in later years surprisingly turned to writing, producing over 40 mystery books, most of them under the pseudonym Lydia Adamson. Included were the Alice Nestleton, Lucy Wayles, and Deirdre Quinn Nightingale series. One classmate said, "Frank turned out to be an all-star off as well as on the court."

For those of us who had the joy of watching him play, his prowess on the hardwood will never be forgotten.

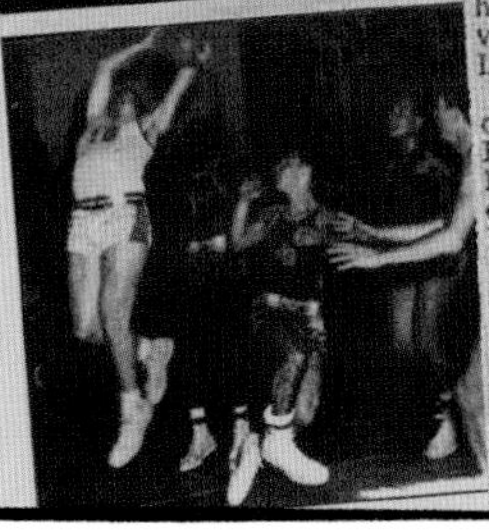

Dick Kossoff was president of an internat... consulting company.

> "...He dribbles the ball in the style of Kenny Sailors, former college and pro star who is recognized as one of the greatest dribblers of all time..."
>
> —*Observation Post* 11/24/54

RONNIE BRESSANT
Boys

TOM HEMANS
Jefferson

FRANK KING
Madison

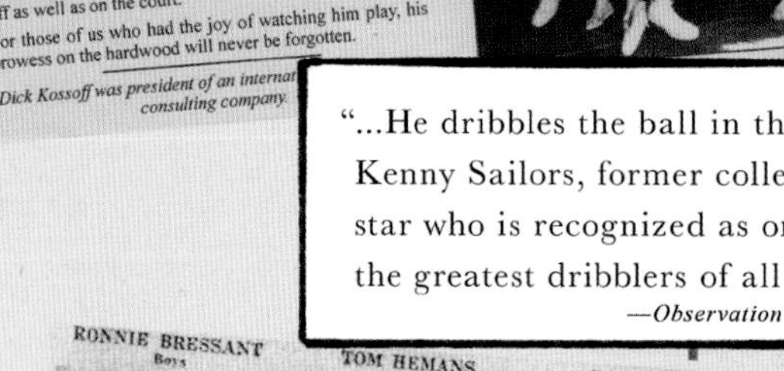

FRANK PETINOS
— New Utrecht

JACK DeFARES
Commerce

Coaches' PSAL All-Scholastic

Brooklyn Boys on J-A ...uches All-Star H.S. Five

It was the ... Fort Hamilton ... 18-8, 39-16, 47-... found the range ... for Fort Ham... Rowan found t... for Grady.

Erasmus Ha... as to the possi... showing Madis... 10, 45-27, 68-45. ... in 38 points to ... all recor... ago. F... jured, h...

...n also h... with M... ree rou... Norman ... had 2... lden an... y Arbeit... ...od.

To keep in ... was also mast... from start to f...

...the lead in the third frame, 46—44 and remained there. Mike Parenti caged 32 points for the Green and White vic-

> "No matter what anyone scribbles, though, Jamie actually has nothing to fear with Frankie boy. For one, consider how this 5'11", 170-pounder treats all the glowing tributes: 'What a lot of bunk. What do they mean by comparing me to such wonderful players ...I'm not that good.'"
>
> —*Brooklyn Eagle* 2/21/53

Eagle's All-Brooklyn Scholastic Cage Teams for 1953

Leading Division Scorers Named To 'Dream' Five

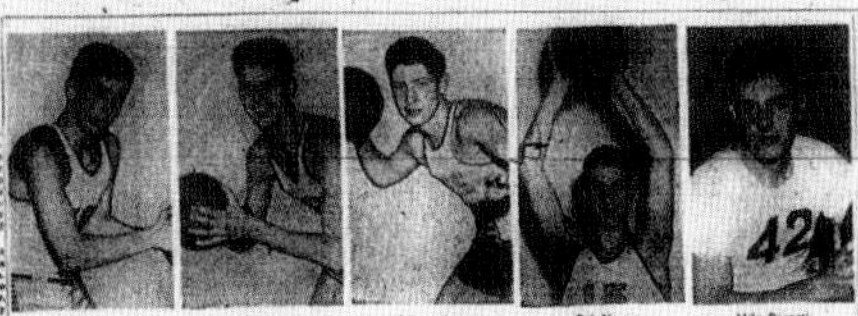

Frank King (James Madison) · Joe Quigg (St. Francis Prep) · Johnny Lee (Erasmus Hall) · Bob Young (Adelphi) · Mike Parenti (New Utrecht)

Brooklyn Eagle's All-Brooklyn Scholastic Fives of 1953

Rex Hasn't Given Up Yet on Barney

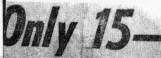

Only 15—

"Frothy comparisons and stunning superlatives are actually odious to Frankie King, a young man whose head can only be turned in one direction—toward the basket… as a 15-year-old Madison High sophomore hailed in one headline or another all around the town, Frankie has Coach Jamie Moskowitz deeply worried over possible repercussions ...

—New York Daily News 2/8/52

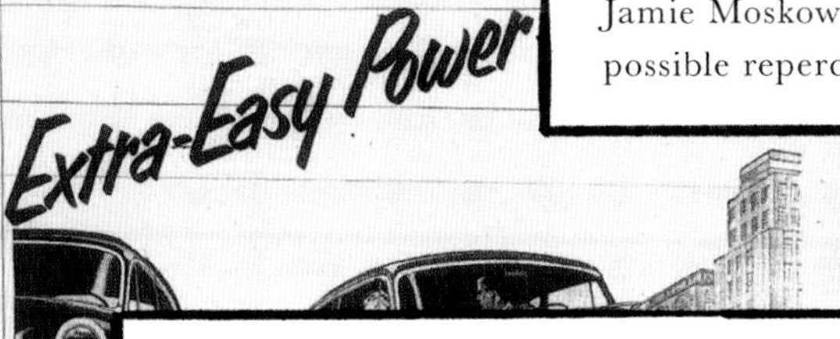

...ped previously unbeaten Fort Hamilton, 51-48 in a PSAL contest, but the talented kid cager turned in a major rebounding and feeding job. He tallied only six points, in contrast to 17 ...t Boys, 19 against St. Aug...s, 18 against Manual and ...against Grady Vocational.

...of a former Haaren and ...nt U. cager, with an older ...r who also played varsity ...ball at Vermont, Frankie ...s hoop heritage. A fast ...performer with good shots, ...cellent floor game, Frankie ...reat future. He packs 171 ... into a solid, lean 5-11

"Citing one overenthusiastic account which likened Frankie and his specialty numbers to some of the top professionals, Moskowitz complained, 'If the newspapers keep it up, they're sure to hurt him, saying such foolish things' ..."

—New York Daily Mirror 5/18/52

Lincoln	G.	F.	P.	Lafayette	G.	F.	P.
Harari	5	1	11	Comito	4	3	11
Serper	3	6	12	Russell	0	1	1
Ostrin	1	1	3	Koufax	10	4	24
Panos	4	3	11	Levine	1	2	4
Storick	7	4	18	Groll	6	1	13
Buch	3	2	8	Lichterman	0	1	1
Koma	0	0	0				
Totals	23	17	63	Totals	21	12	54

Officials—Gleason and Chernick.

Automotive	G.	F.	P.	Alexander Hamilton	G.	F.	P.
Ramos	9	2	20	Walker	3	1	
Rogers	4	2	10	Ballard	1	1	
Auletti	4	1	9	Nivelier	4	4	1
Watson	1	2	5	McLaughlin	0	1	
Mallory	3	1	7	N. Robinson	2	3	
Ackerman	0	0	0	Sullivan	0		
Mantel	4	1	9	Goldsmith	3		
Davis	2	3	7	Pokorny	3		
Gottfried	2	2	6	Evans	0		
Totals	32	27	91	Totals	20	2	

Only a Baby-Faced Soph of 15, But How He Pours the Points In!

By ZANDER HOLLANDER.

Frothy comparisons and stunning superlatives are actually odious to Frankie King, a young man whose head can only be turned in one direction—toward the basket.

As a 15-year-old Madison High sophomore hailed in one headline or another all around the town, Frankie has Coach Jamie Moskowitz deeply worried over possible repercussions. The printed word can be dangerous, theorizes Jamie.

Citing one overenthusiastic account which likened Frankie and his specialty numbers to some of the top professionals, Moskowitz complained, "If the newspapers keep it up, they're sure to hurt him, saying such foolish things."

No matter what anyone scribbles, though, Jamie actually has nothing to fear with Frankie boy. For one ... how this 5-11, 170-pounder ... tributes: "What a lot of ... mean by comparing me to ...s . . I'm not that good."

"This baby-faced boy ... has a long shot, a short one, a smooth, deceitful dribble, a light touch, a cool manner and a way with the crowd. They are vividly aware of him, but he seemingly not of them ..."

—New York Journal-American 4/2/53

...y wears long pants, has a ... a smooth, deceitful dribble, ...ol manner and a way with ... vividly aware of him, but ...em. He still needs lots of ...nly experience can teach ...e stratagems that go into ...e star.

...r Frankie like a lioness ...'s only a baby," Jamie ...now the Highwaymen ...im to grow up.

... Smith, Arch Solomon ...me a few, think King ... play with him in Kelly Park on Ave. S and E. 14th St. and such competition can only lead to cage worldliness. King has learned so well and so swiftly that this season, his first on the Madison team, he's twice scored 26 points, marking a new one-game record for the school.

Along with Fred Lane, Stu Gottlieb, Roy Kieval and Milt Winawer, King has put together a 6-0 slate in Brooklyn II PSAL play. Since Gottlieb is the only midyear grad, Madison won't be drastically affected as it shoots for all the marbles in the second half.

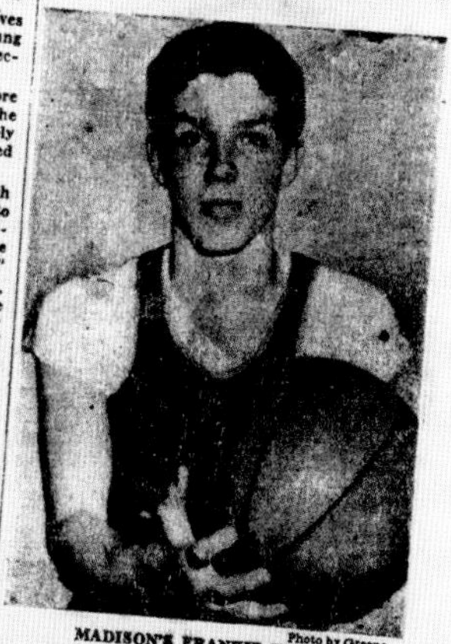

Photo by Greene.

MADISON'S FRANKIE KING.

The Highwaymen say it's more than King and mates who are responsible for their high mark. They couldn't do it without the father of Winawer, a baker who attends all the games and rewards the players with cakes afterward, win or lose. By way of appreciation, though, they never lose.

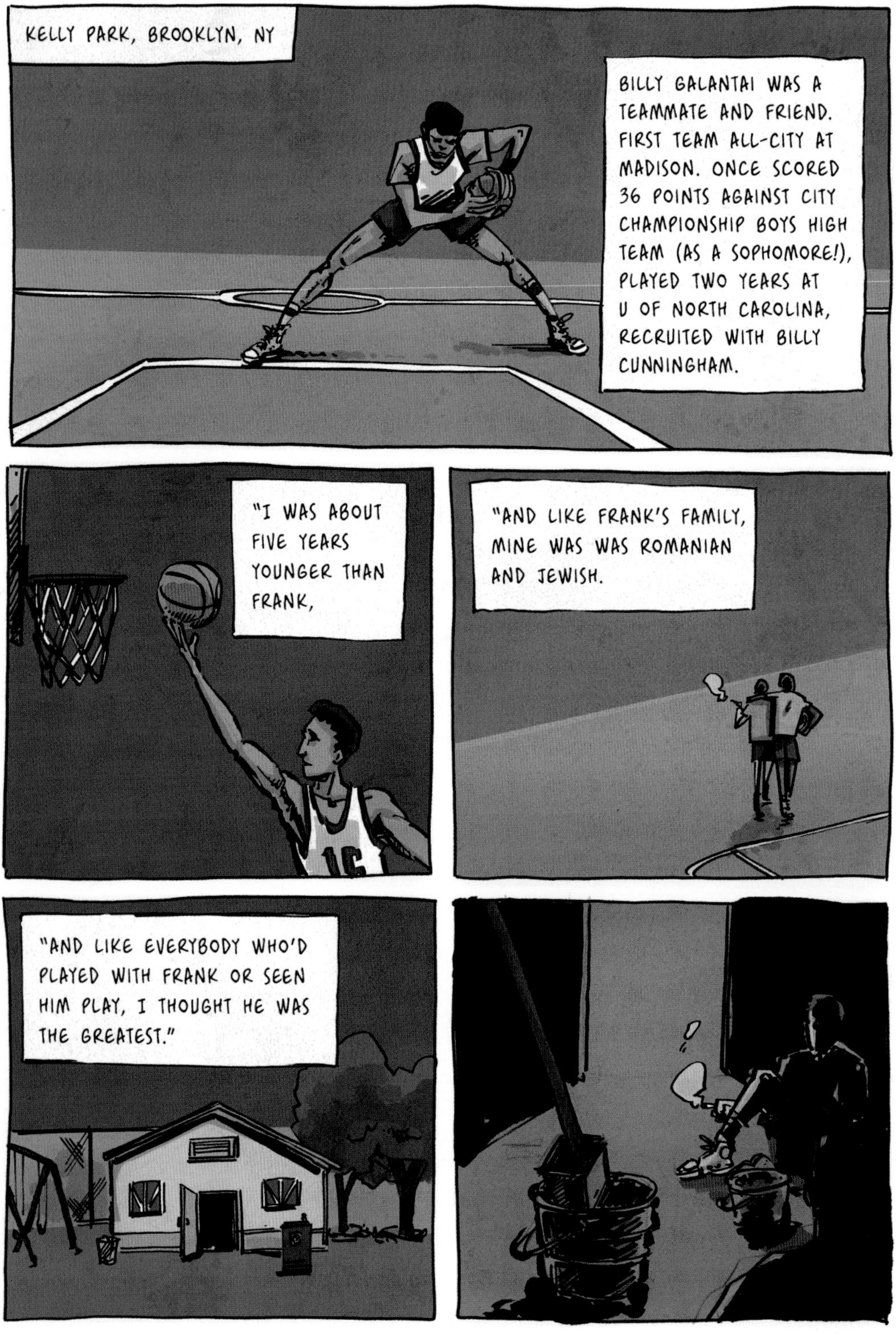

KELLY PARK, BROOKLYN, NY
BILLY GALANTAI WAS A TEAMMATE AND FRIEND. FIRST TEAM ALL-CITY AT MADISON. ONCE SCORED 36 POINTS AGAINST CITY CHAMPIONSHIP BOYS HIGH TEAM (AS A SOPHOMORE!), PLAYED TWO YEARS AT U OF NORTH CAROLINA, RECRUITED WITH BILLY CUNNINGHAM.
"I WAS ABOUT FIVE YEARS YOUNGER THAN FRANK,
"AND LIKE FRANK'S FAMILY, MINE WAS WAS ROMANIAN AND JEWISH.
"AND LIKE EVERYBODY WHO'D PLAYED WITH FRANK OR SEEN HIM PLAY, I THOUGHT HE WAS THE GREATEST."
!

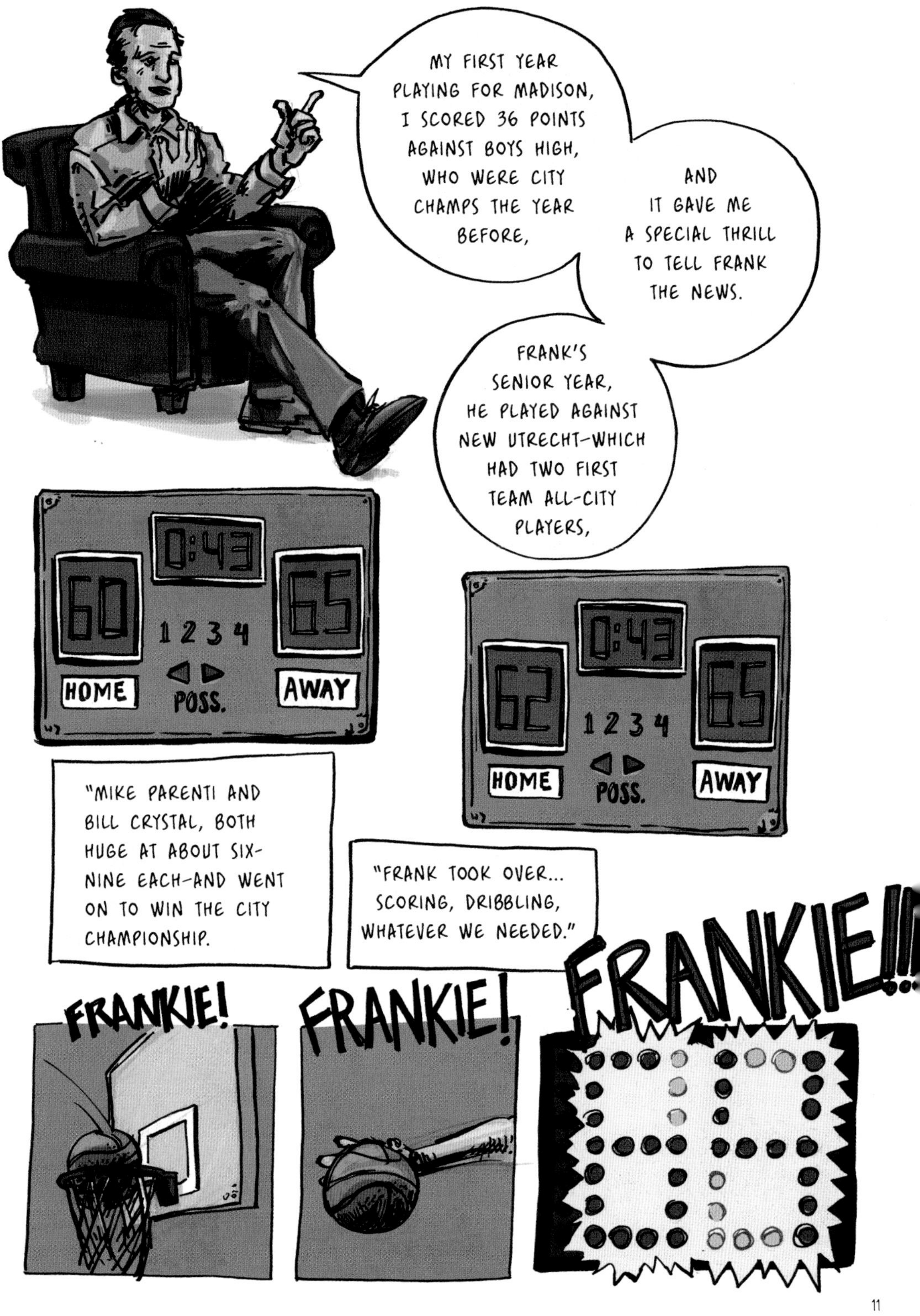
MY FIRST YEAR PLAYING FOR MADISON, I SCORED 36 POINTS AGAINST BOYS HIGH, WHO WERE CITY CHAMPS THE YEAR BEFORE,
AND IT GAVE ME A SPECIAL THRILL TO TELL FRANK THE NEWS.
FRANK'S SENIOR YEAR, HE PLAYED AGAINST NEW UTRECHT—WHICH HAD TWO FIRST TEAM ALL-CITY PLAYERS,
0:43
60
65
1 2 3 4
HOME
POSS.
AWAY
0:43
62
65
1 2 3 4
HOME
POSS.
AWAY
"MIKE PARENTI AND BILL CRYSTAL, BOTH HUGE AT ABOUT SIX-NINE EACH—AND WENT ON TO WIN THE CITY CHAMPIONSHIP.
"FRANK TOOK OVER... SCORING, DRIBBLING, WHATEVER WE NEEDED."
FRANKIE!
FRANKIE!
FRANKIE!!!

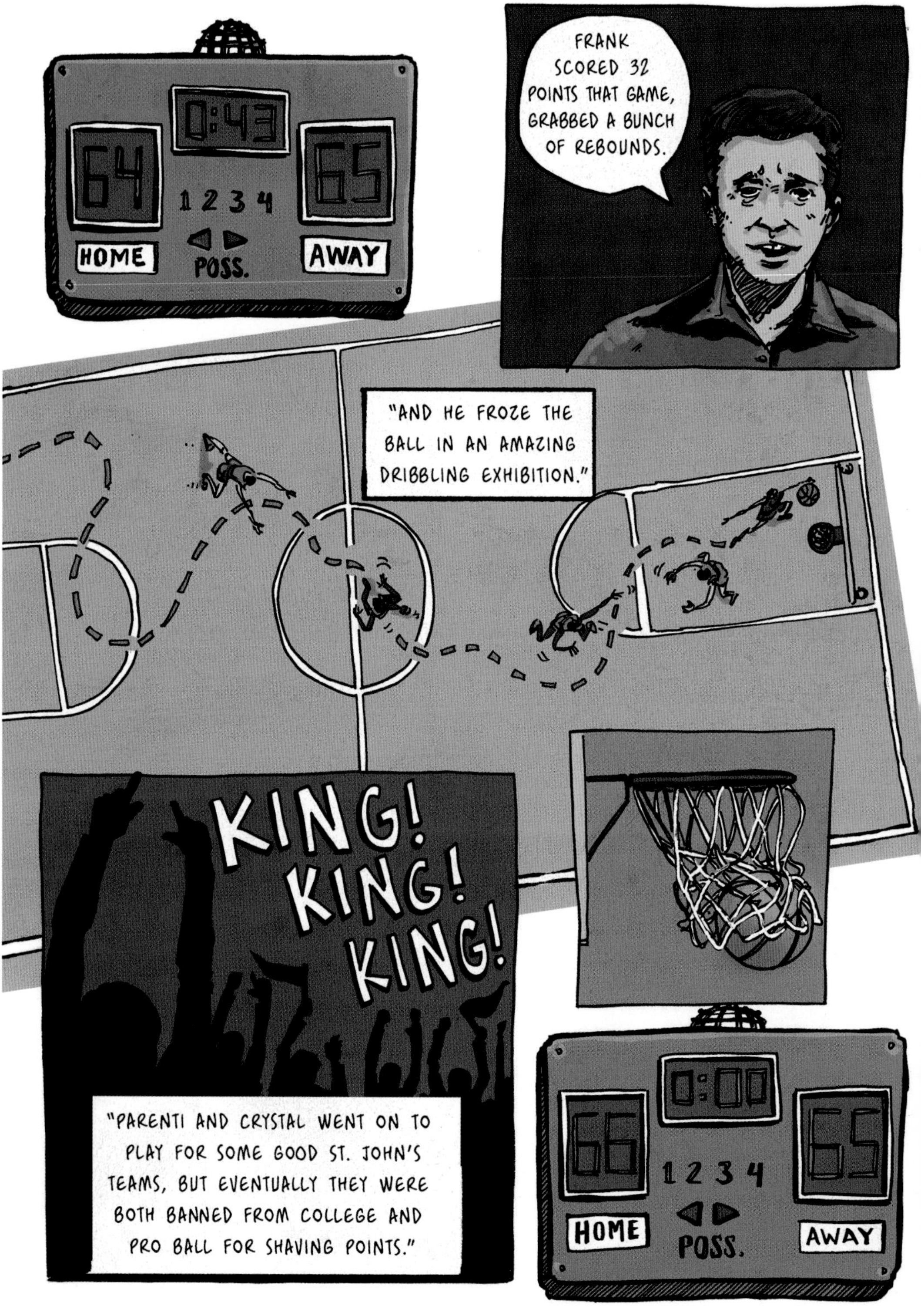
0:43
64
65
1 2 3 4
HOME
POSS.
AWAY
FRANK SCORED 32 POINTS THAT GAME, GRABBED A BUNCH OF REBOUNDS.
"AND HE FROZE THE BALL IN AN AMAZING DRIBBLING EXHIBITION."
KING! KING! KING!
"PARENTI AND CRYSTAL WENT ON TO PLAY FOR SOME GOOD ST. JOHN'S TEAMS, BUT EVENTUALLY THEY WERE BOTH BANNED FROM COLLEGE AND PRO BALL FOR SHAVING POINTS."
0:00
66
65
1 2 3 4
HOME
POSS.
AWAY

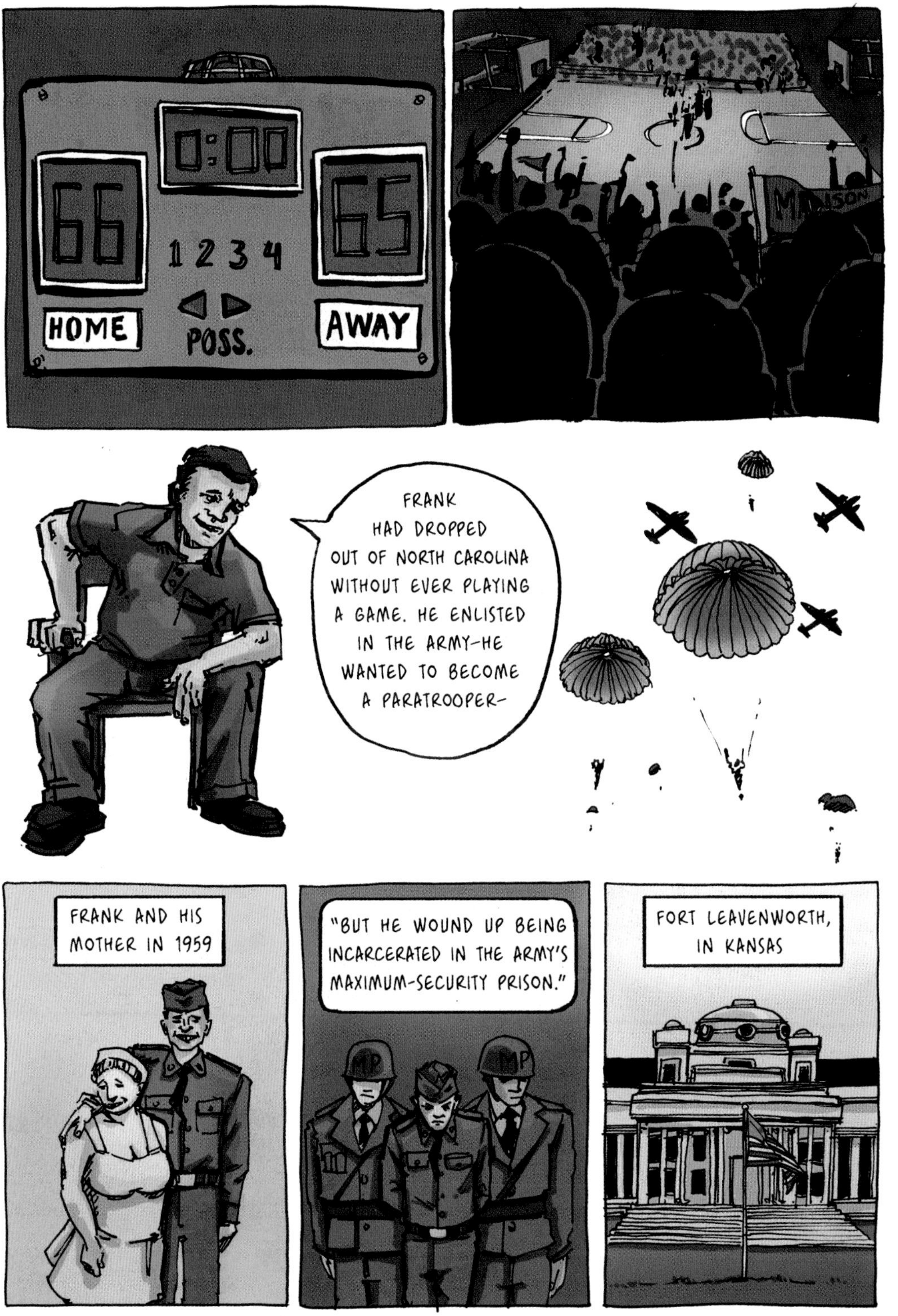
0:00
66
65
1 2 3 4
HOME
POSS.
AWAY
MADISON
FRANK HAD DROPPED OUT OF NORTH CAROLINA WITHOUT EVER PLAYING A GAME. HE ENLISTED IN THE ARMY–HE WANTED TO BECOME A PARATROOPER–
FRANK AND HIS MOTHER IN 1959
"BUT HE WOUND UP BEING INCARCERATED IN THE ARMY'S MAXIMUM-SECURITY PRISON."
MP
MP
FORT LEAVENWORTH, IN KANSAS

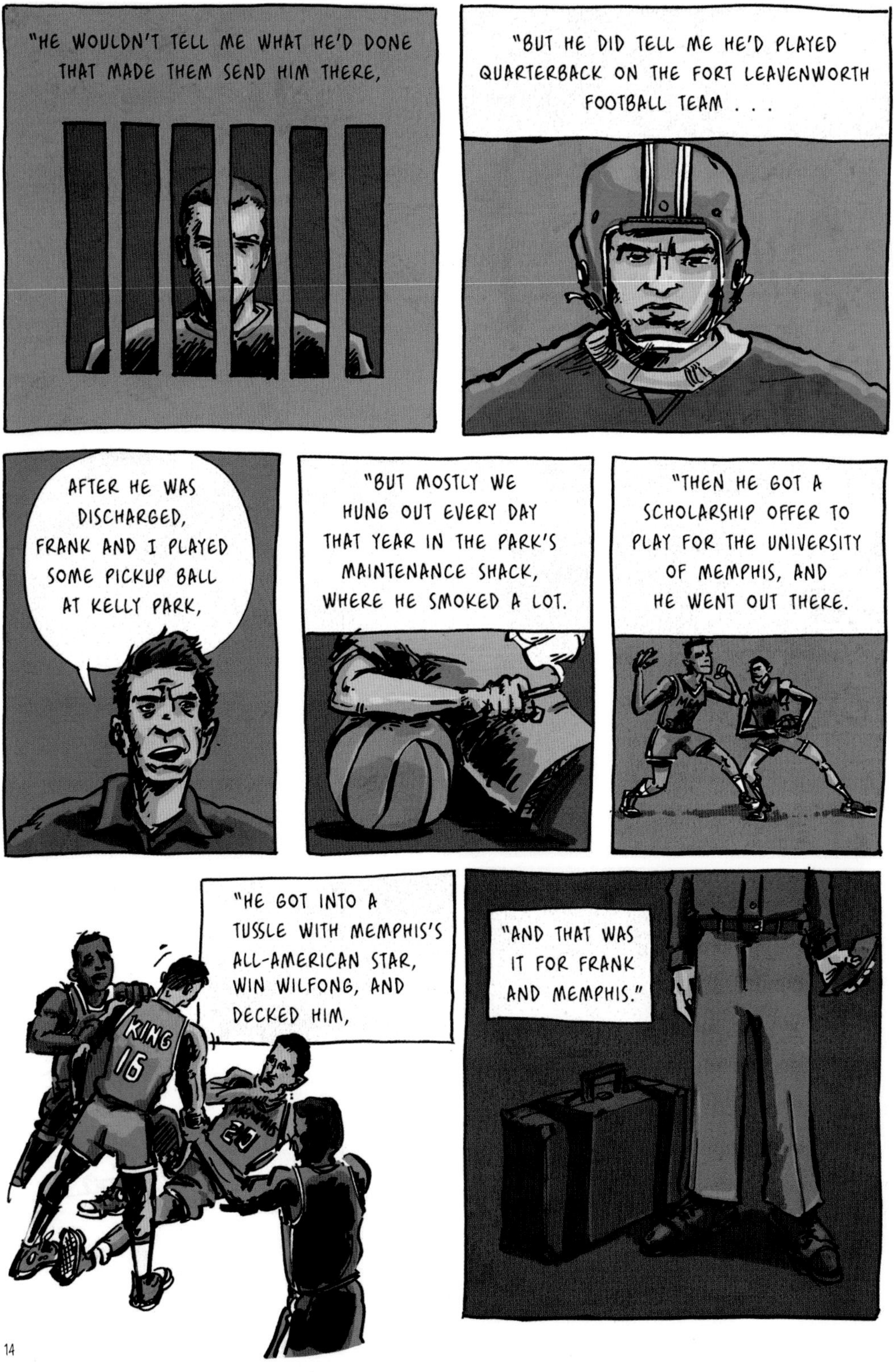
"HE WOULDN'T TELL ME WHAT HE'D DONE THAT MADE THEM SEND HIM THERE,
"BUT HE DID TELL ME HE'D PLAYED QUARTERBACK ON THE FORT LEAVENWORTH FOOTBALL TEAM . . .
AFTER HE WAS DISCHARGED, FRANK AND I PLAYED SOME PICKUP BALL AT KELLY PARK,
"BUT MOSTLY WE HUNG OUT EVERY DAY THAT YEAR IN THE PARK'S MAINTENANCE SHACK, WHERE HE SMOKED A LOT.
"THEN HE GOT A SCHOLARSHIP OFFER TO PLAY FOR THE UNIVERSITY OF MEMPHIS, AND HE WENT OUT THERE.
"HE GOT INTO A TUSSLE WITH MEMPHIS'S ALL-AMERICAN STAR, WIN WILFONG, AND DECKED HIM,
KING
16
"AND THAT WAS IT FOR FRANK AND MEMPHIS."

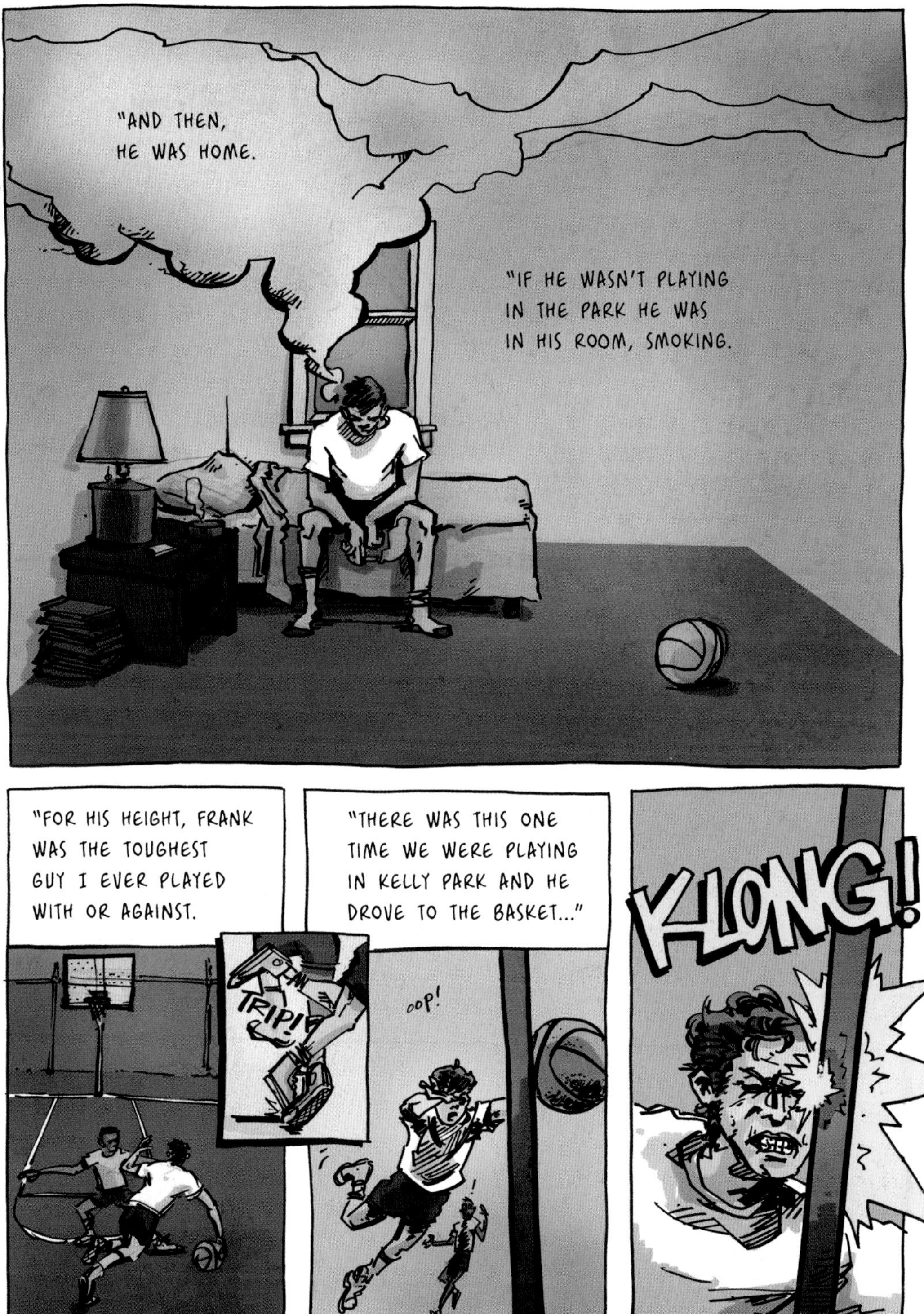
"AND THEN,
HE WAS HOME.
"IF HE WASN'T PLAYING
IN THE PARK HE WAS
IN HIS ROOM, SMOKING.
"FOR HIS HEIGHT, FRANK
WAS THE TOUGHEST
GUY I EVER PLAYED
WITH OR AGAINST.
TRIP!
"THERE WAS THIS ONE
TIME WE WERE PLAYING
IN KELLY PARK AND HE
DROVE TO THE BASKET..."
OOP!
KLONG!

OH BOY...
SHOULD WE CALL AN AMBULANCE?
I DUNNO... MAYBE?
WHAT HAPPENED?
YOU DROVE STRAIGHT INTO THE POLE!
!!!
THERE IS NO POLE!!!

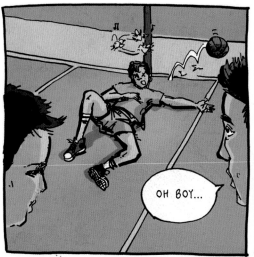

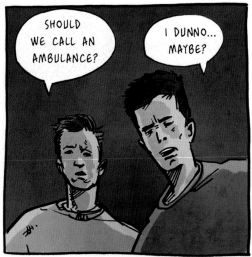

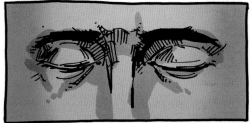

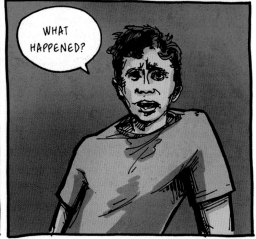

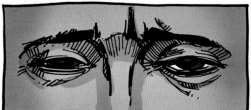

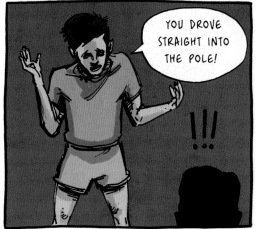

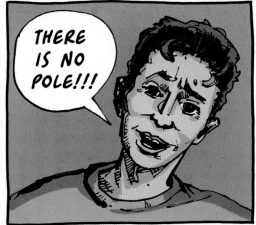

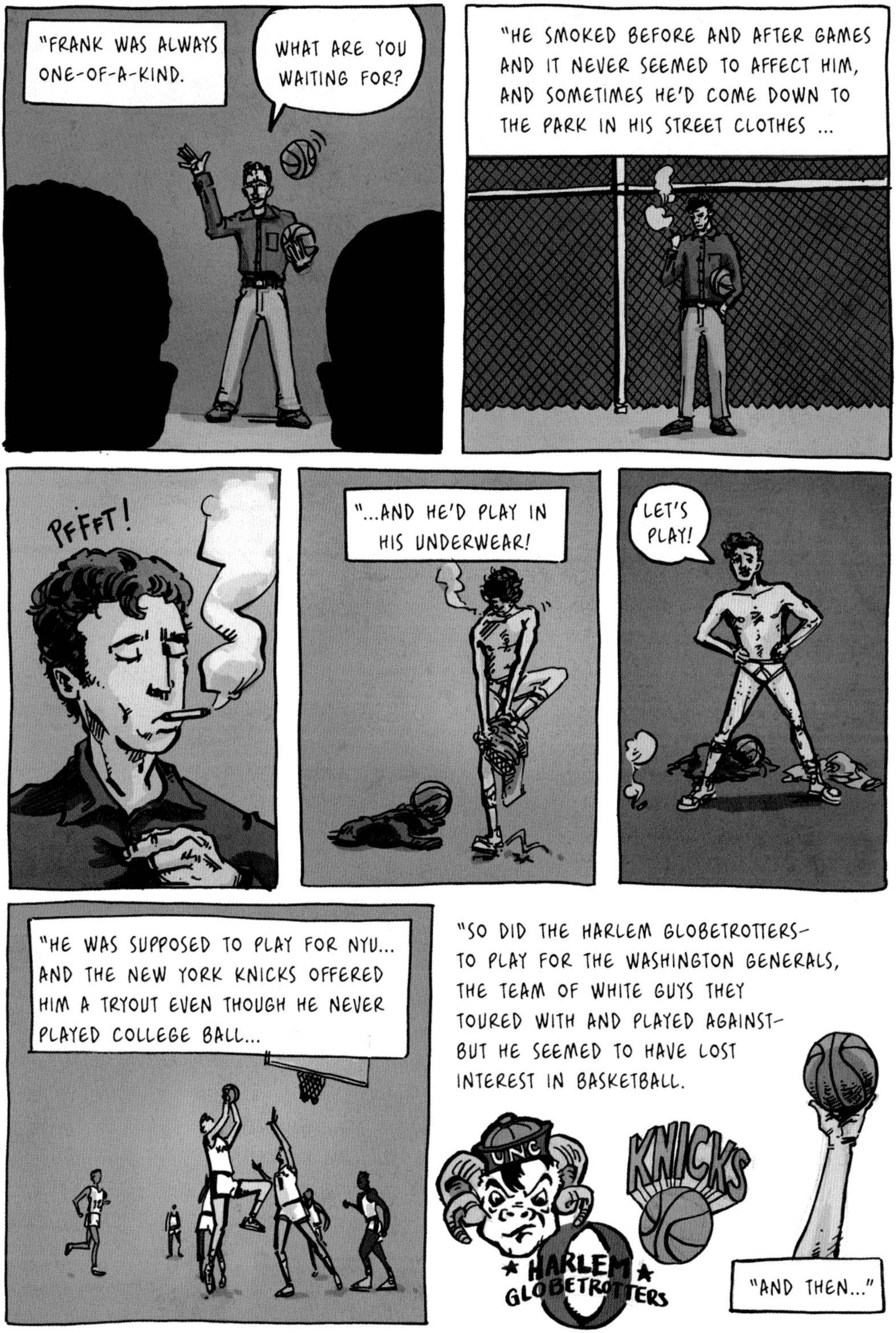
"FRANK WAS ALWAYS ONE-OF-A-KIND.
WHAT ARE YOU WAITING FOR?
"HE SMOKED BEFORE AND AFTER GAMES AND IT NEVER SEEMED TO AFFECT HIM, AND SOMETIMES HE'D COME DOWN TO THE PARK IN HIS STREET CLOTHES ...
PFFFT!
"...AND HE'D PLAY IN HIS UNDERWEAR!
LET'S PLAY!
"HE WAS SUPPOSED TO PLAY FOR NYU... AND THE NEW YORK KNICKS OFFERED HIM A TRYOUT EVEN THOUGH HE NEVER PLAYED COLLEGE BALL...
"SO DID THE HARLEM GLOBETROTTERS- TO PLAY FOR THE WASHINGTON GENERALS, THE TEAM OF WHITE GUYS THEY TOURED WITH AND PLAYED AGAINST- BUT HE SEEMED TO HAVE LOST INTEREST IN BASKETBALL.
UNC
KNICKS
HARLEM GLOBETROTTERS
"AND THEN..."

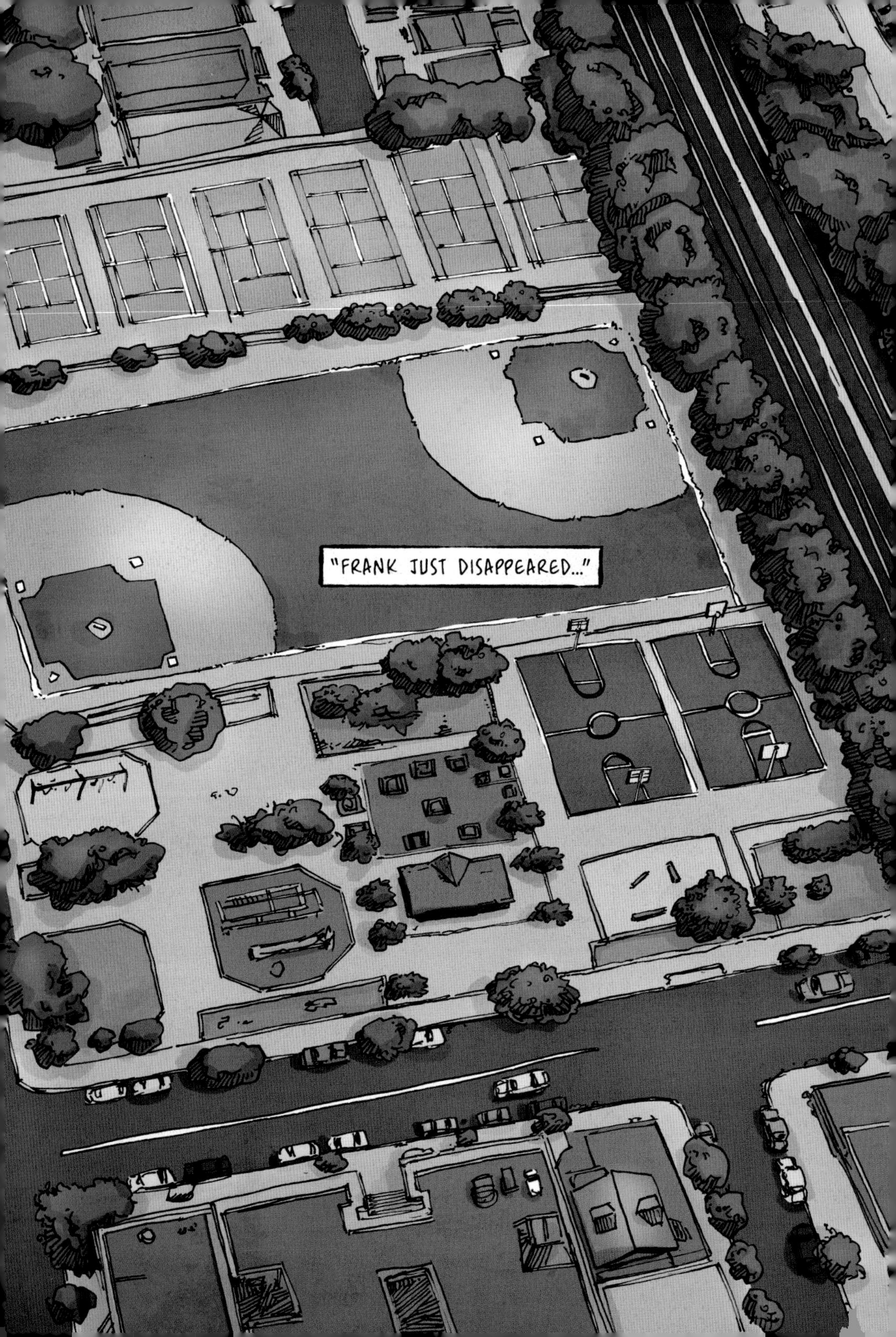
"FRANK JUST DISAPPEARED..."

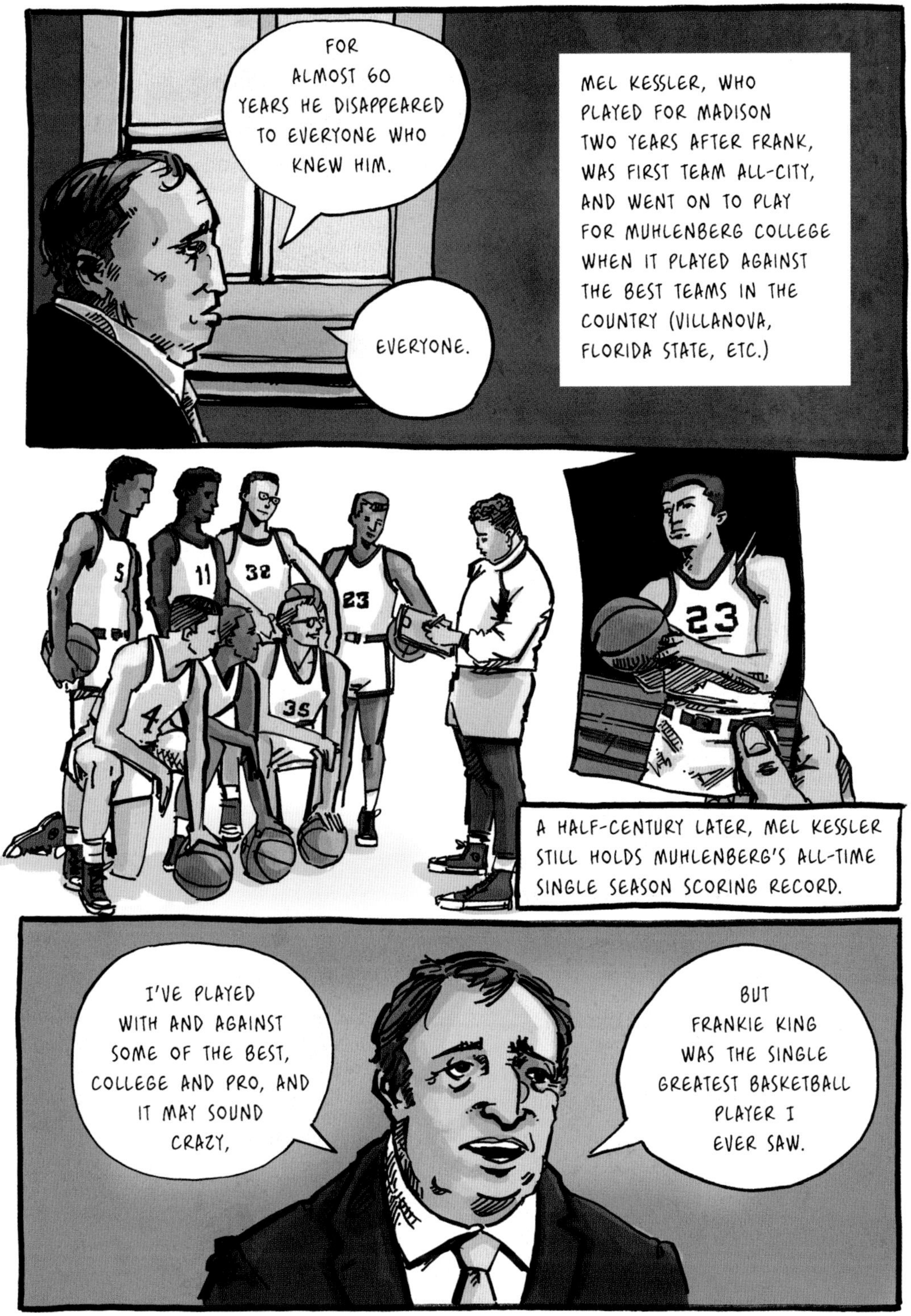

FOR ALMOST 60 YEARS HE DISAPPEARED TO EVERYONE WHO KNEW HIM.
EVERYONE.
MEL KESSLER, WHO PLAYED FOR MADISON TWO YEARS AFTER FRANK, WAS FIRST TEAM ALL-CITY, AND WENT ON TO PLAY FOR MUHLENBERG COLLEGE WHEN IT PLAYED AGAINST THE BEST TEAMS IN THE COUNTRY (VILLANOVA, FLORIDA STATE, ETC.)
5
11
32
23
4
35
23
A HALF-CENTURY LATER, MEL KESSLER STILL HOLDS MUHLENBERG'S ALL-TIME SINGLE SEASON SCORING RECORD.
I'VE PLAYED WITH AND AGAINST SOME OF THE BEST, COLLEGE AND PRO, AND IT MAY SOUND CRAZY,
BUT FRANKIE KING WAS THE SINGLE GREATEST BASKETBALL PLAYER I EVER SAW.

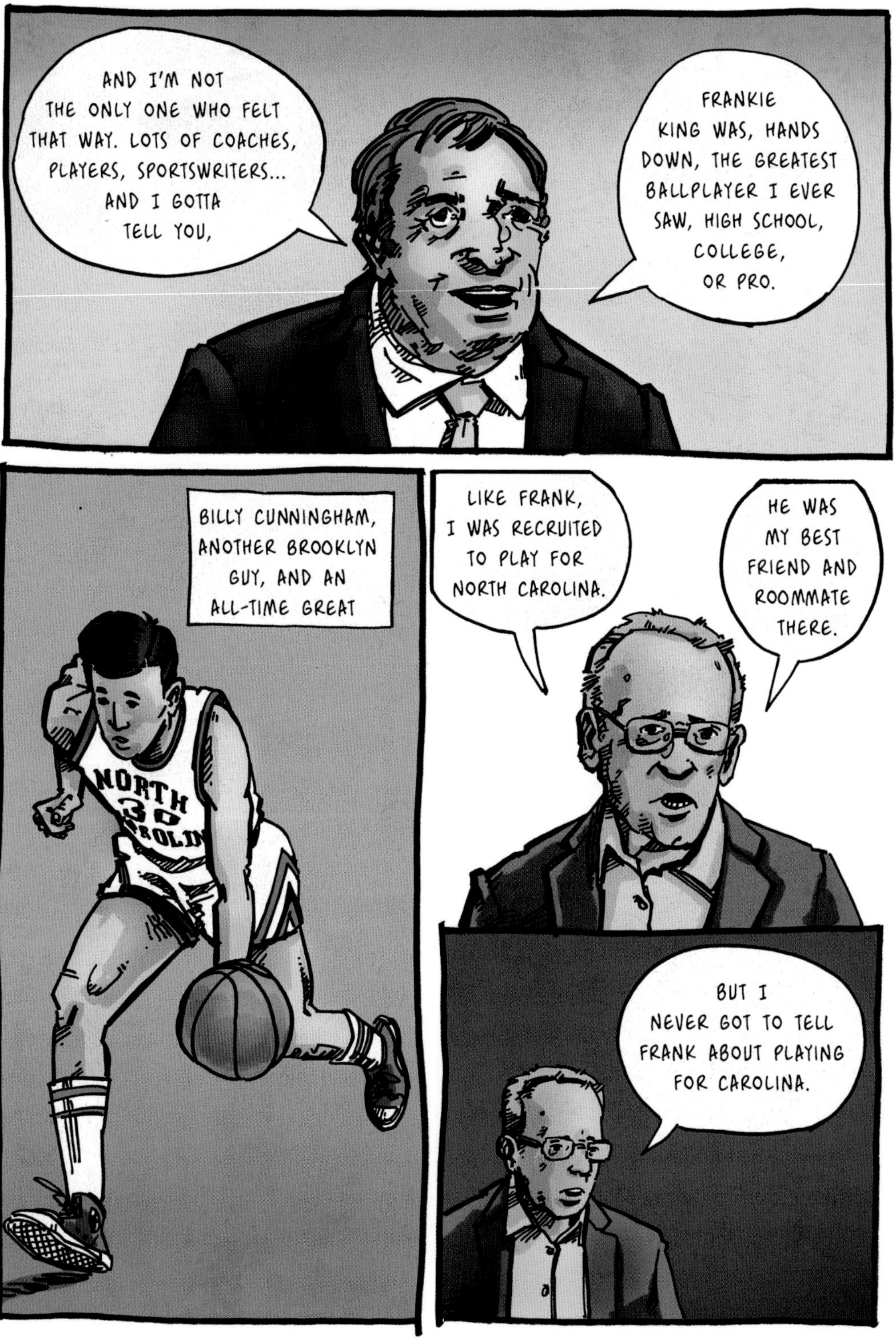
AND I'M NOT THE ONLY ONE WHO FELT THAT WAY. LOTS OF COACHES, PLAYERS, SPORTSWRITERS... AND I GOTTA TELL YOU,
FRANKIE KING WAS, HANDS DOWN, THE GREATEST BALLPLAYER I EVER SAW, HIGH SCHOOL, COLLEGE, OR PRO.
BILLY CUNNINGHAM, ANOTHER BROOKLYN GUY, AND AN ALL-TIME GREAT
NORTH CAROLINA
30
LIKE FRANK, I WAS RECRUITED TO PLAY FOR NORTH CAROLINA.
HE WAS MY BEST FRIEND AND ROOMMATE THERE.
BUT I NEVER GOT TO TELL FRANK ABOUT PLAYING FOR CAROLINA.

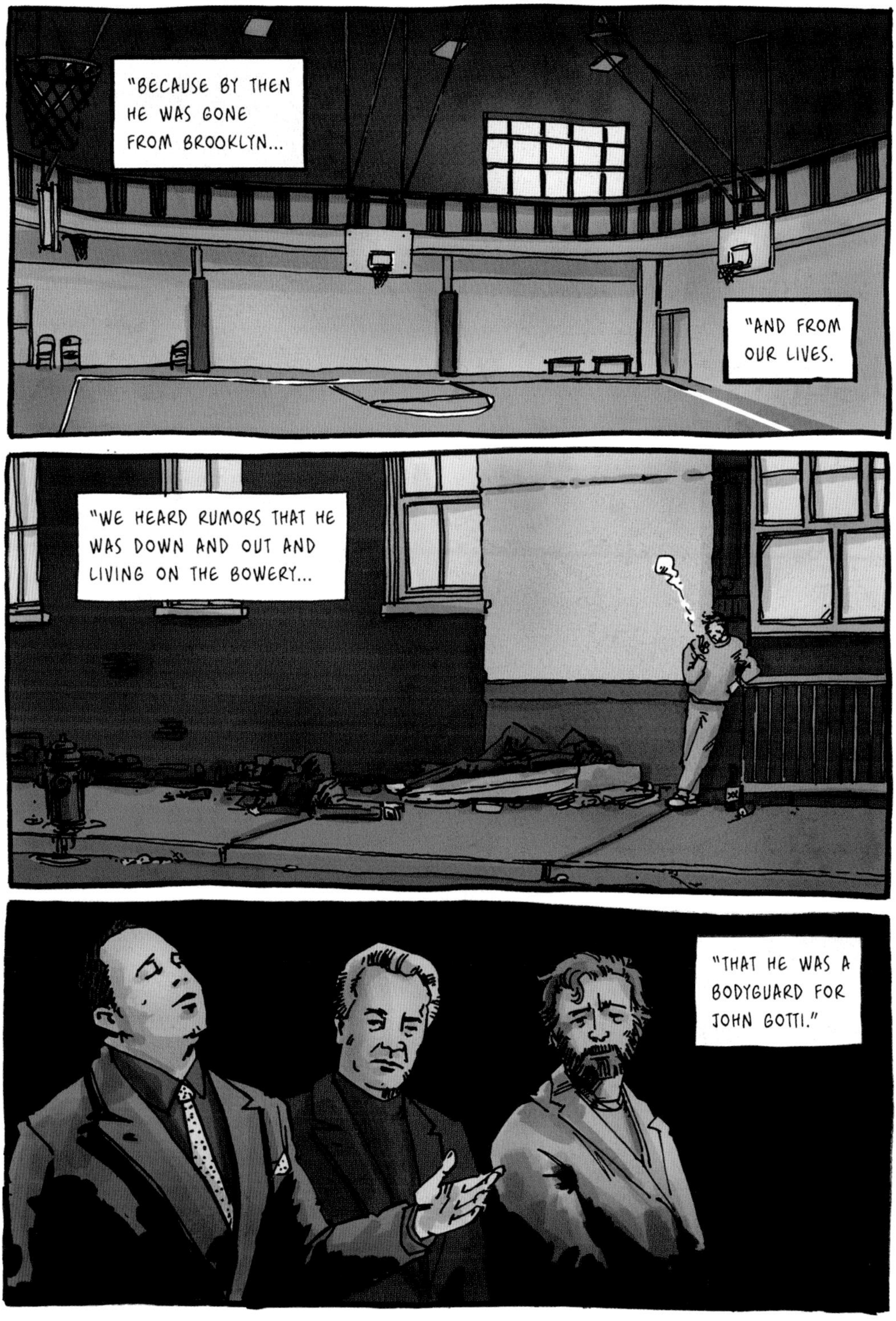
"BECAUSE BY THEN HE WAS GONE FROM BROOKLYN...
"AND FROM OUR LIVES.
"WE HEARD RUMORS THAT HE WAS DOWN AND OUT AND LIVING ON THE BOWERY...
"THAT HE WAS A BODYGUARD FOR JOHN GOTTI."

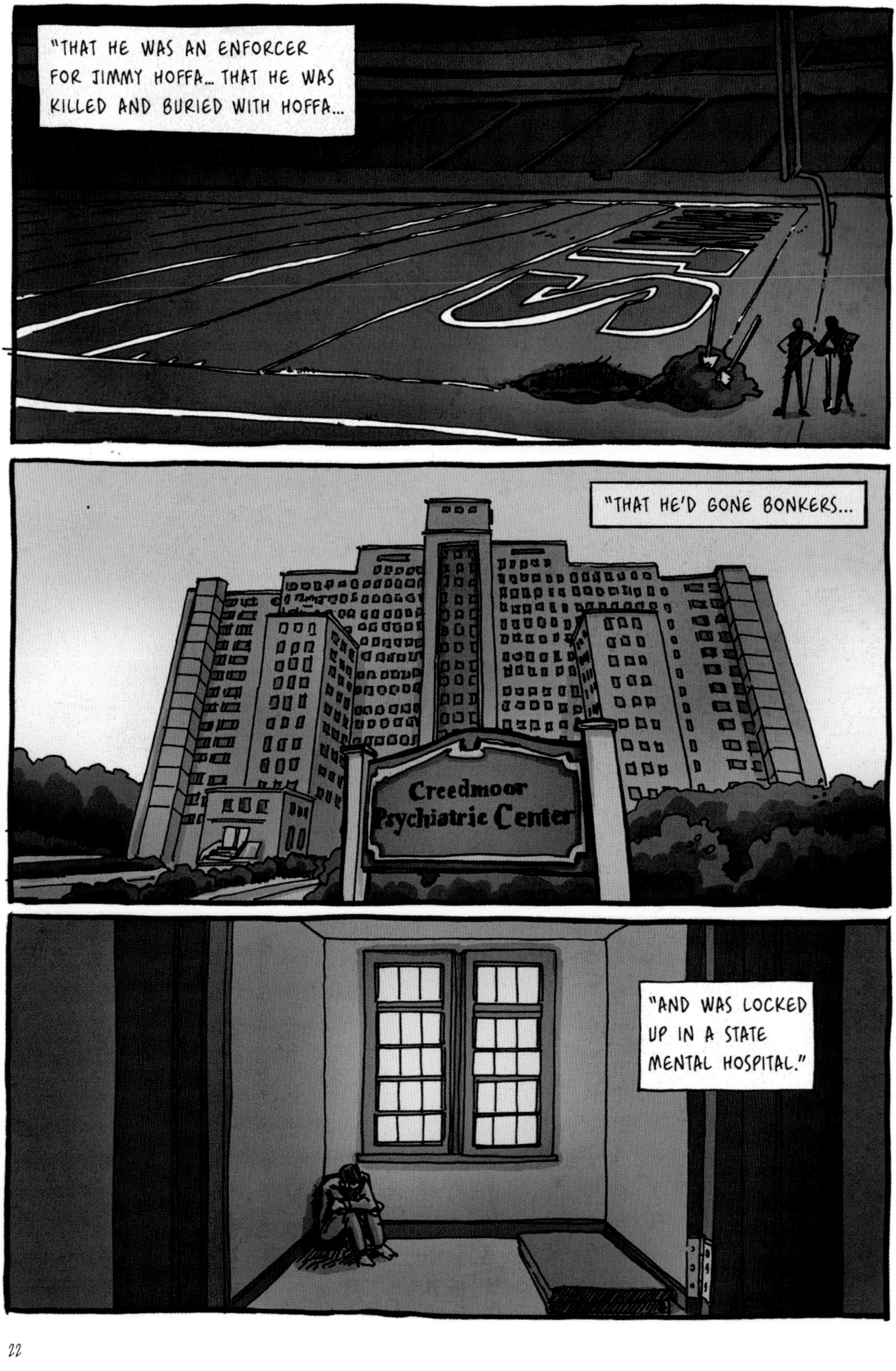
"THAT HE WAS AN ENFORCER FOR JIMMY HOFFA... THAT HE WAS KILLED AND BURIED WITH HOFFA...
"THAT HE'D GONE BONKERS...
Creedmoor Psychiatric Center
"AND WAS LOCKED UP IN A STATE MENTAL HOSPITAL."

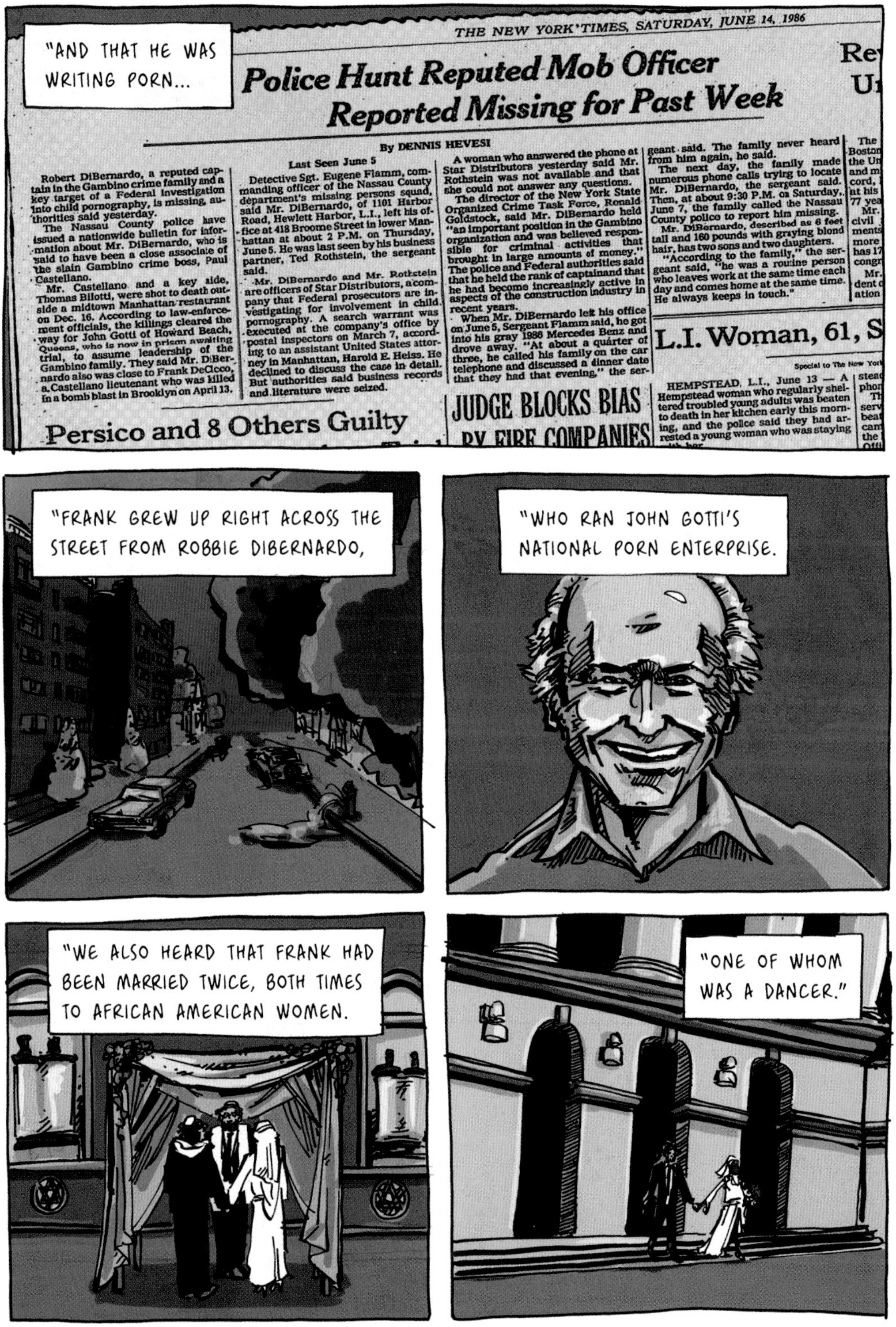
"AND THAT HE WAS WRITING PORN...
THE NEW YORK TIMES, SATURDAY, JUNE 14, 1986
Police Hunt Reputed Mob Officer Reported Missing for Past Week
By DENNIS HEVESI
Robert DiBernardo, a reputed captain in the Gambino crime family and a key target of a Federal investigation into child pornography, is missing, authorities said yesterday.
The Nassau County police have issued a nationwide bulletin for information about Mr. DiBernardo, who is said to have been a close associate of the slain Gambino crime boss, Paul Castellano.
Mr. Castellano and a key aide, Thomas Bilotti, were shot to death outside a midtown Manhattan restaurant on Dec. 16. According to law-enforcement officials, the killings cleared the way for John Gotti of Howard Beach, Queens, who is now in prison awaiting trial, to assume leadership of the Gambino family. They said Mr. DiBernardo also was close to Frank DeCicco, a Castellano lieutenant who was killed in a bomb blast in Brooklyn on April 13.
Last Seen June 5
Detective Sgt. Eugene Flamm, commanding officer of the Nassau County department's missing persons squad, said Mr. DiBernardo, of 1101 Harbor Road, Hewlett Harbor, L.I., left his office at 418 Broome Street in lower Manhattan at about 2 P.M. on Thursday, June 5. He was last seen by his business partner, Ted Rothstein, the sergeant said.
Mr. DiBernardo and Mr. Rothstein are officers of Star Distributors, a company that Federal prosecutors are investigating for involvement in child pornography. A search warrant was executed at the company's office by postal inspectors on March 7, according to an assistant United States attorney in Manhattan, Harold E. Heiss. He declined to discuss the case in detail. But authorities said business records and literature were seized.
A woman who answered the phone at Star Distributors yesterday said Mr. Rothstein was not available and that she could not answer any questions.
The director of the New York State Organized Crime Task Force, Ronald Goldstock, said Mr. DiBernardo held "an important position in the Gambino organization and was believed responsible for criminal activities that brought in large amounts of money." The police and Federal authorities said that he held the rank of captainand that he had become increasingly active in aspects of the construction industry in recent years.
When Mr. DiBernardo left his office on June 5, Sergeant Flamm said, he got into his gray 1986 Mercedes Benz and drove away. "At about a quarter of three, he called his family on the car telephone and discussed a dinner date that they had that evening," the sergeant said. The family never heard from him again, he said.
The next day, the family made numerous phone calls trying to locate Mr. DiBernardo, the sergeant said. Then, at about 9:30 P.M. on Saturday, June 7, the family called the Nassau County police to report him missing.
Mr. DiBernardo, described as 6 feet tall and 160 pounds with graying blond hair, has two sons and two daughters.
"According to the family," the sergeant said, "he was a routine person who leaves work at the same time each day and comes home at the same time. He always keeps in touch."
Persico and 8 Others Guilty
JUDGE BLOCKS BIAS
L.I. Woman, 61,
HEMPSTEAD, L.I., June 13 — A Hempstead woman who regularly sheltered troubled young adults was beaten to death in her kitchen early this morning, and the police said they had arrested a young woman who was staying
"FRANK GREW UP RIGHT ACROSS THE STREET FROM ROBBIE DIBERNARDO,
"WHO RAN JOHN GOTTI'S NATIONAL PORN ENTERPRISE.
"WE ALSO HEARD THAT FRANK HAD BEEN MARRIED TWICE, BOTH TIMES TO AFRICAN AMERICAN WOMEN.
"ONE OF WHOM WAS A DANCER."

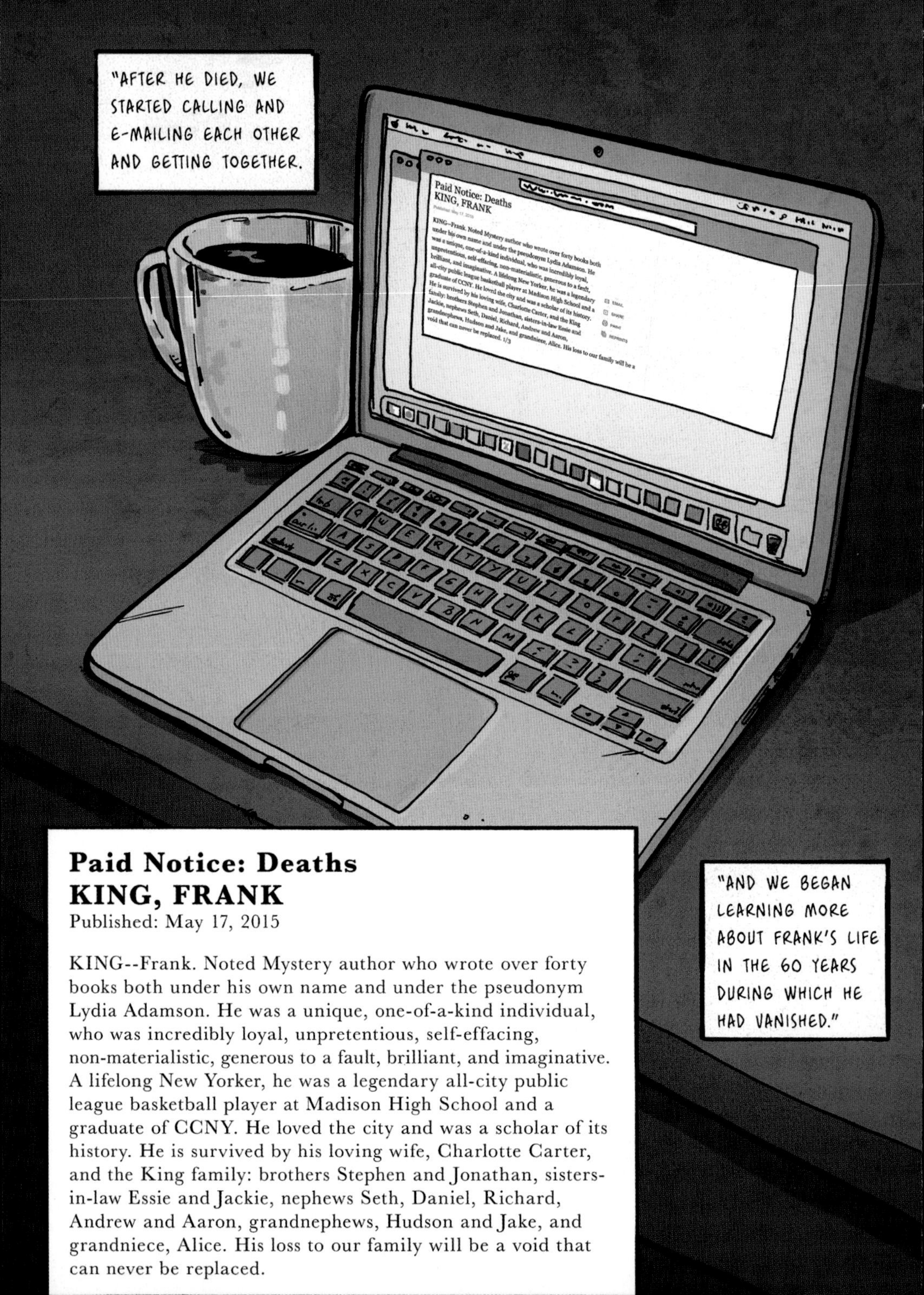
"AFTER HE DIED, WE STARTED CALLING AND E-MAILING EACH OTHER AND GETTING TOGETHER.
Paid Notice: Deaths
KING, FRANK
Published: May 17, 2015
KING--Frank. Noted Mystery author who wrote over forty books both under his own name and under the pseudonym Lydia Adamson. He was a unique, one-of-a-kind individual, who was incredibly loyal, unpretentious, self-effacing, non-materialistic, generous to a fault, brilliant, and imaginative. A lifelong New Yorker, he was a legendary all-city public league basketball player at Madison High School and a graduate of CCNY. He loved the city and was a scholar of its history. He is survived by his loving wife, Charlotte Carter, and the King family: brothers Stephen and Jonathan, sisters-in-law Essie and Jackie, nephews Seth, Daniel, Richard, Andrew and Aaron, grandnephews, Hudson and Jake, and grandniece, Alice. His loss to our family will be a void that can never be replaced.
"AND WE BEGAN LEARNING MORE ABOUT FRANK'S LIFE IN THE 60 YEARS DURING WHICH HE HAD VANISHED."

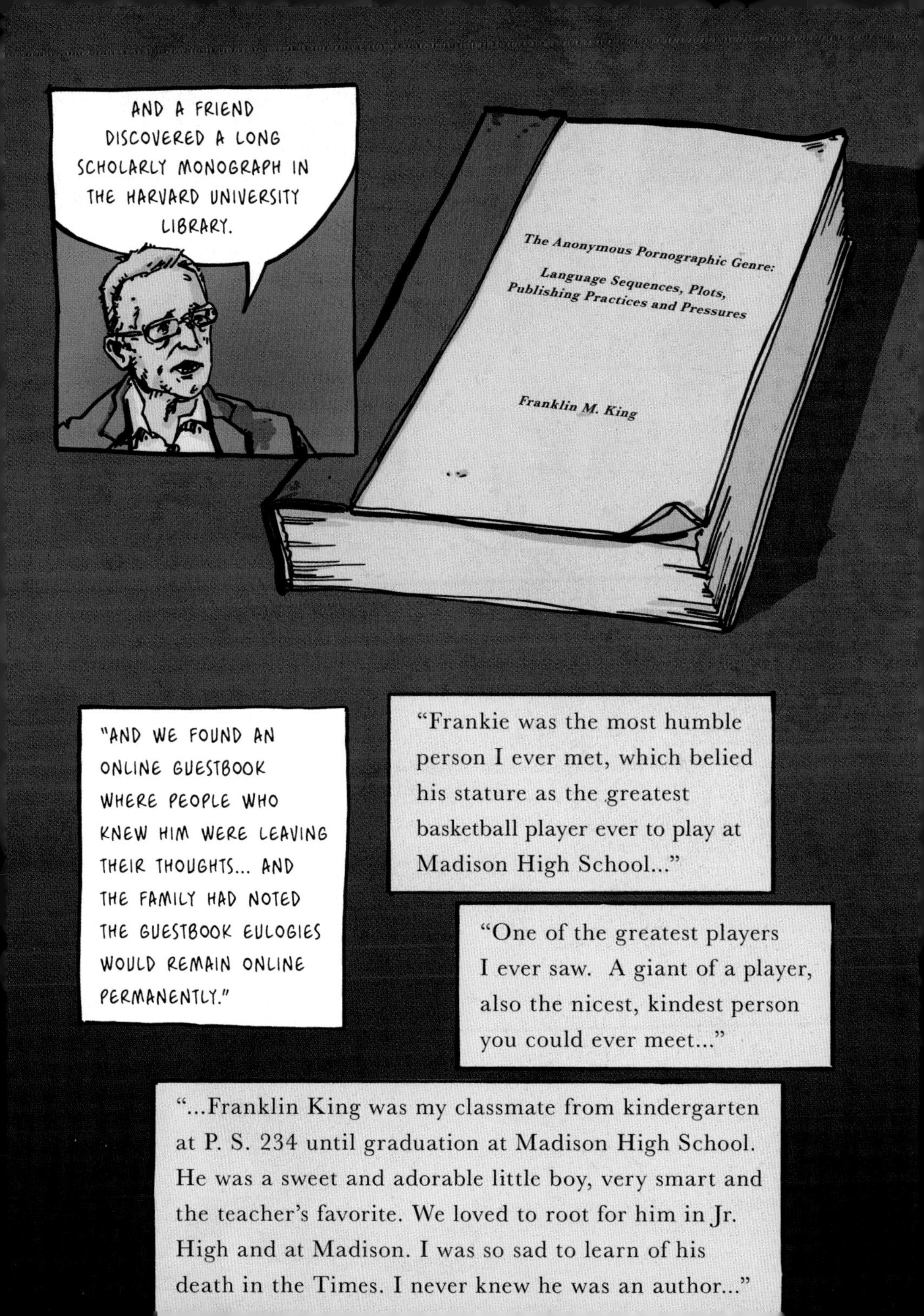
AND A FRIEND DISCOVERED A LONG SCHOLARLY MONOGRAPH IN THE HARVARD UNIVERSITY LIBRARY.
The Anonymous Pornographic Genre: Language Sequences, Plots, Publishing Practices and Pressures
Franklin M. King
"AND WE FOUND AN ONLINE GUESTBOOK WHERE PEOPLE WHO KNEW HIM WERE LEAVING THEIR THOUGHTS... AND THE FAMILY HAD NOTED THE GUESTBOOK EULOGIES WOULD REMAIN ONLINE PERMANENTLY."
"Frankie was the most humble person I ever met, which belied his stature as the greatest basketball player ever to play at Madison High School..."
"One of the greatest players I ever saw. A giant of a player, also the nicest, kindest person you could ever meet..."
"...Franklin King was my classmate from kindergarten at P. S. 234 until graduation at Madison High School. He was a sweet and adorable little boy, very smart and the teacher's favorite. We loved to root for him in Jr. High and at Madison. I was so sad to learn of his death in the Times. I never knew he was an author..."

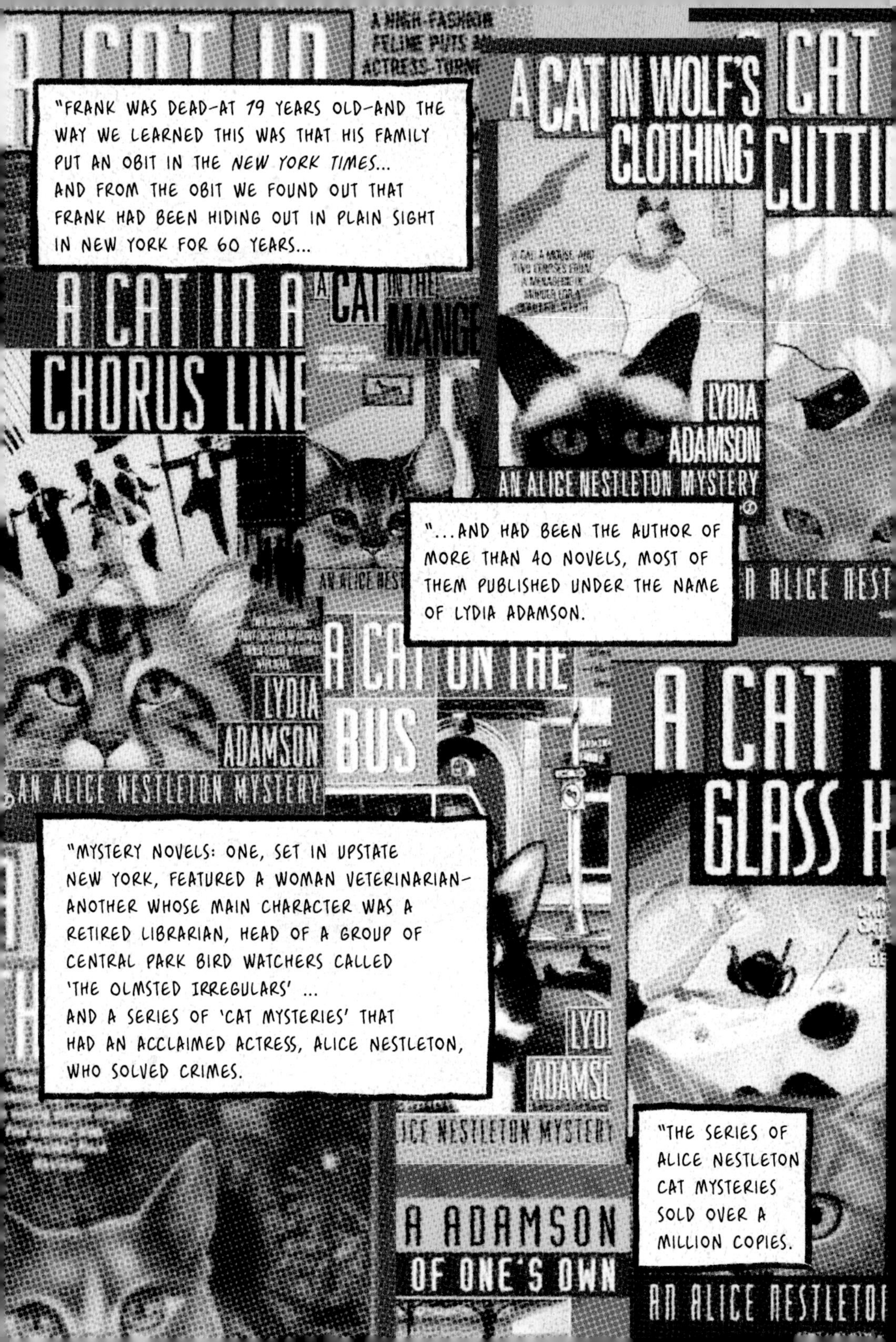
"FRANK WAS DEAD—AT 79 YEARS OLD—AND THE WAY WE LEARNED THIS WAS THAT HIS FAMILY PUT AN OBIT IN THE *NEW YORK TIMES*... AND FROM THE OBIT WE FOUND OUT THAT FRANK HAD BEEN HIDING OUT IN PLAIN SIGHT IN NEW YORK FOR 60 YEARS...
A CAT IN WOLF'S CLOTHING
LYDIA ADAMSON
AN ALICE NESTLETON MYSTERY
A CAT IN A CHORUS LINE
"...AND HAD BEEN THE AUTHOR OF MORE THAN 40 NOVELS, MOST OF THEM PUBLISHED UNDER THE NAME OF LYDIA ADAMSON.
LYDIA ADAMSON
AN ALICE NESTLETON MYSTERY
A CAT ON THE BUS
"MYSTERY NOVELS: ONE, SET IN UPSTATE NEW YORK, FEATURED A WOMAN VETERINARIAN—ANOTHER WHOSE MAIN CHARACTER WAS A RETIRED LIBRARIAN, HEAD OF A GROUP OF CENTRAL PARK BIRD WATCHERS CALLED 'THE OLMSTED IRREGULARS' ... AND A SERIES OF 'CAT MYSTERIES' THAT HAD AN ACCLAIMED ACTRESS, ALICE NESTLETON, WHO SOLVED CRIMES.
A ADAMSON
OF ONE'S OWN
"THE SERIES OF ALICE NESTLETON CAT MYSTERIES SOLD OVER A MILLION COPIES.

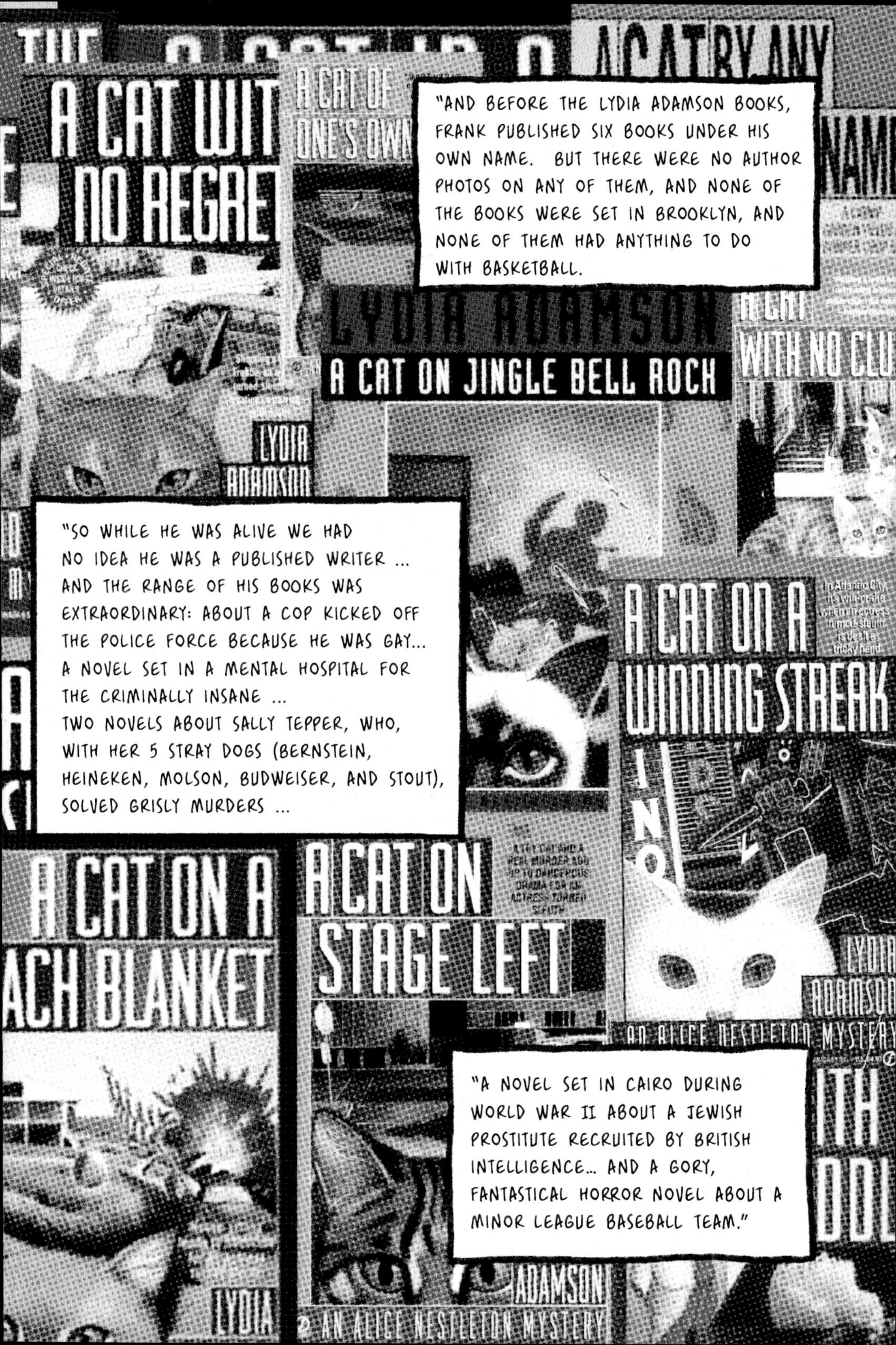
"AND BEFORE THE LYDIA ADAMSON BOOKS, FRANK PUBLISHED SIX BOOKS UNDER HIS OWN NAME. BUT THERE WERE NO AUTHOR PHOTOS ON ANY OF THEM, AND NONE OF THE BOOKS WERE SET IN BROOKLYN, AND NONE OF THEM HAD ANYTHING TO DO WITH BASKETBALL.
"SO WHILE HE WAS ALIVE WE HAD NO IDEA HE WAS A PUBLISHED WRITER ... AND THE RANGE OF HIS BOOKS WAS EXTRAORDINARY: ABOUT A COP KICKED OFF THE POLICE FORCE BECAUSE HE WAS GAY... A NOVEL SET IN A MENTAL HOSPITAL FOR THE CRIMINALLY INSANE ... TWO NOVELS ABOUT SALLY TEPPER, WHO, WITH HER 5 STRAY DOGS (BERNSTEIN, HEINEKEN, MOLSON, BUDWEISER, AND STOUT), SOLVED GRISLY MURDERS ...
"A NOVEL SET IN CAIRO DURING WORLD WAR II ABOUT A JEWISH PROSTITUTE RECRUITED BY BRITISH INTELLIGENCE... AND A GORY, FANTASTICAL HORROR NOVEL ABOUT A MINOR LEAGUE BASEBALL TEAM."
A CAT OF ONE'S OWN
LYDIA ADAMSON
A CAT ON JINGLE BELL ROCK
A CAT ON A WINNING STREAK
A CAT ON STAGE LEFT
AN ALICE NESTLETON MYSTERY

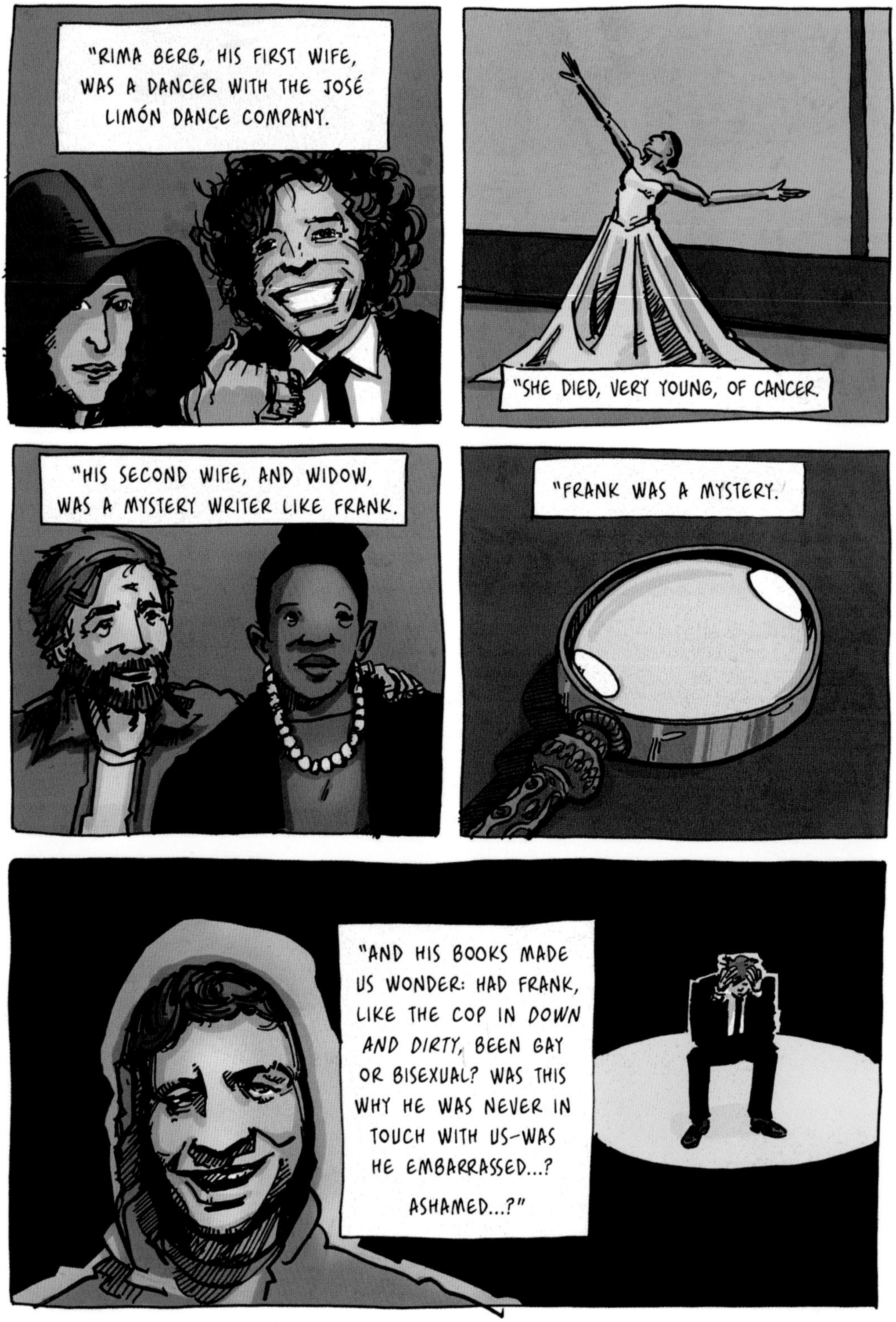
"RIMA BERG, HIS FIRST WIFE, WAS A DANCER WITH THE JOSÉ LIMÓN DANCE COMPANY.
"SHE DIED, VERY YOUNG, OF CANCER.
"HIS SECOND WIFE, AND WIDOW, WAS A MYSTERY WRITER LIKE FRANK.
"FRANK WAS A MYSTERY.
"AND HIS BOOKS MADE US WONDER: HAD FRANK, LIKE THE COP IN *DOWN AND DIRTY*, BEEN GAY OR BISEXUAL? WAS THIS WHY HE WAS NEVER IN TOUCH WITH US—WAS HE EMBARRASSED...?
ASHAMED...?"

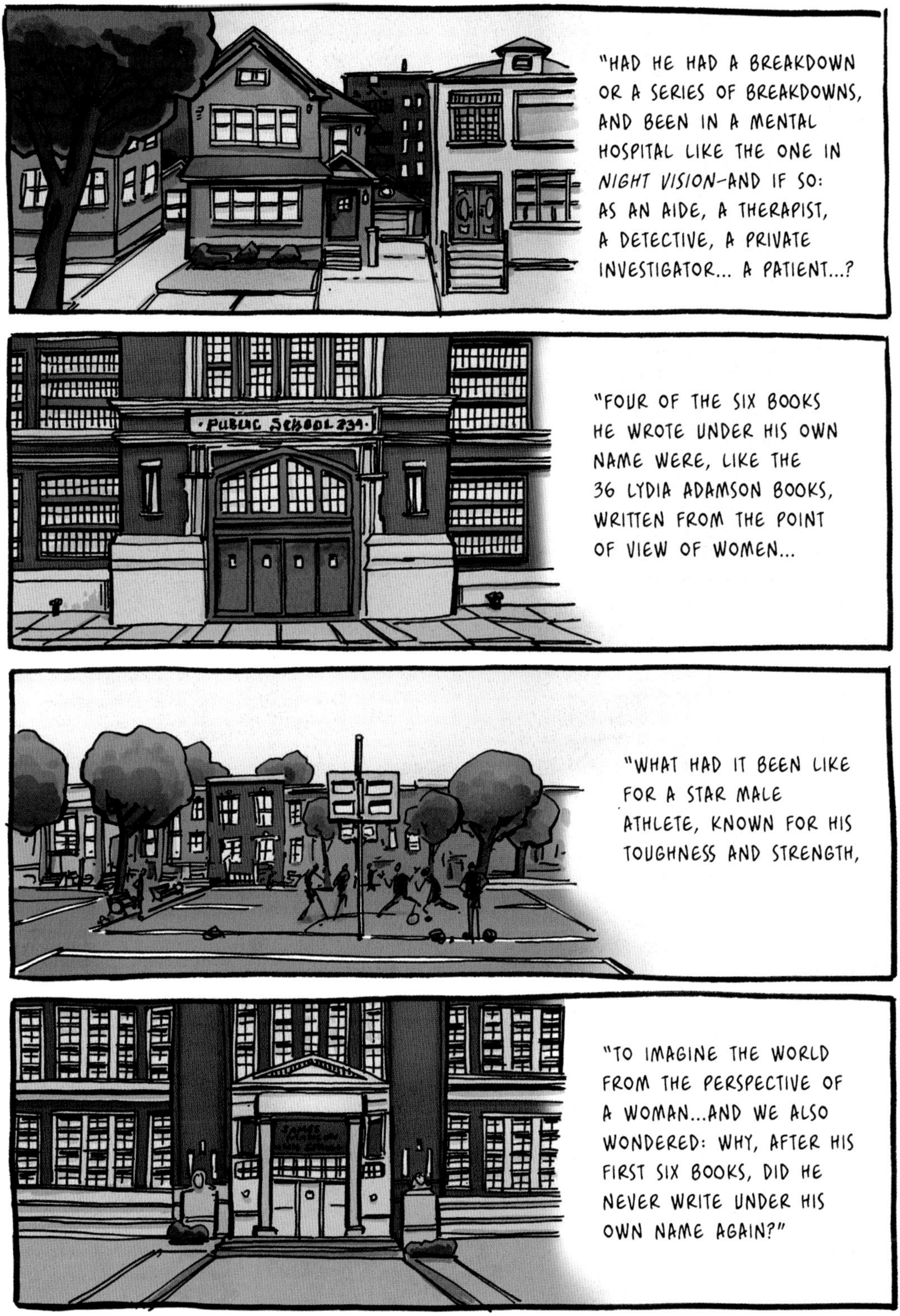
"HAD HE HAD A BREAKDOWN OR A SERIES OF BREAKDOWNS, AND BEEN IN A MENTAL HOSPITAL LIKE THE ONE IN *NIGHT VISION*–AND IF SO: AS AN AIDE, A THERAPIST, A DETECTIVE, A PRIVATE INVESTIGATOR... A PATIENT...?
PUBLIC SCHOOL 234
"FOUR OF THE SIX BOOKS HE WROTE UNDER HIS OWN NAME WERE, LIKE THE 36 LYDIA ADAMSON BOOKS, WRITTEN FROM THE POINT OF VIEW OF WOMEN...
"WHAT HAD IT BEEN LIKE FOR A STAR MALE ATHLETE, KNOWN FOR HIS TOUGHNESS AND STRENGTH,
"TO IMAGINE THE WORLD FROM THE PERSPECTIVE OF A WOMAN...AND WE ALSO WONDERED: WHY, AFTER HIS FIRST SIX BOOKS, DID HE NEVER WRITE UNDER HIS OWN NAME AGAIN?"

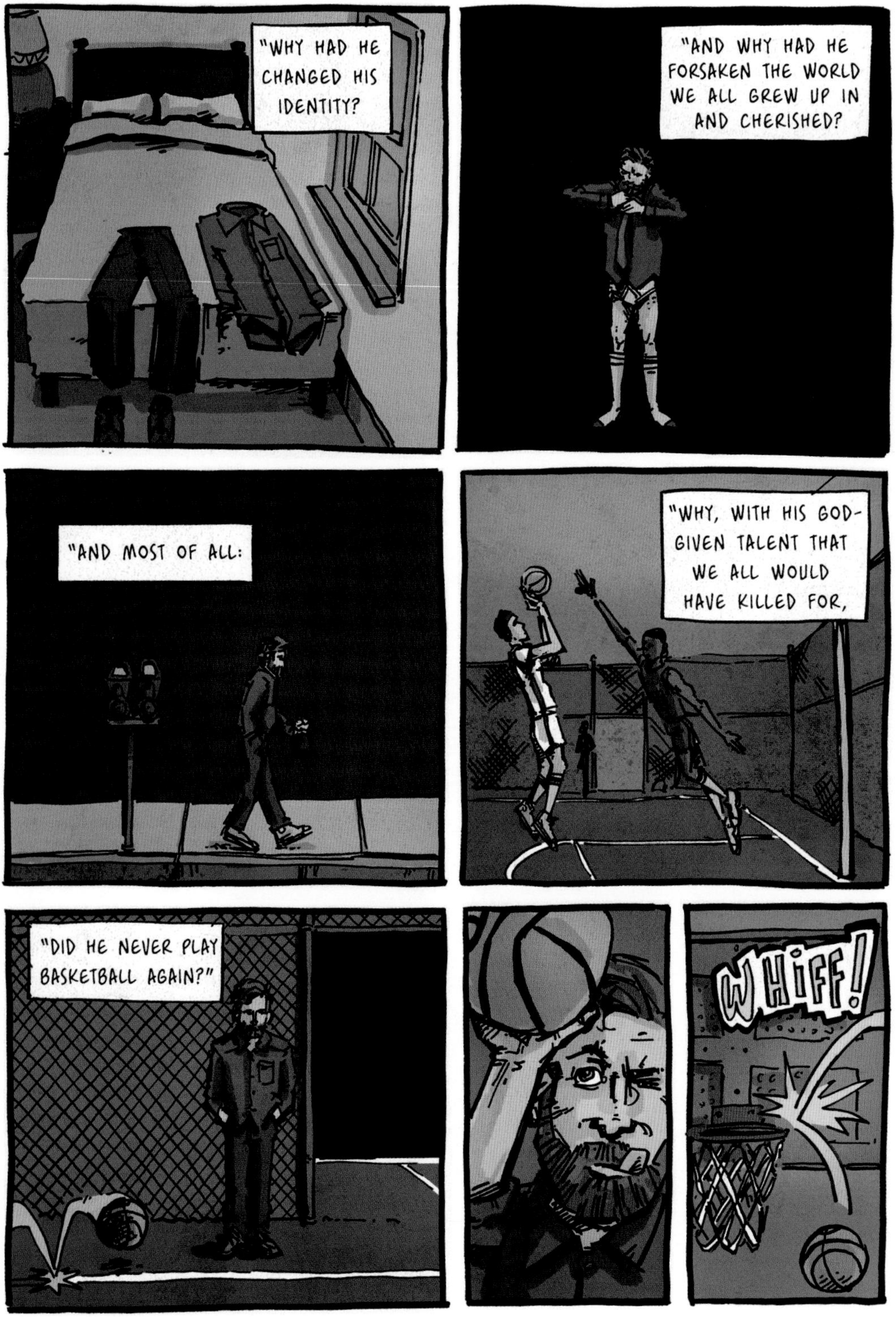
"WHY HAD HE CHANGED HIS IDENTITY?
"AND WHY HAD HE FORSAKEN THE WORLD WE ALL GREW UP IN AND CHERISHED?
"AND MOST OF ALL:
"WHY, WITH HIS GOD-GIVEN TALENT THAT WE ALL WOULD HAVE KILLED FOR,
"DID HE NEVER PLAY BASKETBALL AGAIN?"
WHIFF!

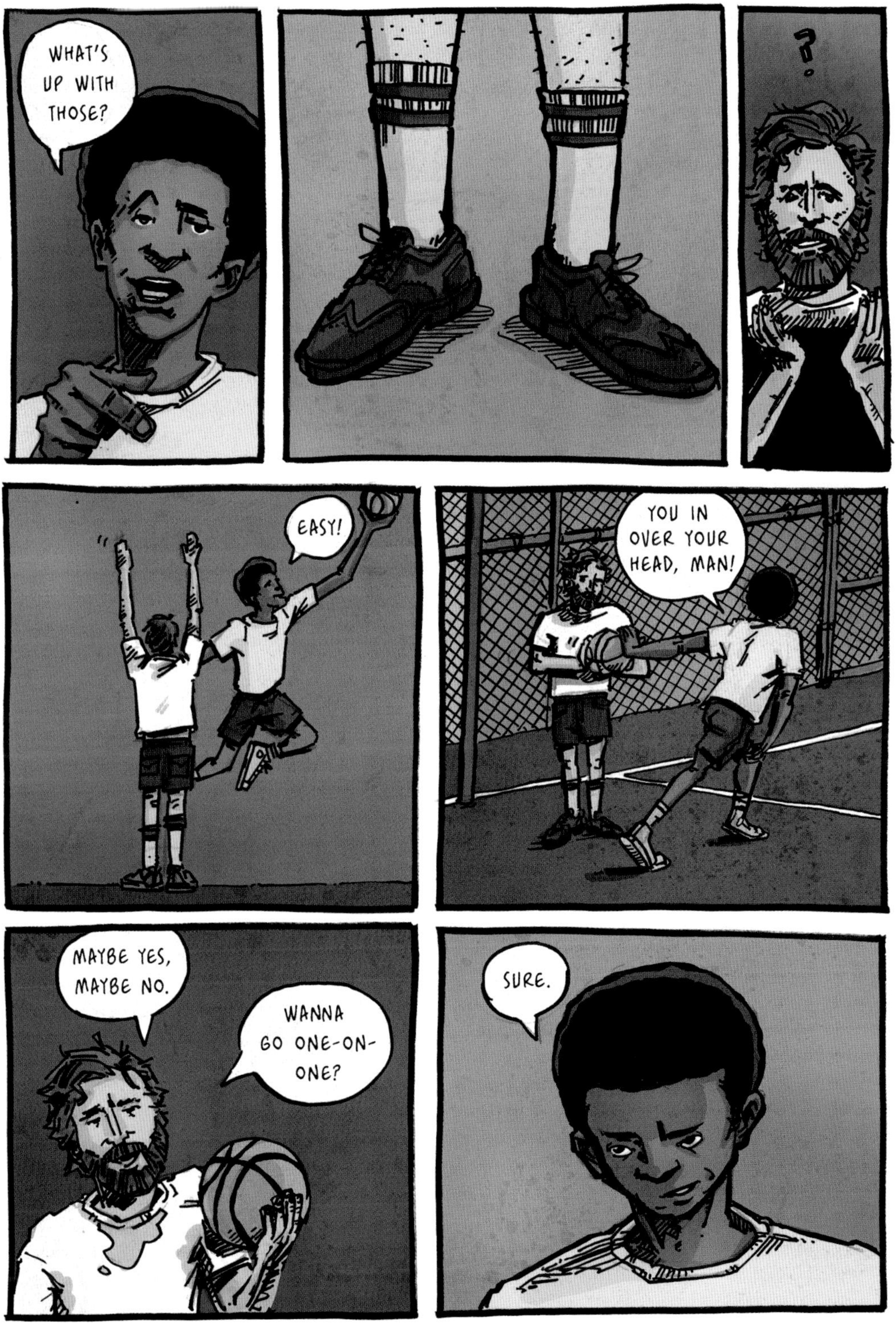
WHAT'S UP WITH THOSE?
?
EASY!
YOU IN OVER YOUR HEAD, MAN!
MAYBE YES, MAYBE NO.
WANNA GO ONE-ON-ONE?
SURE.

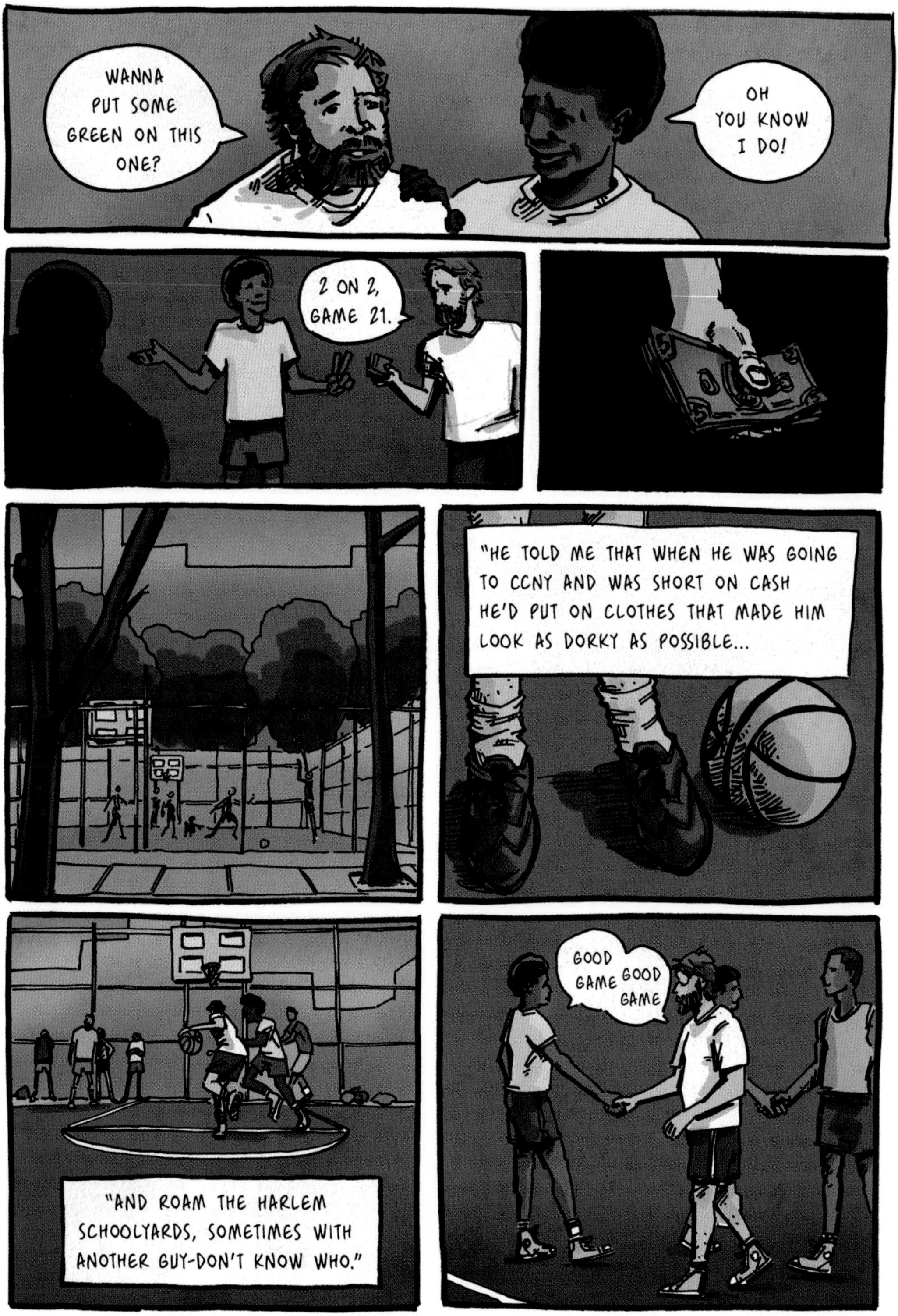
WANNA PUT SOME GREEN ON THIS ONE?
OH YOU KNOW I DO!
2 ON 2, GAME 21.
"HE TOLD ME THAT WHEN HE WAS GOING TO CCNY AND WAS SHORT ON CASH HE'D PUT ON CLOTHES THAT MADE HIM LOOK AS DORKY AS POSSIBLE...
"AND ROAM THE HARLEM SCHOOLYARDS, SOMETIMES WITH ANOTHER GUY-DON'T KNOW WHO."
GOOD GAME
GOOD GAME

"AND PLAY BADLY FOR A FEW GAMES—THE OLD POOL PLAYER GRIFT—

"AND THEN TURN IT UP WHEN THE BETS WERE PLACED."

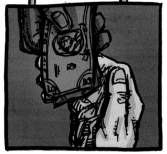 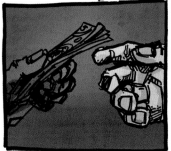 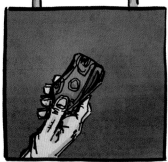

YOU MUST BE THE WHITE GUY WE HEARD OF...

BEEN PULLING A CON JOB ON US!

WHOA, WHOA...

GET HIM!

SETH KING: "MY DAD STEVE—FRANK'S OLDER BROTHER—BECAME WORRIED ABOUT FRANK—THAT FRANK WAS SUICIDAL—SO I MOVED IN WITH HIM AND WOUND UP LIVING WITH HIM FOR THREE YEARS.

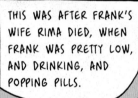

THIS WAS AFTER FRANK'S WIFE RIMA DIED, WHEN FRANK WAS PRETTY LOW, AND DRINKING, AND POPPING PILLS.

[SETH KING, FRANK'S NEPHEW]

"BY THE TIME I CAME INTO THE PICTURE HE WAS DONE WITH BASKETBALL.

"EXCEPT FOR WATCHING IT ON TV, MOSTLY COLLEGE, AND SOMETIMES THE KNICKS.

"I NEVER SAW FRANK SO MUCH AS HOLD A BASKETBALL.

"AS FAR AS I KNOW HE NEVER PLAYED AGAIN FOR THE REST OF HIS LIFE."

201

OTB OFF-TRACK BETTING

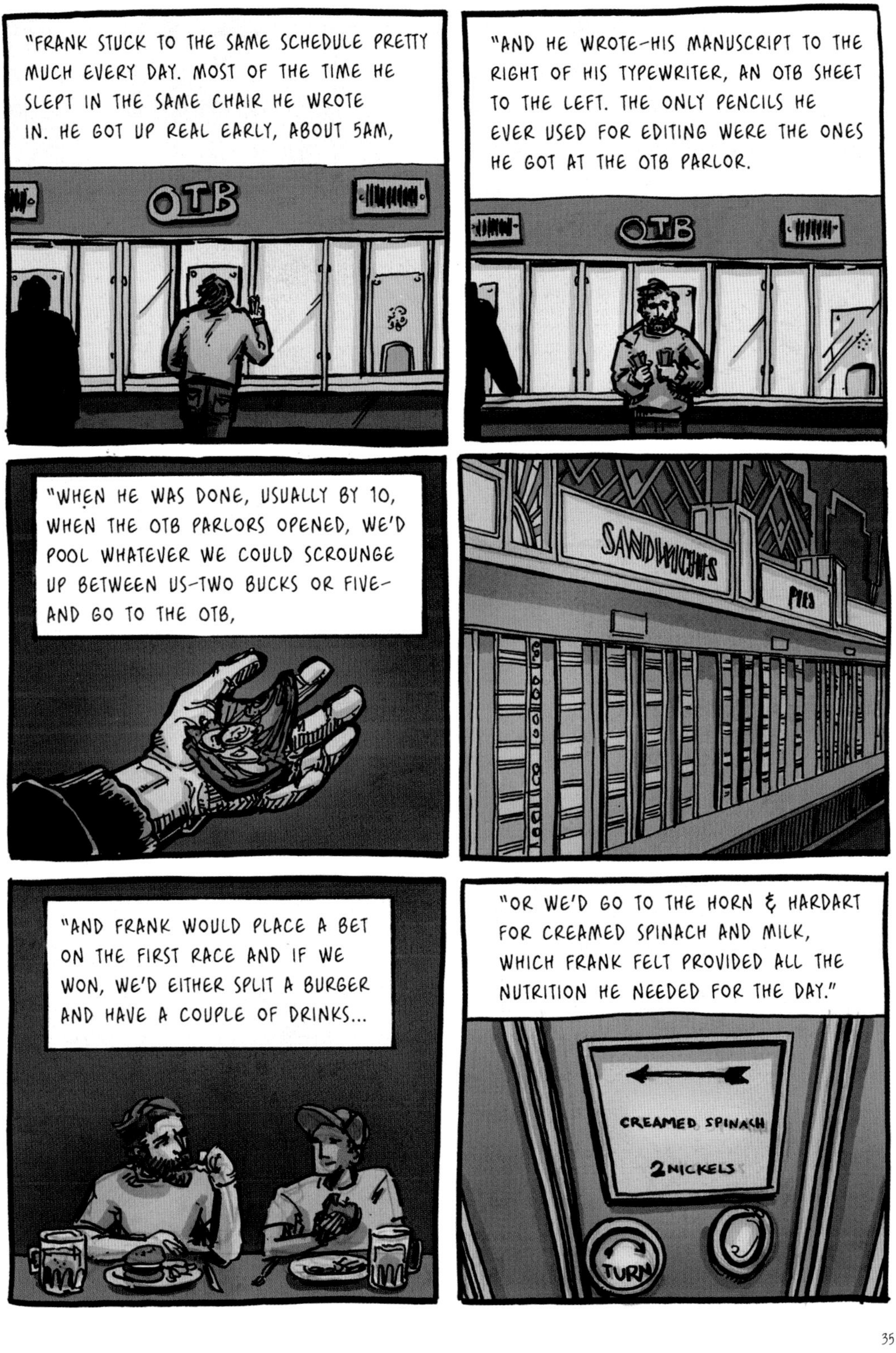
"FRANK STUCK TO THE SAME SCHEDULE PRETTY MUCH EVERY DAY. MOST OF THE TIME HE SLEPT IN THE SAME CHAIR HE WROTE IN. HE GOT UP REAL EARLY, ABOUT 5AM,
OTB
"AND HE WROTE—HIS MANUSCRIPT TO THE RIGHT OF HIS TYPEWRITER, AN OTB SHEET TO THE LEFT. THE ONLY PENCILS HE EVER USED FOR EDITING WERE THE ONES HE GOT AT THE OTB PARLOR.
OTB
"WHEN HE WAS DONE, USUALLY BY 10, WHEN THE OTB PARLORS OPENED, WE'D POOL WHATEVER WE COULD SCROUNGE UP BETWEEN US—TWO BUCKS OR FIVE—AND GO TO THE OTB,
SANDWICHES
PIES
"AND FRANK WOULD PLACE A BET ON THE FIRST RACE AND IF WE WON, WE'D EITHER SPLIT A BURGER AND HAVE A COUPLE OF DRINKS...
"OR WE'D GO TO THE HORN & HARDART FOR CREAMED SPINACH AND MILK, WHICH FRANK FELT PROVIDED ALL THE NUTRITION HE NEEDED FOR THE DAY."
CREAMED SPINACH
2 NICKELS
TURN

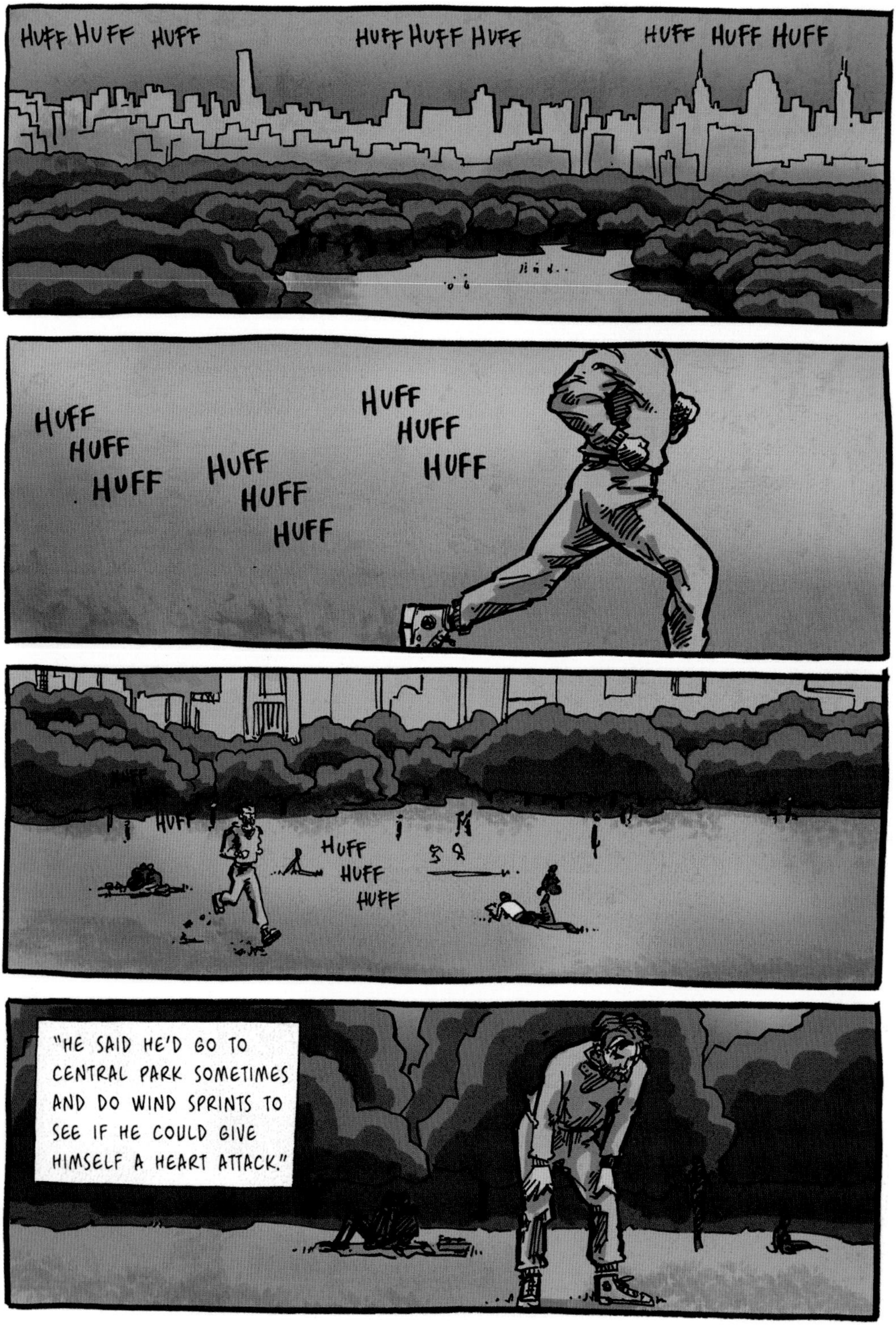
HUFF HUFF HUFF
HUFF HUFF HUFF
HUFF HUFF HUFF
HUFF HUFF HUFF
HUFF HUFF HUFF
HUFF HUFF HUFF
HUFF
HUFF HUFF HUFF
"HE SAID HE'D GO TO CENTRAL PARK SOMETIMES AND DO WIND SPRINTS TO SEE IF HE COULD GIVE HIMSELF A HEART ATTACK."

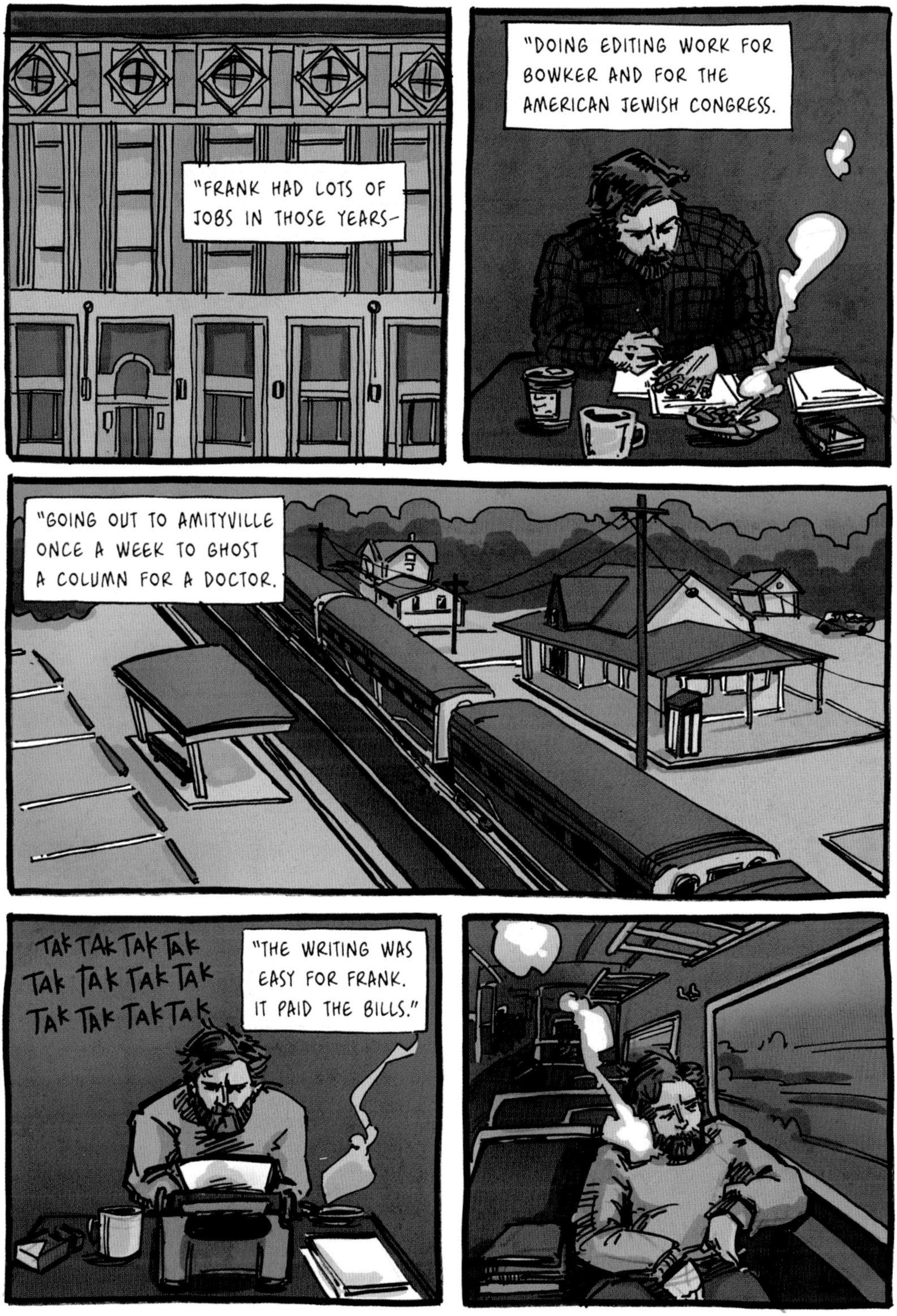
"FRANK HAD LOTS OF JOBS IN THOSE YEARS-
"DOING EDITING WORK FOR BOWKER AND FOR THE AMERICAN JEWISH CONGRESS.
"GOING OUT TO AMITYVILLE ONCE A WEEK TO GHOST A COLUMN FOR A DOCTOR.
TAK TAK TAK TAK TAK TAK TAK TAK TAK TAK TAK TAK
"THE WRITING WAS EASY FOR FRANK. IT PAID THE BILLS."

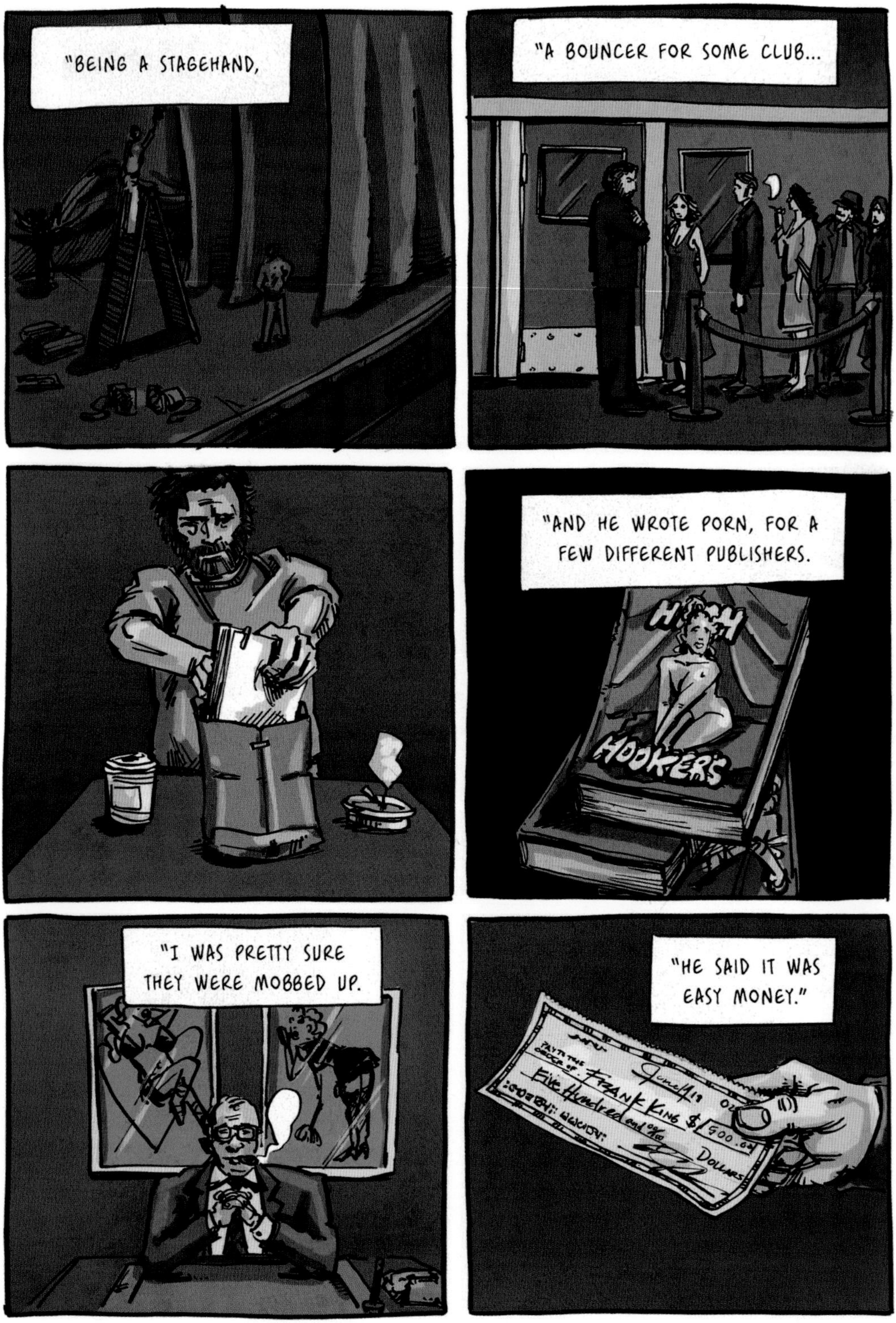
"BEING A STAGEHAND,
"A BOUNCER FOR SOME CLUB...
"AND HE WROTE PORN, FOR A FEW DIFFERENT PUBLISHERS.
HOOKERS
"I WAS PRETTY SURE THEY WERE MOBBED UP.
"HE SAID IT WAS EASY MONEY."
FRANK KING
Five Hundred and 00/100
500.00
DOLLARS

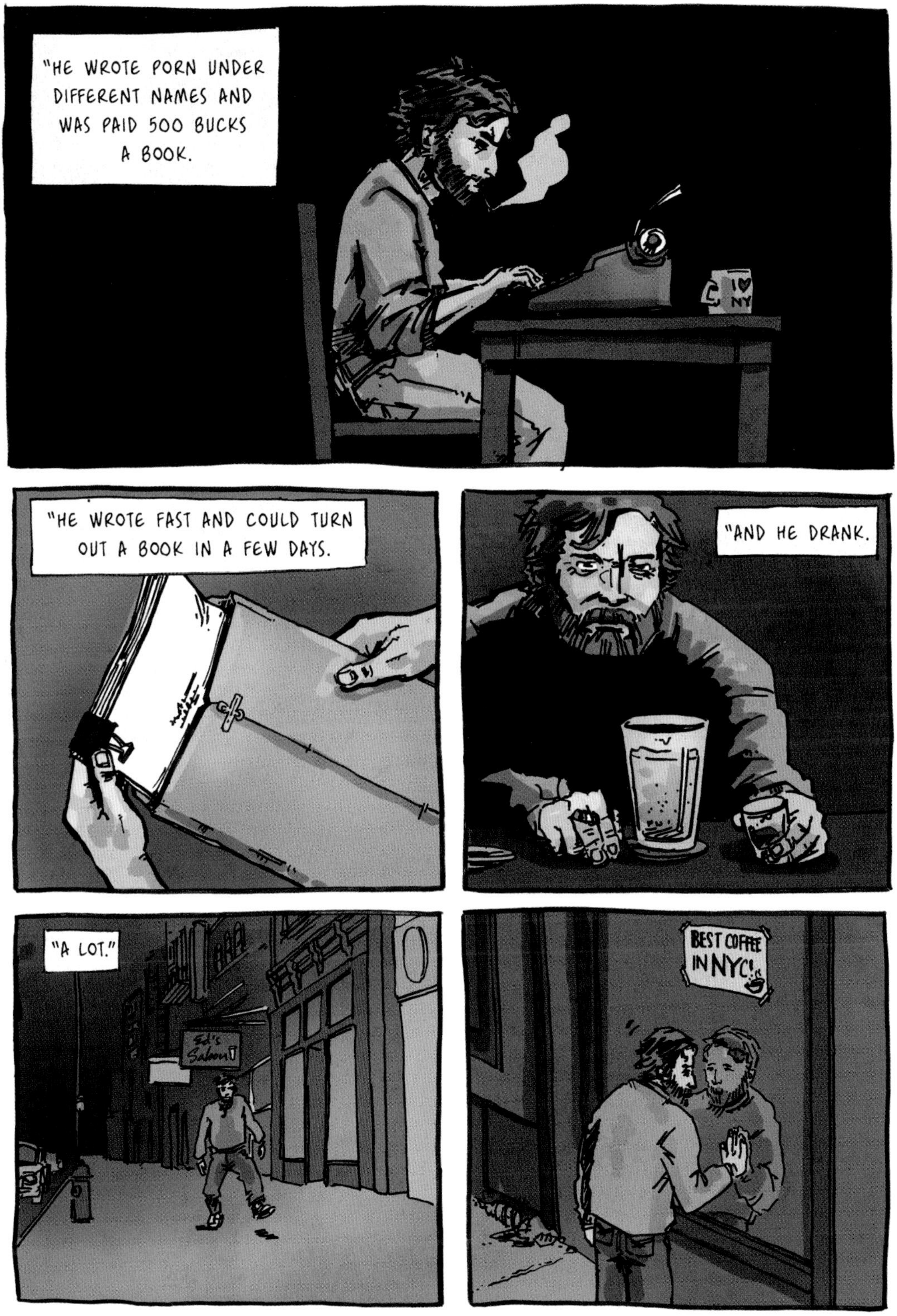
"HE WROTE PORN UNDER DIFFERENT NAMES AND WAS PAID 500 BUCKS A BOOK.
I ♥ NY
"HE WROTE FAST AND COULD TURN OUT A BOOK IN A FEW DAYS.
"AND HE DRANK.
"A LOT."
Ed's Saloon
BEST COFFEE IN NYC!

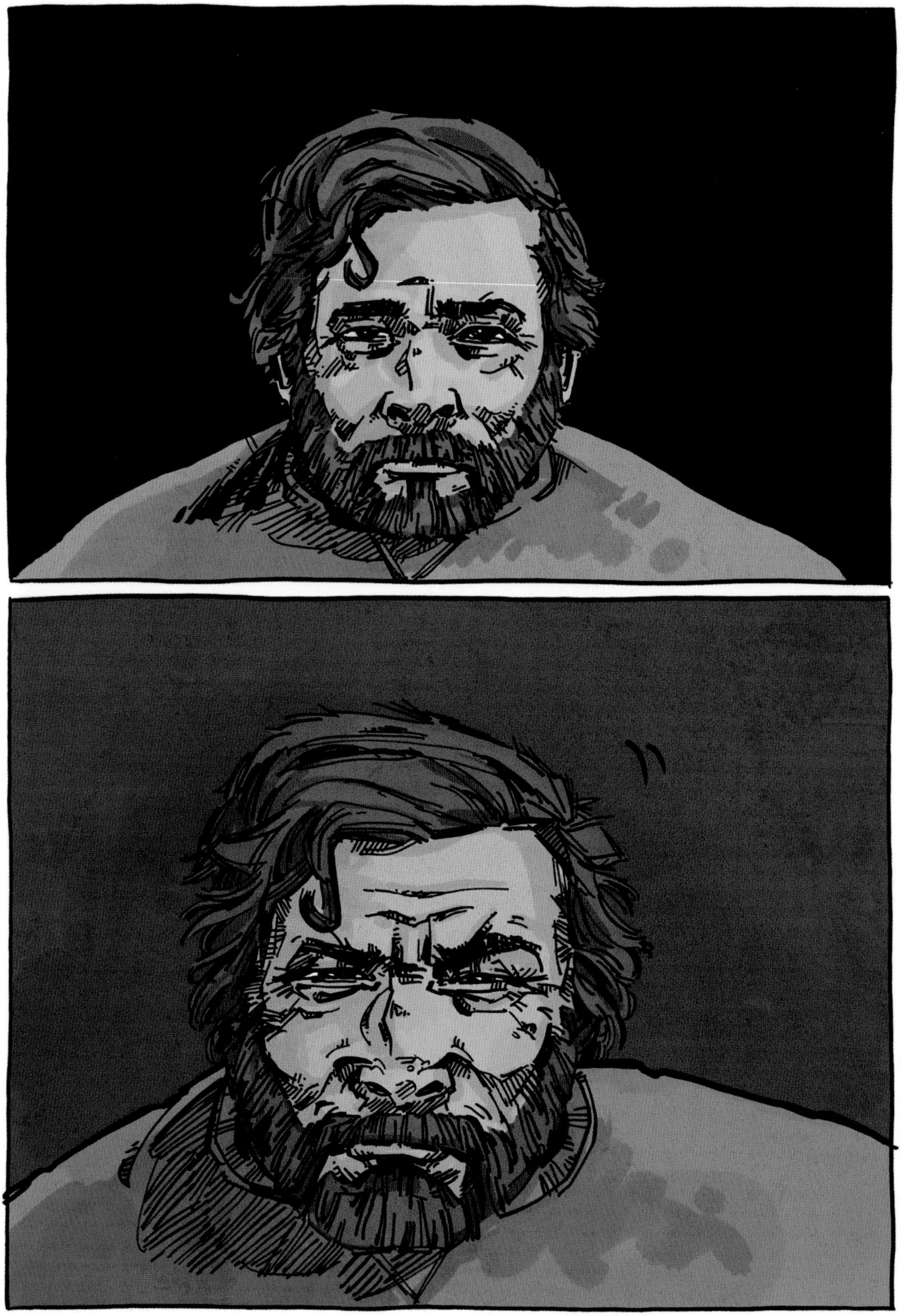

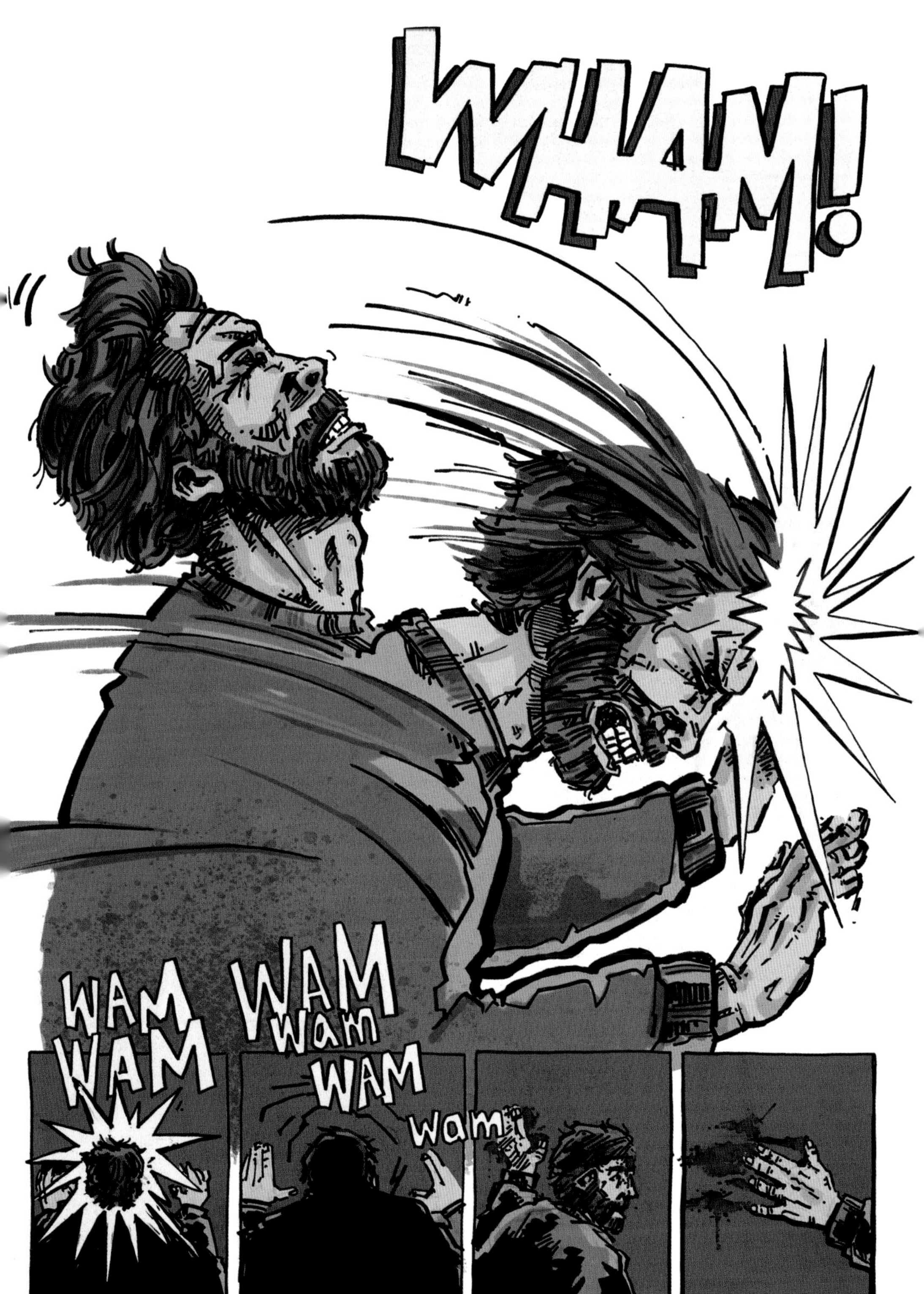
WHAM!
WAM WAM
WAM wam WAM
wam

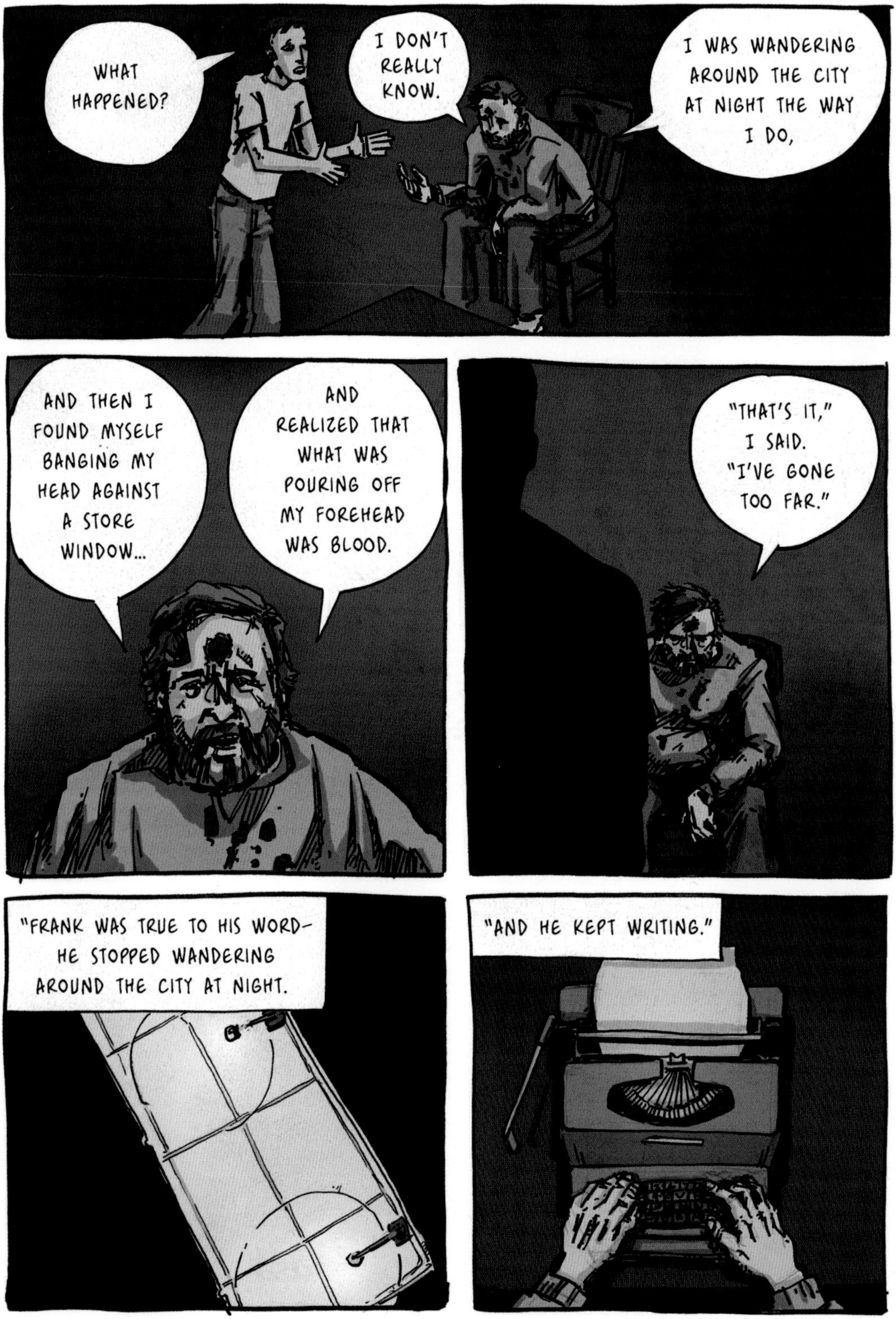
WHAT HAPPENED?
I DON'T REALLY KNOW.
I WAS WANDERING AROUND THE CITY AT NIGHT THE WAY I DO,
AND THEN I FOUND MYSELF BANGING MY HEAD AGAINST A STORE WINDOW...
AND REALIZED THAT WHAT WAS POURING OFF MY FOREHEAD WAS BLOOD.
"THAT'S IT," I SAID. "I'VE GONE TOO FAR."
"FRANK WAS TRUE TO HIS WORD- HE STOPPED WANDERING AROUND THE CITY AT NIGHT.
"AND HE KEPT WRITING."

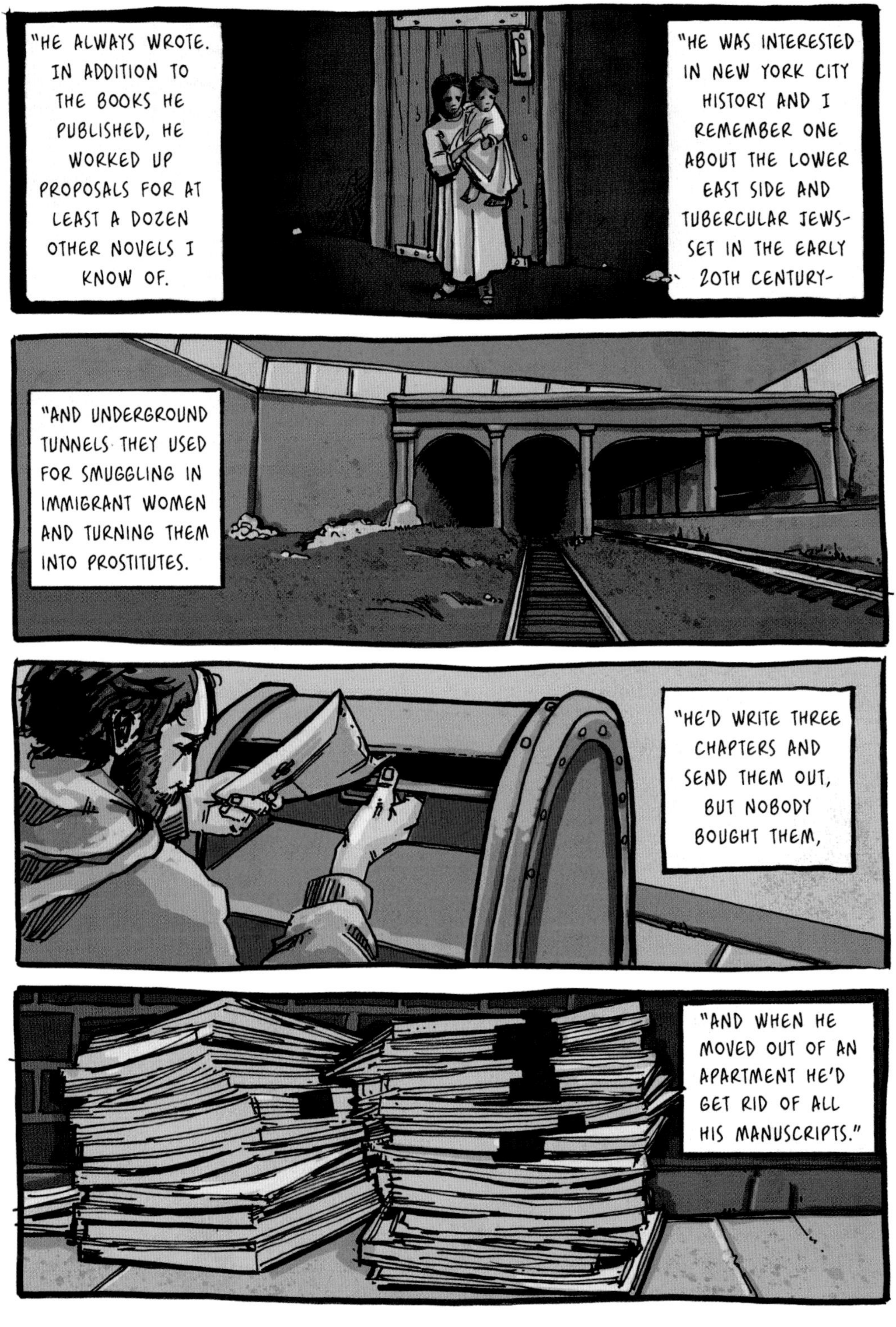
"HE ALWAYS WROTE. IN ADDITION TO THE BOOKS HE PUBLISHED, HE WORKED UP PROPOSALS FOR AT LEAST A DOZEN OTHER NOVELS I KNOW OF.
"HE WAS INTERESTED IN NEW YORK CITY HISTORY AND I REMEMBER ONE ABOUT THE LOWER EAST SIDE AND TUBERCULAR JEWS- SET IN THE EARLY 20TH CENTURY-
"AND UNDERGROUND TUNNELS THEY USED FOR SMUGGLING IN IMMIGRANT WOMEN AND TURNING THEM INTO PROSTITUTES.
"HE'D WRITE THREE CHAPTERS AND SEND THEM OUT, BUT NOBODY BOUGHT THEM,
"AND WHEN HE MOVED OUT OF AN APARTMENT HE'D GET RID OF ALL HIS MANUSCRIPTS."

"HE'D SIT AT HIS DESK AND GO THROUGH BOXES OF LETTERS, READING THEM.

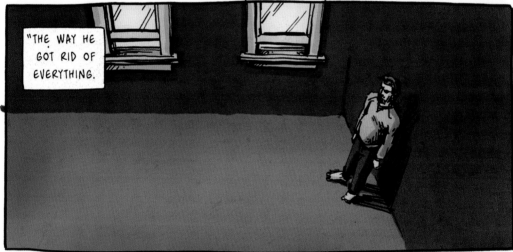

"THE WAY HE GOT RID OF EVERYTHING.

"THROWING AWAY THE LETTERS, AND THEN THE SAME WITH HIS MANUSCRIPTS.

"IT WAS AS IF, I SOMETIMES THINK, FRANK SPENT HIS ENTIRE LIFE PREPARING TO DIE."

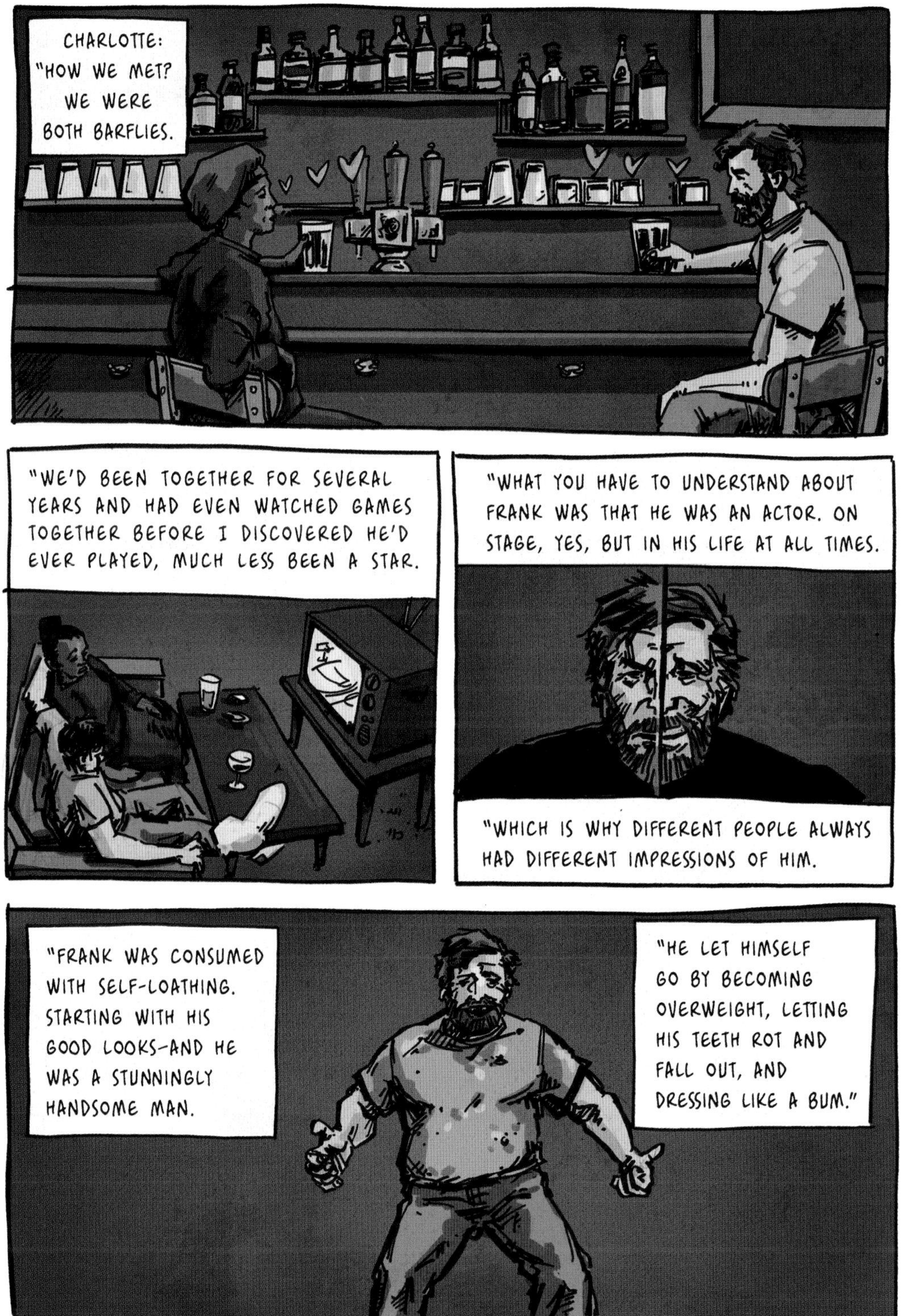
CHARLOTTE: "HOW WE MET? WE WERE BOTH BARFLIES.
"WE'D BEEN TOGETHER FOR SEVERAL YEARS AND HAD EVEN WATCHED GAMES TOGETHER BEFORE I DISCOVERED HE'D EVER PLAYED, MUCH LESS BEEN A STAR.
"WHAT YOU HAVE TO UNDERSTAND ABOUT FRANK WAS THAT HE WAS AN ACTOR. ON STAGE, YES, BUT IN HIS LIFE AT ALL TIMES.
"WHICH IS WHY DIFFERENT PEOPLE ALWAYS HAD DIFFERENT IMPRESSIONS OF HIM.
"FRANK WAS CONSUMED WITH SELF-LOATHING. STARTING WITH HIS GOOD LOOKS–AND HE WAS A STUNNINGLY HANDSOME MAN.
"HE LET HIMSELF GO BY BECOMING OVERWEIGHT, LETTING HIS TEETH ROT AND FALL OUT, AND DRESSING LIKE A BUM."

"HE WAS DETERMINED TO SPEND HIS LIFE ERASING HIMSELF.

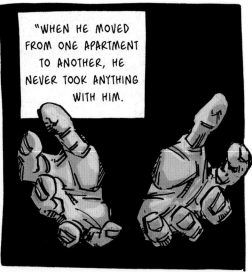

"WHEN HE MOVED FROM ONE APARTMENT TO ANOTHER, HE NEVER TOOK ANYTHING WITH HIM.

"HE DESTROYED EVERYTHING HE COULD ABOUT HIMSELF...

"HIS AWARDS AND MEDALS, AND DOZENS OF UNPUBLISHED NOVELS, PLAYS, POEMS, AND BOOK AND MOVIE PROPOSALS."

STEVE: "I WAS FOUR YEARS OLDER THAN FRANK, AND DESPITE ALL HIS TALENTS, HE WAS A TROUBLED GUY. HE WAS A CHAIN-SMOKER, AND HE LIKED TO DRINK, AND TO GAMBLE.

"FROM THE TIME HE LEFT THE ARMY UNTIL HE DIED–FOR 60 YEARS–HE REFUSED TO SEE A DOCTOR OR A DENTIST. BY THE END OF HIS LIFE, HE'D LOST ALL HIS TEETH.

"I GRADUATED FROM MADISON WHEN I WAS 16, AND WENT TO THE U OF VERMONT. AFTER I SCORED 36 POINTS IN AN INTRAMURAL GAME, THE VARSITY COACH ASKED ME TO BE ON THE FRESHMAN TEAM.

"WHICH I DID...
BUT I TRANSFERRED TO THE UNIVERSITY OF PENNSYLVANIA THE NEXT YEAR, AND HAVING TO WORK MY WAY THROUGH, I DIDN'T HAVE TIME FOR BASKETBALL...

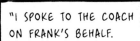

"I SPOKE TO THE COACH ON FRANK'S BEHALF.

I TOLD COACH DALMAR I COULDN'T COME OUT FOR THE TEAM, BUT THAT MY BROTHER FRANK WAS FIRST TEAM ALL-CITY...

"AND THOUGH HE HAD LOTS OF OFFERS I'D HAVE LIKED TO SEE HIM THERE AT PENN...

UNDERSIZED BUT I INSISTED HE HAD TO SEE HIM PLAY IN PERSON."

47

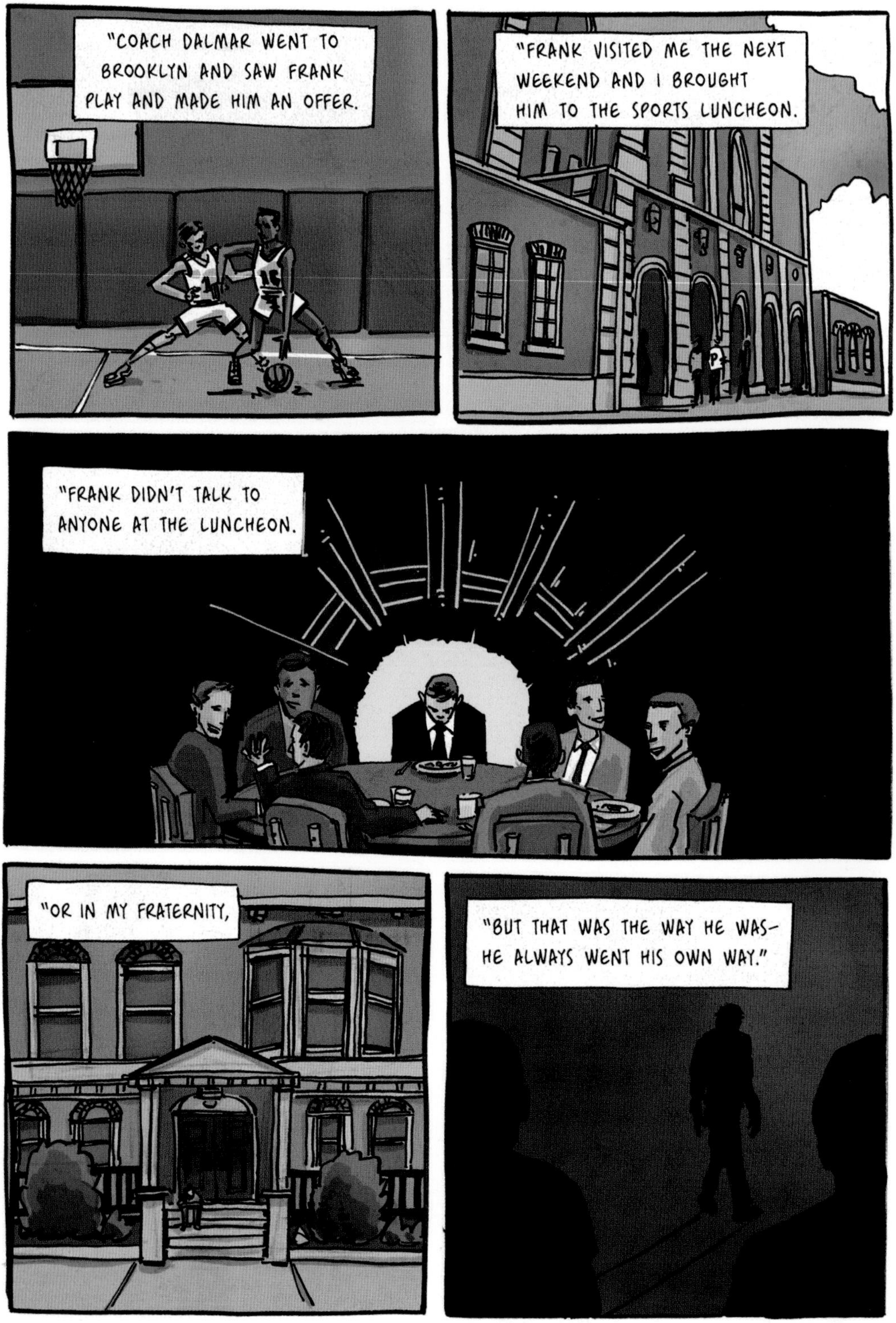
"COACH DALMAR WENT TO BROOKLYN AND SAW FRANK PLAY AND MADE HIM AN OFFER.
"FRANK VISITED ME THE NEXT WEEKEND AND I BROUGHT HIM TO THE SPORTS LUNCHEON.
"FRANK DIDN'T TALK TO ANYONE AT THE LUNCHEON.
"OR IN MY FRATERNITY,
"BUT THAT WAS THE WAY HE WAS–HE ALWAYS WENT HIS OWN WAY."

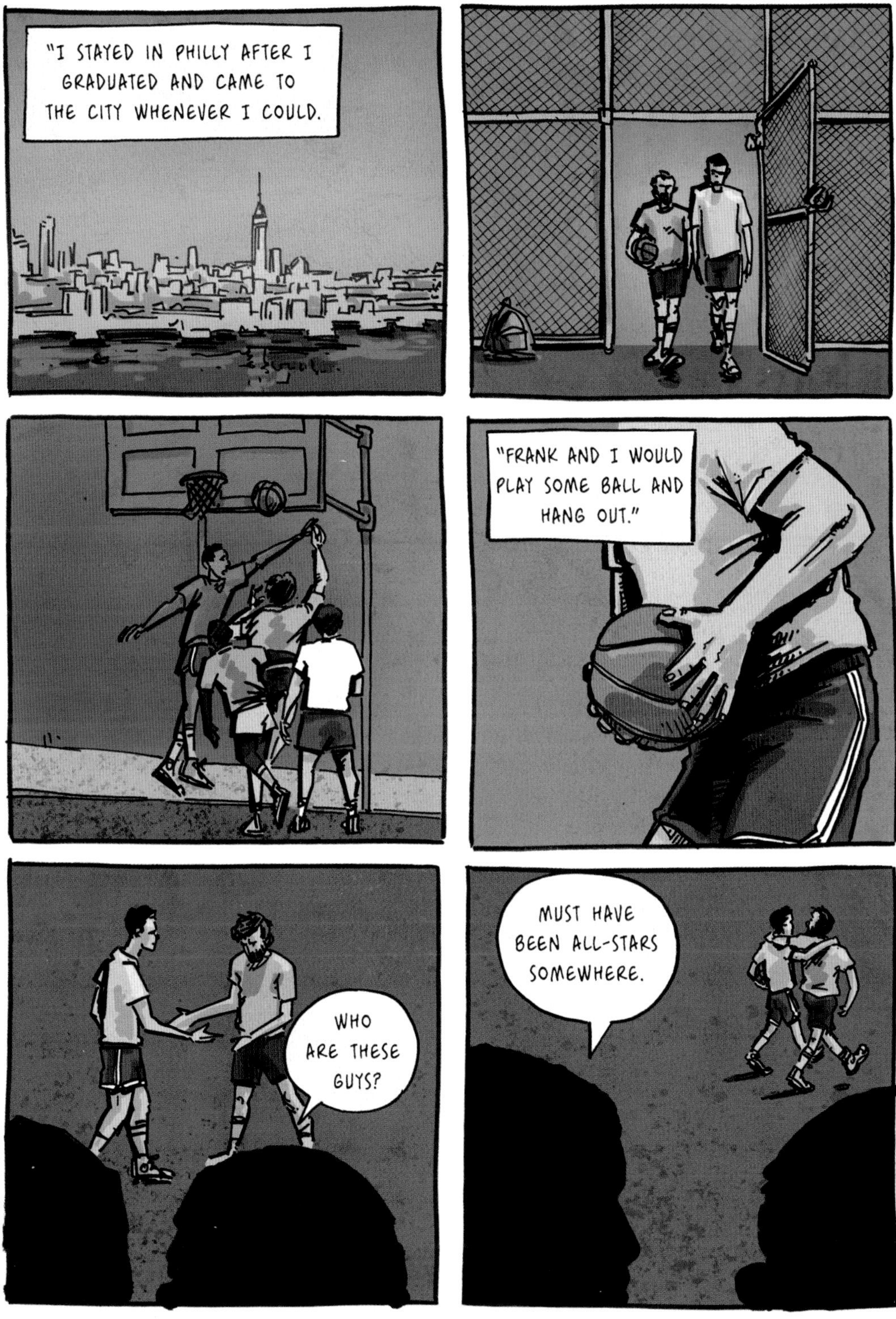
"I STAYED IN PHILLY AFTER I GRADUATED AND CAME TO THE CITY WHENEVER I COULD.
"FRANK AND I WOULD PLAY SOME BALL AND HANG OUT."
WHO ARE THESE GUYS?
MUST HAVE BEEN ALL-STARS SOMEWHERE.

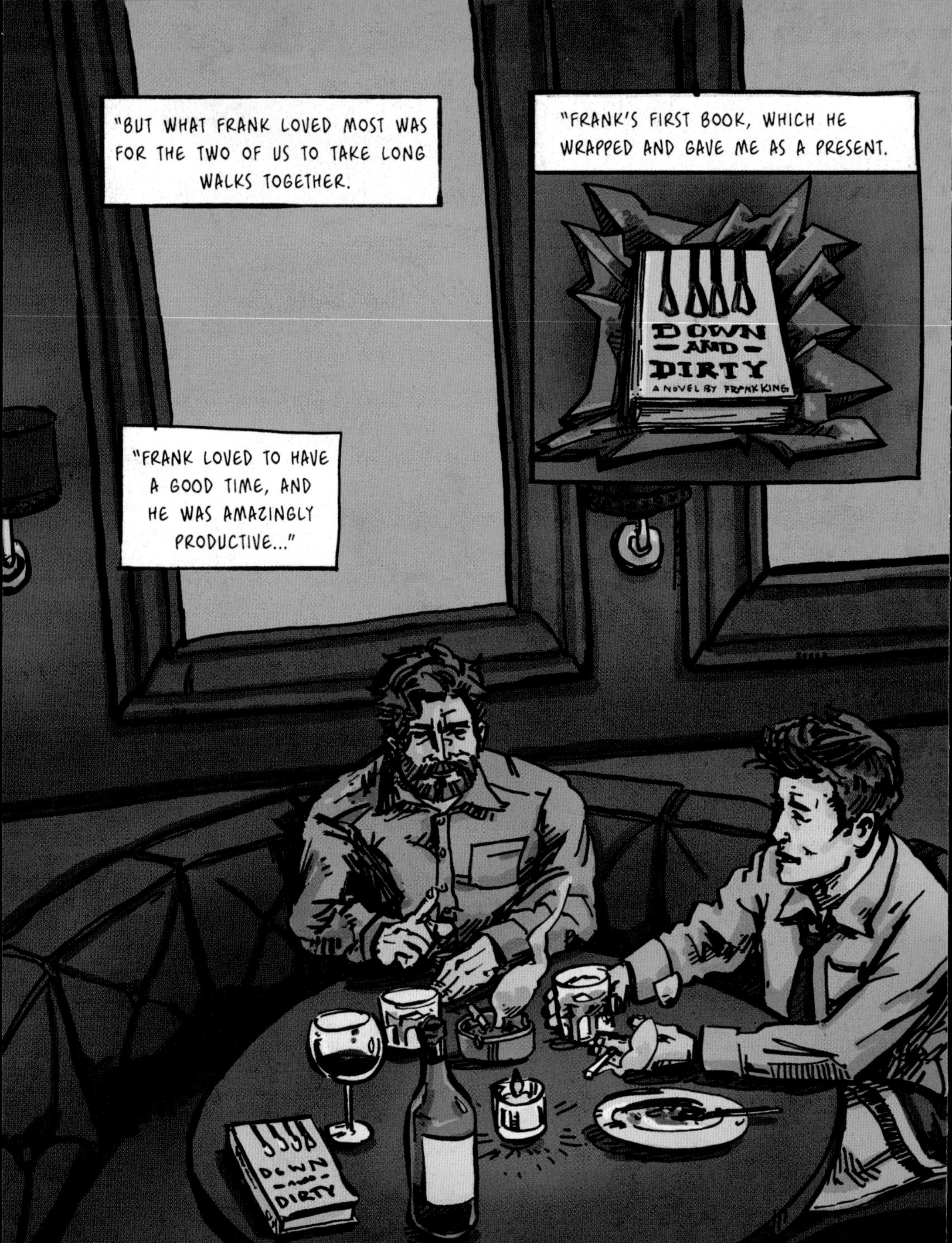
"BUT WHAT FRANK LOVED MOST WAS FOR THE TWO OF US TO TAKE LONG WALKS TOGETHER.
"FRANK'S FIRST BOOK, WHICH HE WRAPPED AND GAVE ME AS A PRESENT.
DOWN AND DIRTY
A NOVEL BY FRANK KING
"FRANK LOVED TO HAVE A GOOD TIME, AND HE WAS AMAZINGLY PRODUCTIVE..."
DOWN AND DIRTY

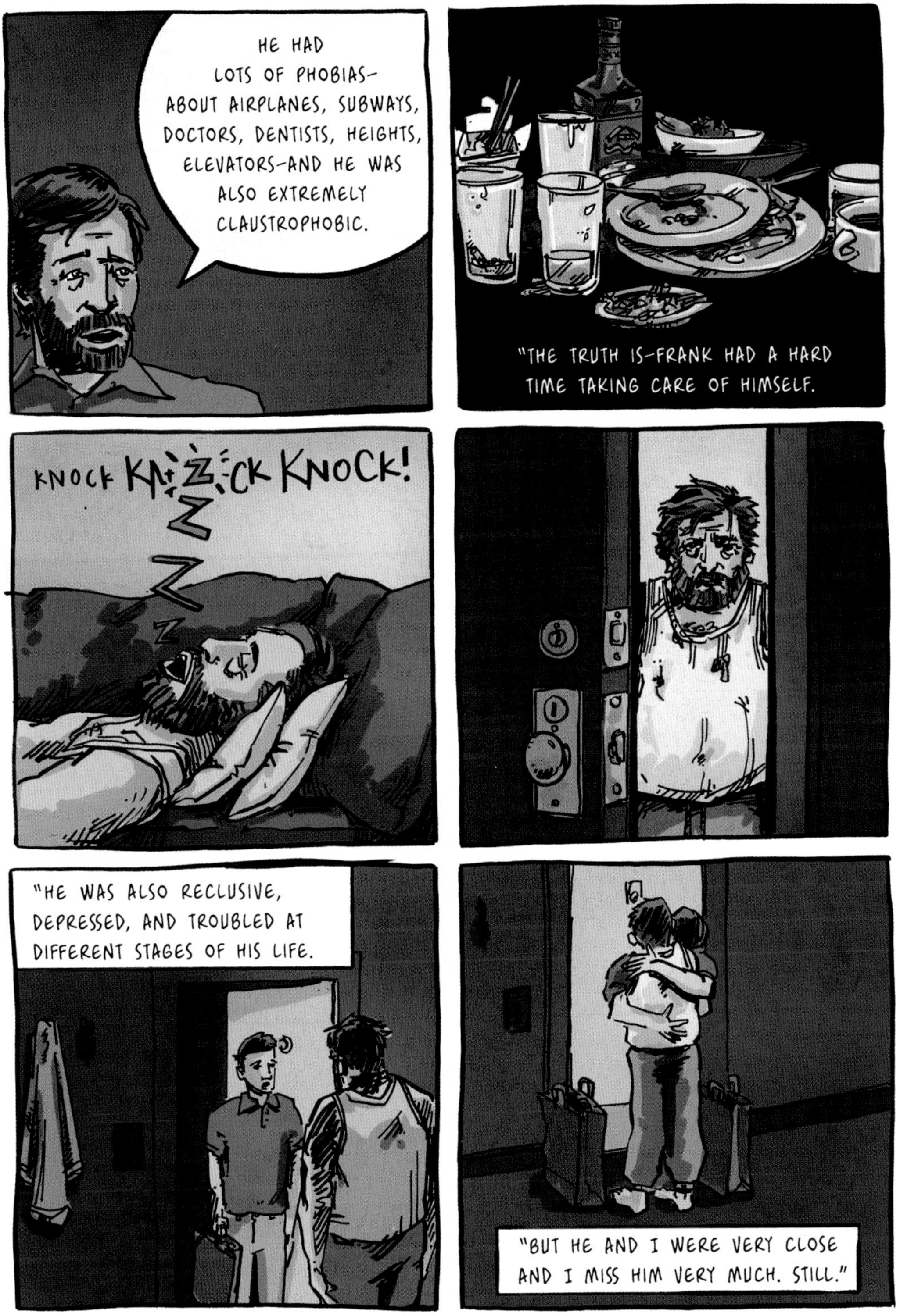
HE HAD LOTS OF PHOBIAS—ABOUT AIRPLANES, SUBWAYS, DOCTORS, DENTISTS, HEIGHTS, ELEVATORS—AND HE WAS ALSO EXTREMELY CLAUSTROPHOBIC.
"THE TRUTH IS—FRANK HAD A HARD TIME TAKING CARE OF HIMSELF.
KNOCK
KNOCK!
Z
Z
Z
"HE WAS ALSO RECLUSIVE, DEPRESSED, AND TROUBLED AT DIFFERENT STAGES OF HIS LIFE.
"BUT HE AND I WERE VERY CLOSE AND I MISS HIM VERY MUCH. STILL."

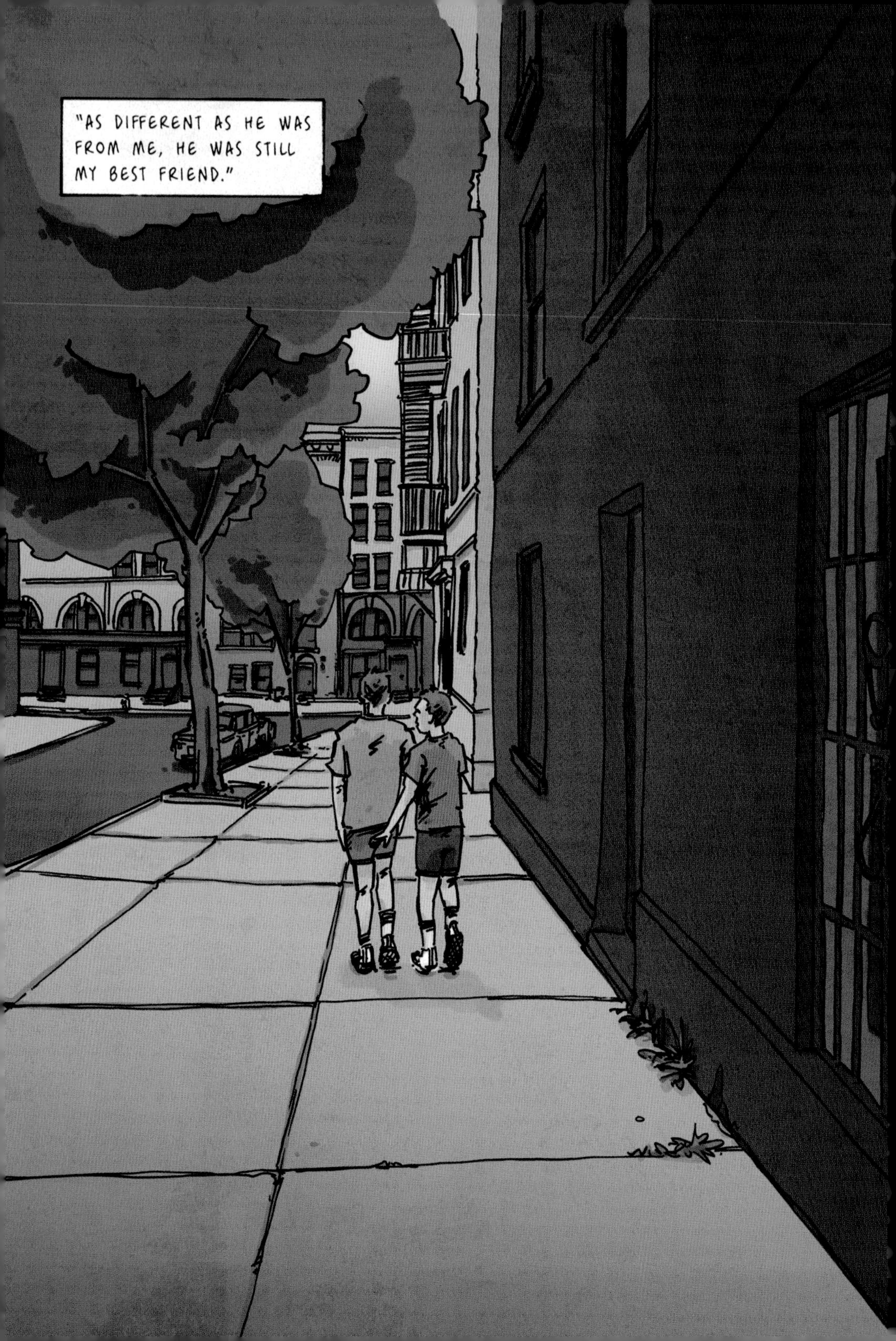
"AS DIFFERENT AS HE WAS FROM ME, HE WAS STILL MY BEST FRIEND."

1953 NYC
HIGH SCHOOL
ALL-STAR GAME

BROOKLYN & QUEENS
VS.
MANHATTAN, BRONX
& STATEN ISLAND

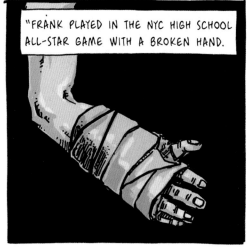

"FRANK PLAYED IN THE NYC HIGH SCHOOL ALL-STAR GAME WITH A BROKEN HAND.

"MOST PLAYERS WOULDN'T HAVE EVEN PLAYED, BUT WITH HIS DRIBBLING SKILLS, HE DOMINATED!

"AND THERE WERE A LOT OF COLLEGE COACHES THERE TAKING NOTICE..."

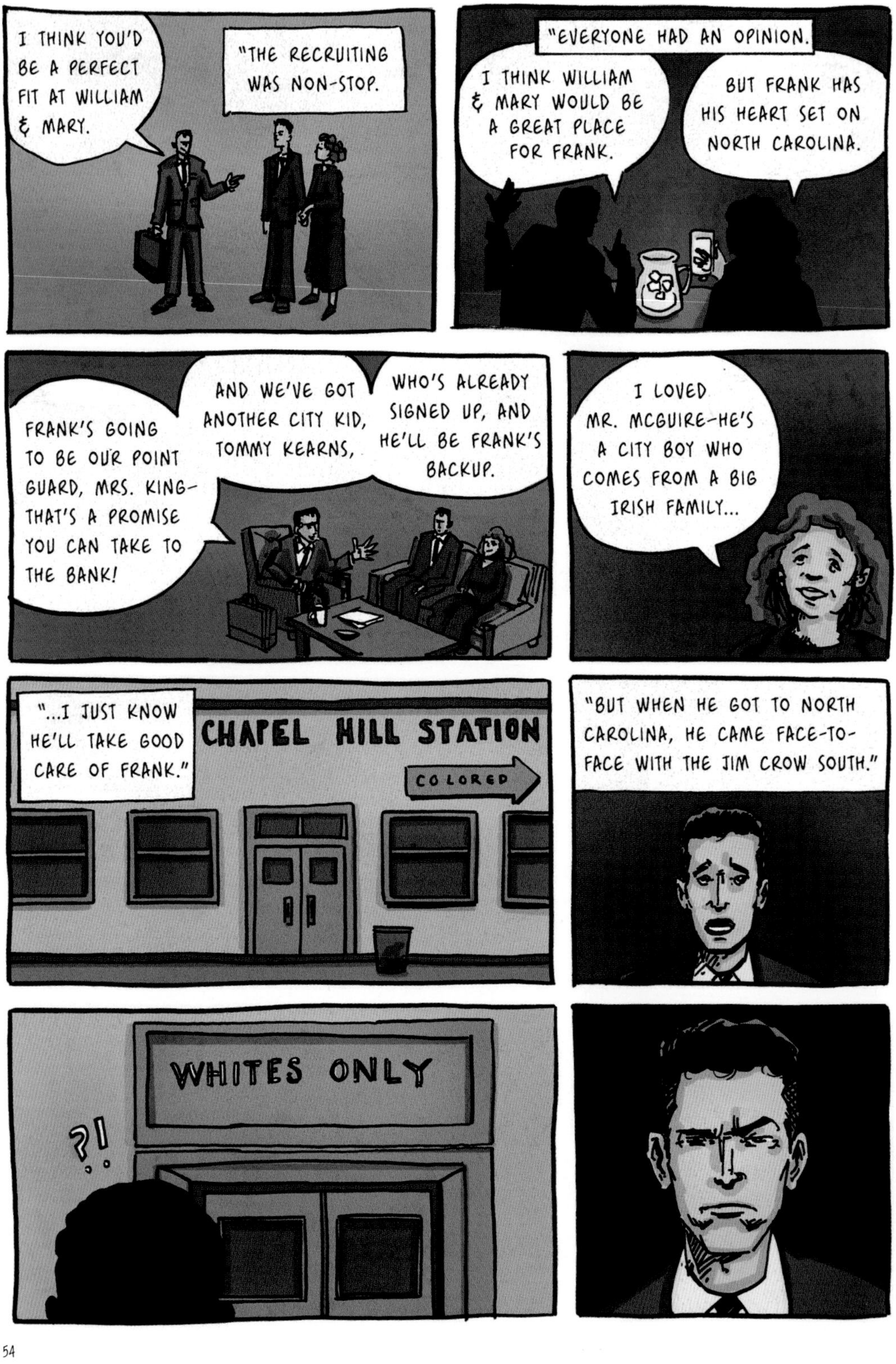
"THE RECRUITING WAS NON-STOP.
I THINK YOU'D BE A PERFECT FIT AT WILLIAM & MARY.
"EVERYONE HAD AN OPINION.
I THINK WILLIAM & MARY WOULD BE A GREAT PLACE FOR FRANK.
BUT FRANK HAS HIS HEART SET ON NORTH CAROLINA.
FRANK'S GOING TO BE OUR POINT GUARD, MRS. KING-THAT'S A PROMISE YOU CAN TAKE TO THE BANK!
AND WE'VE GOT ANOTHER CITY KID, TOMMY KEARNS,
WHO'S ALREADY SIGNED UP, AND HE'LL BE FRANK'S BACKUP.
I LOVED MR. MCGUIRE-HE'S A CITY BOY WHO COMES FROM A BIG IRISH FAMILY...
"...I JUST KNOW HE'LL TAKE GOOD CARE OF FRANK."
CHAPEL HILL STATION
COLORED
"BUT WHEN HE GOT TO NORTH CAROLINA, HE CAME FACE-TO-FACE WITH THE JIM CROW SOUTH."
WHITES ONLY
?!

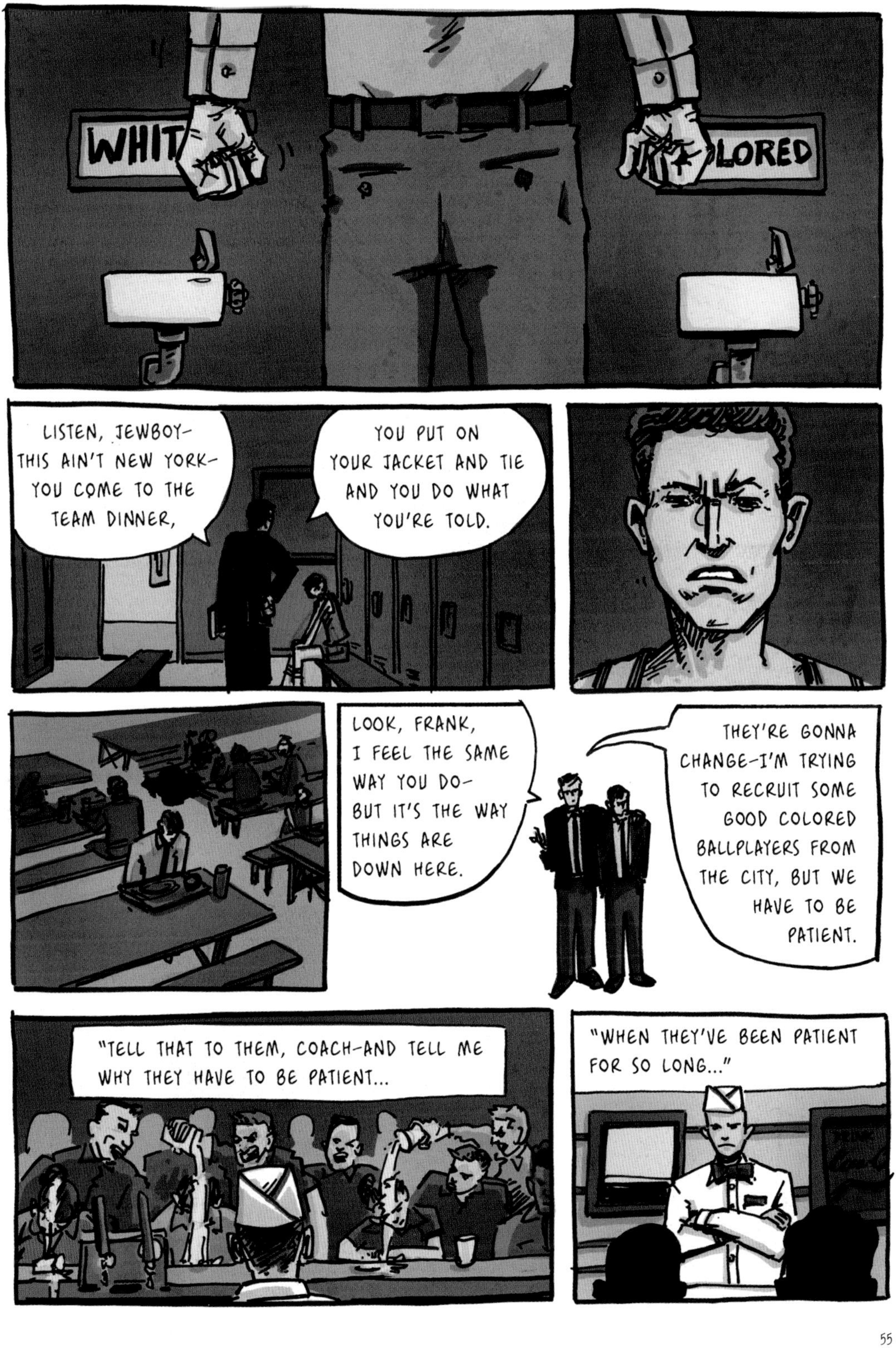
WHIT
LORED
LISTEN, JEWBOY-THIS AIN'T NEW YORK-YOU COME TO THE TEAM DINNER,
YOU PUT ON YOUR JACKET AND TIE AND YOU DO WHAT YOU'RE TOLD.
LOOK, FRANK, I FEEL THE SAME WAY YOU DO-BUT IT'S THE WAY THINGS ARE DOWN HERE.
THEY'RE GONNA CHANGE-I'M TRYING TO RECRUIT SOME GOOD COLORED BALLPLAYERS FROM THE CITY, BUT WE HAVE TO BE PATIENT.
"TELL THAT TO THEM, COACH-AND TELL ME WHY THEY HAVE TO BE PATIENT...
"WHEN THEY'VE BEEN PATIENT FOR SO LONG..."

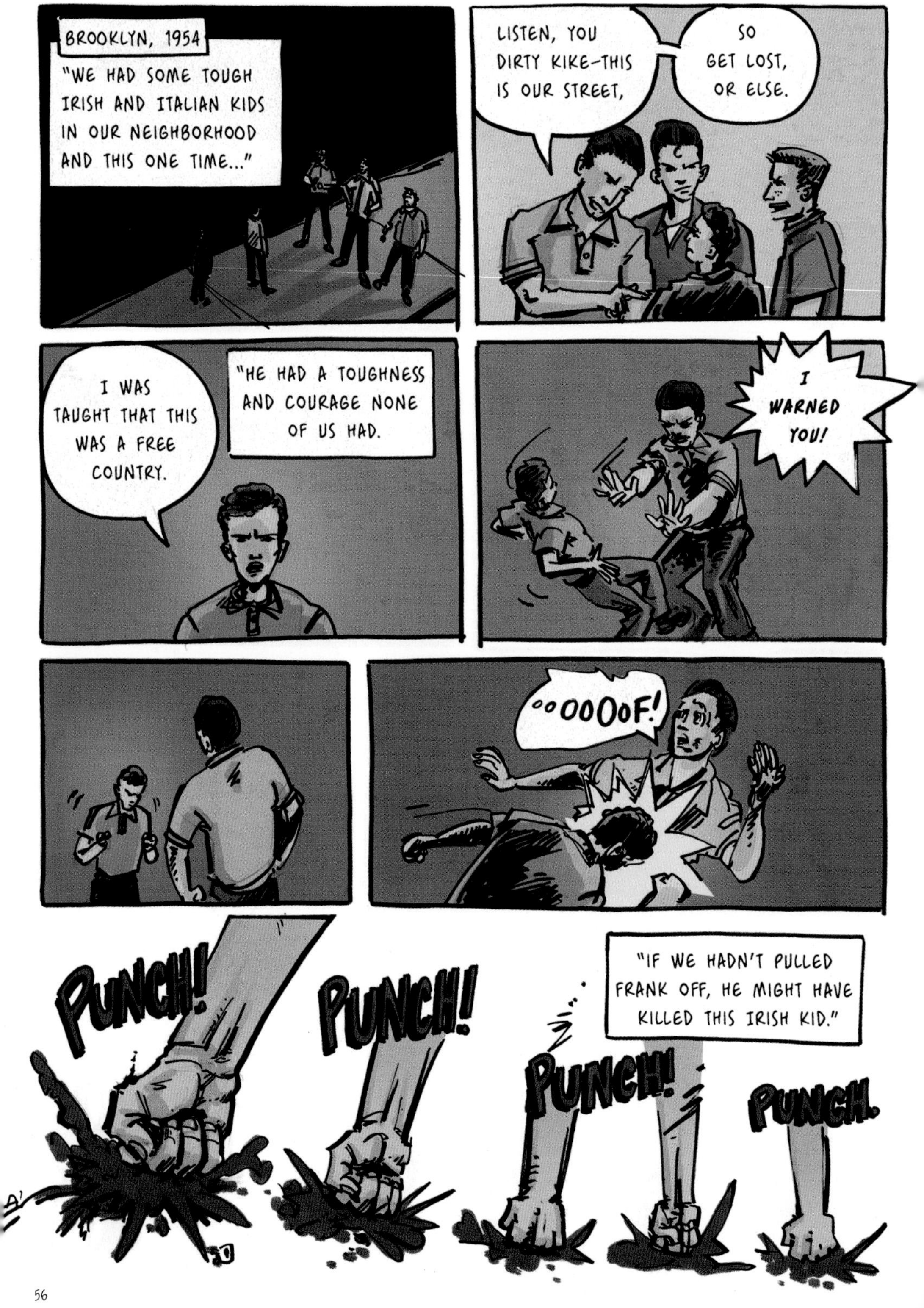

BROOKLYN, 1954
"WE HAD SOME TOUGH IRISH AND ITALIAN KIDS IN OUR NEIGHBORHOOD AND THIS ONE TIME..."
LISTEN, YOU DIRTY KIKE–THIS IS OUR STREET,
SO GET LOST, OR ELSE.
I WAS TAUGHT THAT THIS WAS A FREE COUNTRY.
"HE HAD A TOUGHNESS AND COURAGE NONE OF US HAD.
I WARNED YOU!
ooOOOoF!
PUNCH!
PUNCH!
"IF WE HADN'T PULLED FRANK OFF, HE MIGHT HAVE KILLED THIS IRISH KID."
PUNCH!
PUNCH.

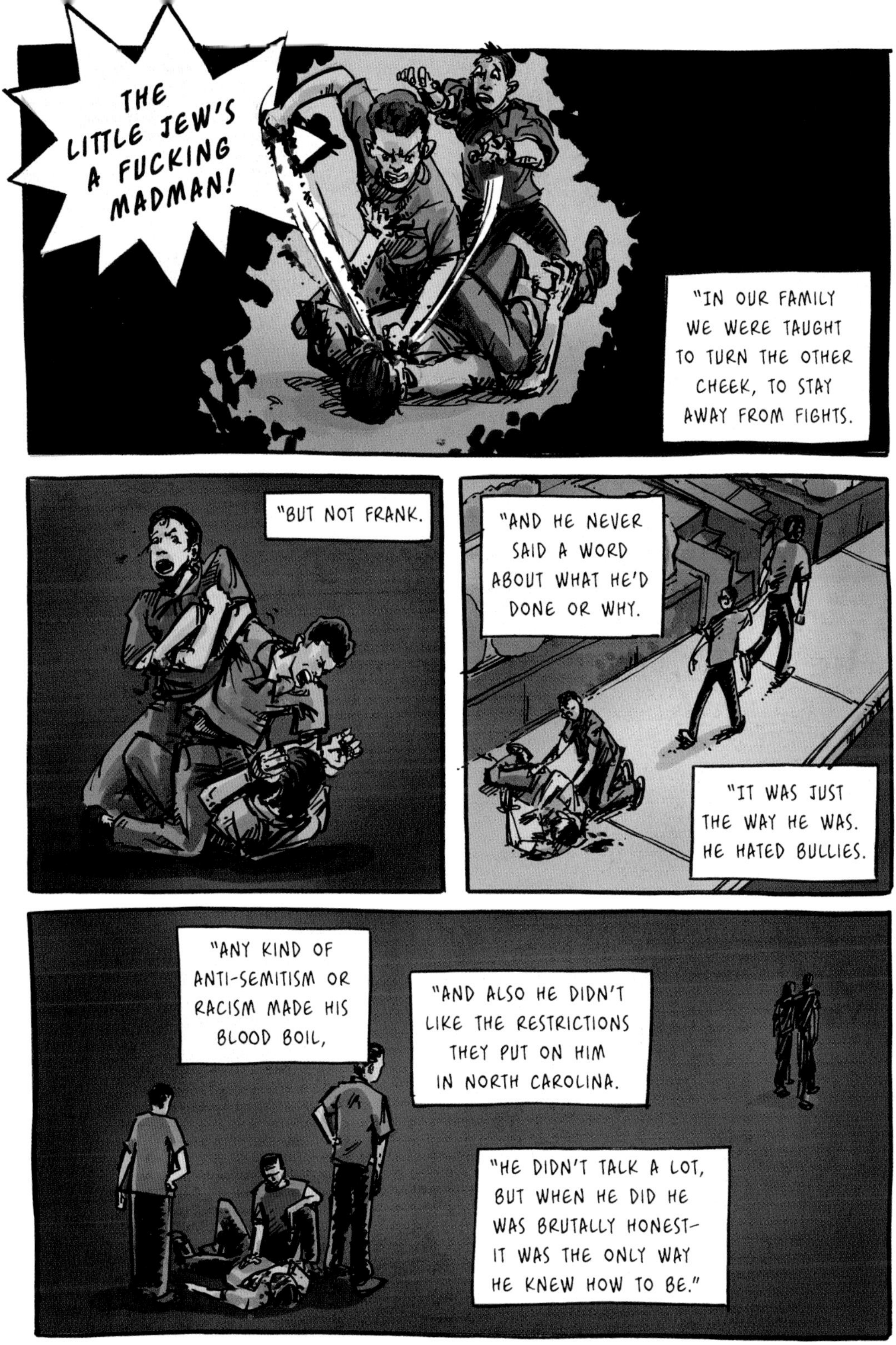
THE LITTLE JEW'S A FUCKING MADMAN!
"IN OUR FAMILY WE WERE TAUGHT TO TURN THE OTHER CHEEK, TO STAY AWAY FROM FIGHTS.
"BUT NOT FRANK.
"AND HE NEVER SAID A WORD ABOUT WHAT HE'D DONE OR WHY.
"IT WAS JUST THE WAY HE WAS. HE HATED BULLIES.
"ANY KIND OF ANTI-SEMITISM OR RACISM MADE HIS BLOOD BOIL,
"AND ALSO HE DIDN'T LIKE THE RESTRICTIONS THEY PUT ON HIM IN NORTH CAROLINA.
"HE DIDN'T TALK A LOT, BUT WHEN HE DID HE WAS BRUTALLY HONEST- IT WAS THE ONLY WAY HE KNEW HOW TO BE."

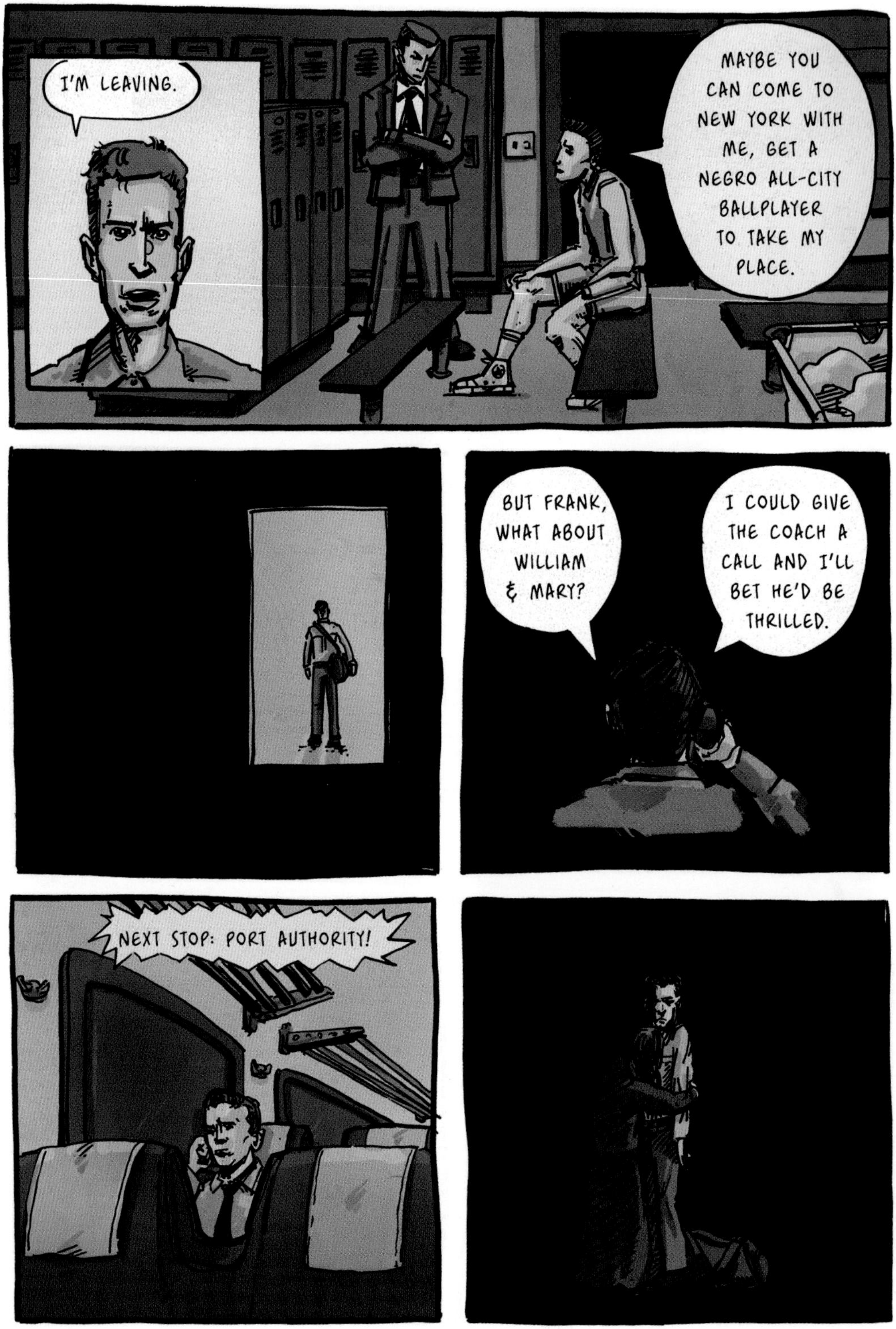
I'M LEAVING.
MAYBE YOU CAN COME TO NEW YORK WITH ME, GET A NEGRO ALL-CITY BALLPLAYER TO TAKE MY PLACE.
BUT FRANK, WHAT ABOUT WILLIAM & MARY?
I COULD GIVE THE COACH A CALL AND I'LL BET HE'D BE THRILLED.
NEXT STOP: PORT AUTHORITY!

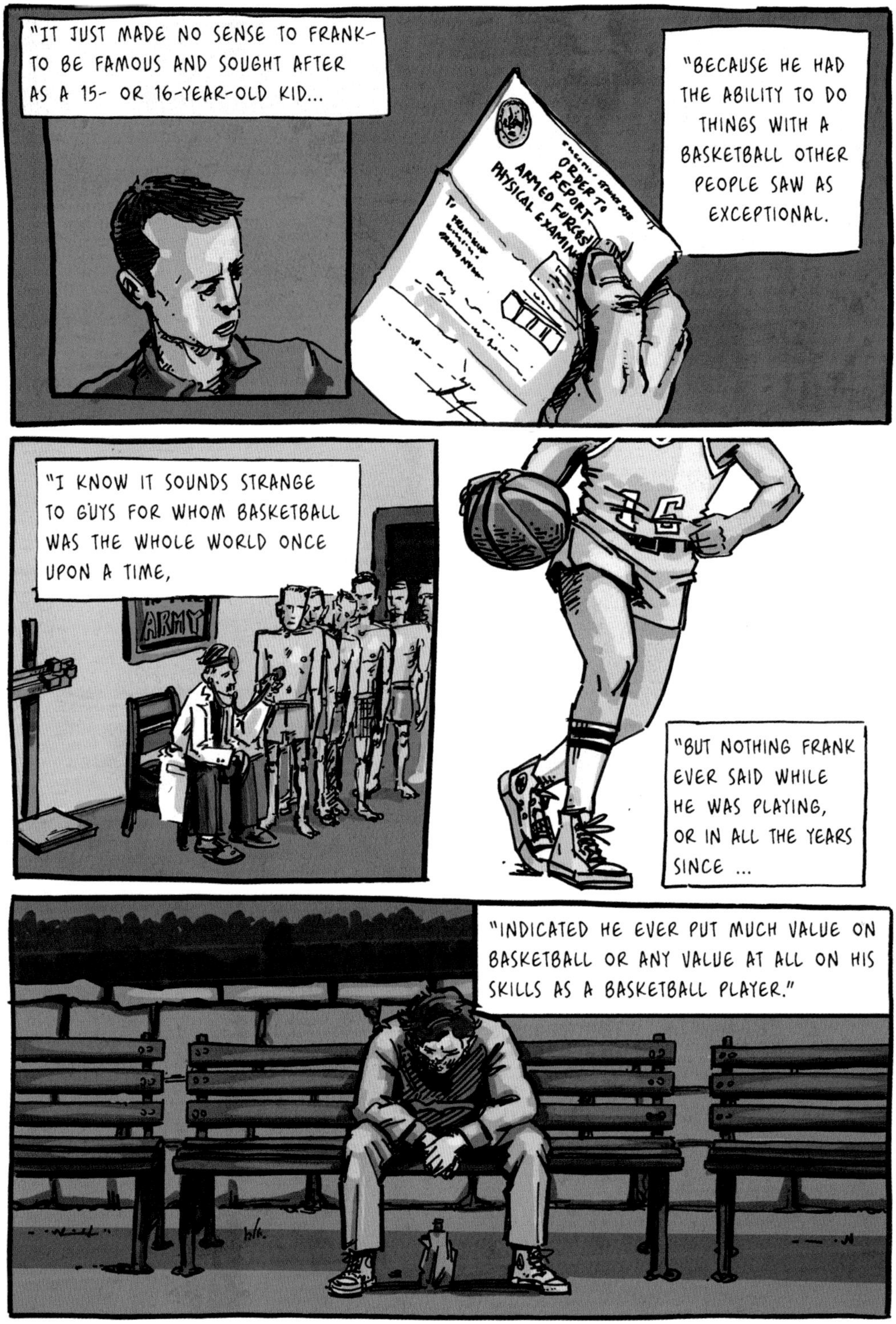
"IT JUST MADE NO SENSE TO FRANK-TO BE FAMOUS AND SOUGHT AFTER AS A 15- OR 16-YEAR-OLD KID...
ORDER TO REPORT
ARMED FORCES
"BECAUSE HE HAD THE ABILITY TO DO THINGS WITH A BASKETBALL OTHER PEOPLE SAW AS EXCEPTIONAL.
"I KNOW IT SOUNDS STRANGE TO GUYS FOR WHOM BASKETBALL WAS THE WHOLE WORLD ONCE UPON A TIME,
ARMY
16
"BUT NOTHING FRANK EVER SAID WHILE HE WAS PLAYING, OR IN ALL THE YEARS SINCE ...
"INDICATED HE EVER PUT MUCH VALUE ON BASKETBALL OR ANY VALUE AT ALL ON HIS SKILLS AS A BASKETBALL PLAYER."

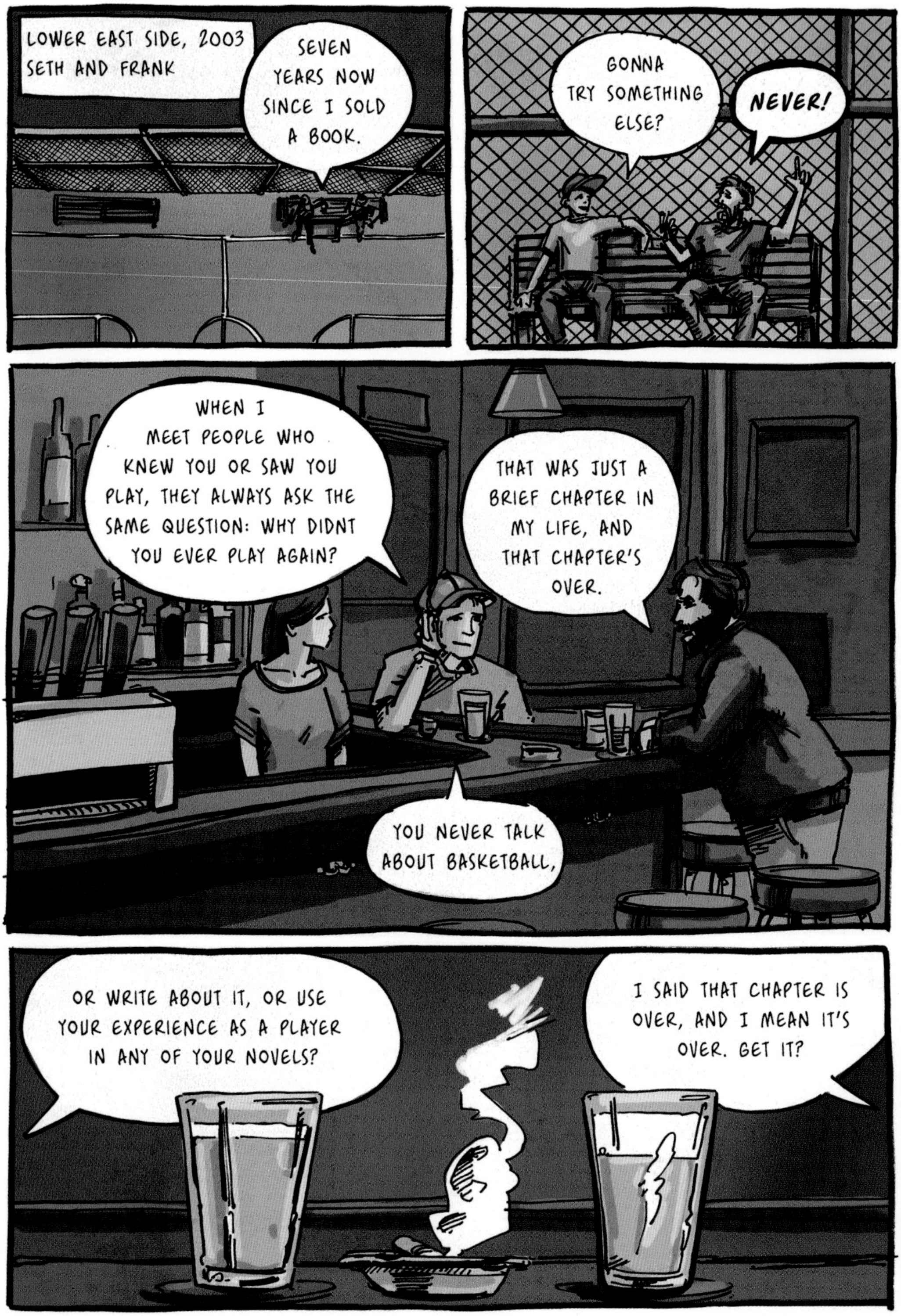
LOWER EAST SIDE, 2003
SETH AND FRANK
SEVEN YEARS NOW SINCE I SOLD A BOOK.
GONNA TRY SOMETHING ELSE?
NEVER!
WHEN I MEET PEOPLE WHO KNEW YOU OR SAW YOU PLAY, THEY ALWAYS ASK THE SAME QUESTION: WHY DIDNT YOU EVER PLAY AGAIN?
THAT WAS JUST A BRIEF CHAPTER IN MY LIFE, AND THAT CHAPTER'S OVER.
YOU NEVER TALK ABOUT BASKETBALL,
OR WRITE ABOUT IT, OR USE YOUR EXPERIENCE AS A PLAYER IN ANY OF YOUR NOVELS?
I SAID THAT CHAPTER IS OVER, AND I MEAN IT'S OVER. GET IT?

"I AGREE WITH MY FATHER THAT FRANK'S GIFTS AS AN ATHLETE...

"AND HIS EARLY FAME...SEEM TO HAVE CARRIED A CURSE WITH THEM.

"IT WAS AS IF, BY BEING A STAR, UNCLE FRANK FELT HE WAS FULFILLING OTHER PEOPLE'S DREAMS AND NOT HIS OWN,

"AND THAT BY DROPPING OUT OF COLLEGE, HE'D LET EVERYBODY DOWN.

LIQUORS

WE'RE GOING TO THE BANK,

WHERE SETH IS GOING TO TAKE CARE OF HIS ALCOHOLIC UNCLE.

"I WAS SO HAPPY WHEN HE AGREED TO MAKE A FILM WITH ME... ABOUT HIM!"

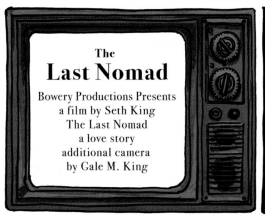

The
Last Nomad
Bowery Productions Presents
a film by Seth King
The Last Nomad
a love story
additional camera
by Gale M. King

FRANK: THIS IS A LETTER MY MOTHER SENT.

"MY SON FRANK HAS HAD NINE LIVES, BUT HE DOESN'T NEED ANOTHER ONE. HE HAS NOTHING TO DO WITH ANYONE ANYMORE.

HIS BLOOD PRESSURE IS A HUNDRED AND NINETY-SIX."

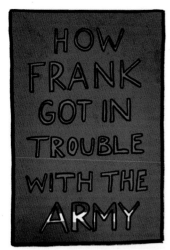

HOW FRANK GOT IN TROUBLE WITH THE ARMY

FRANK'S MOTHER: "HE SPENT OVER A YEAR IN DISCIPLINARY BARRACKS...

OOF!

"FOR ASSAULTING AN MP WITH HIS OWN RIFLE."

"HE WORKS AND SLEEPS AND GOES FROM ONE DAY TO THE NEXT.

"HE SEES NO VISITORS. THIS IS CRUEL AND UNUSUAL PUNISHMENT. AND HE DOESN'T SEE MY LETTERS."

FRANK: "MY HANDS WERE IN INCREDIBLY HOT WATER EVERY DAY ALL DAY FOR A YEAR...

"THEY WERE SCORCHED AND THERE WAS NO RELIEF.

"BUT I FEEL PROUD ABOUT WHAT I DID, AND I AM WITHOUT RANCOR TOWARD THE ARMY."

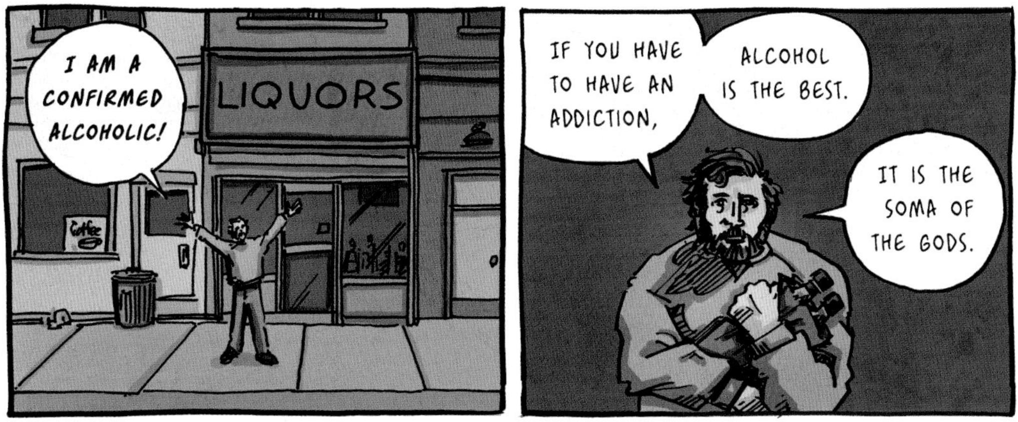
I AM A CONFIRMED ALCOHOLIC!
LIQUORS
IF YOU HAVE TO HAVE AN ADDICTION,
ALCOHOL IS THE BEST.
IT IS THE SOMA OF THE GODS.

HERE'S A LETTER FROM MY SHRINK:

"...AS TO THE SCHIZOPHRENIC PROCESS, WE MIGHT TRACE THE ORIGINS OF FRANK'S CONDITION TO HIS CHILDHOOD...

AND TO HIS GREAT PREOCCUPATION WITH BEING KILLED... AND TO PHILOSOPHICAL DIFFERENCES HE AND I HAD..."

HE DIDN'T KNOW WHAT THE FUCK HE WAS TALKING ABOUT.

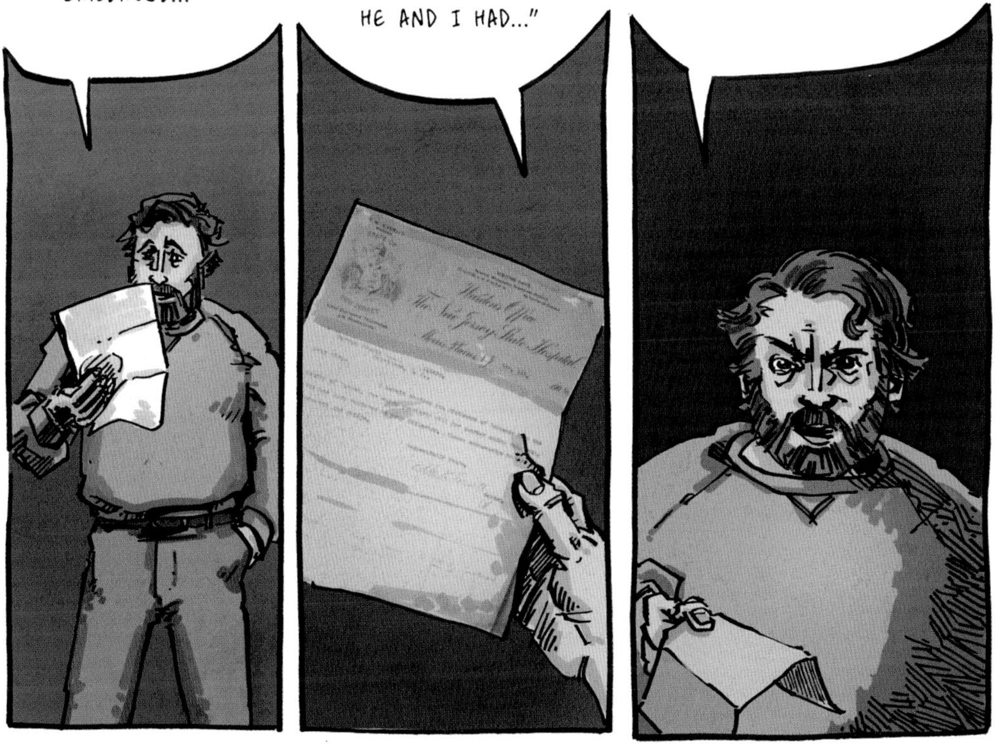

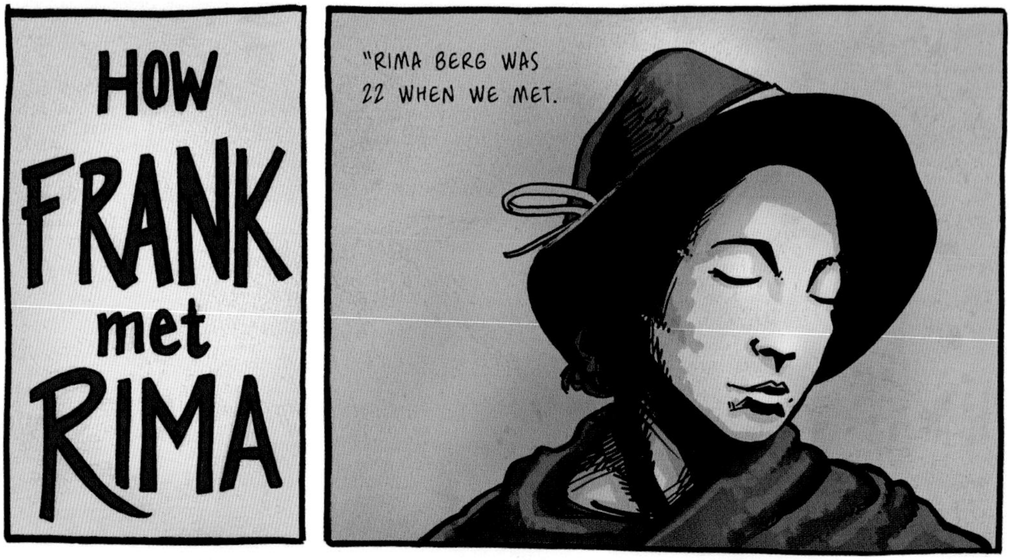
HOW FRANK met RIMA
"RIMA BERG WAS 22 WHEN WE MET.

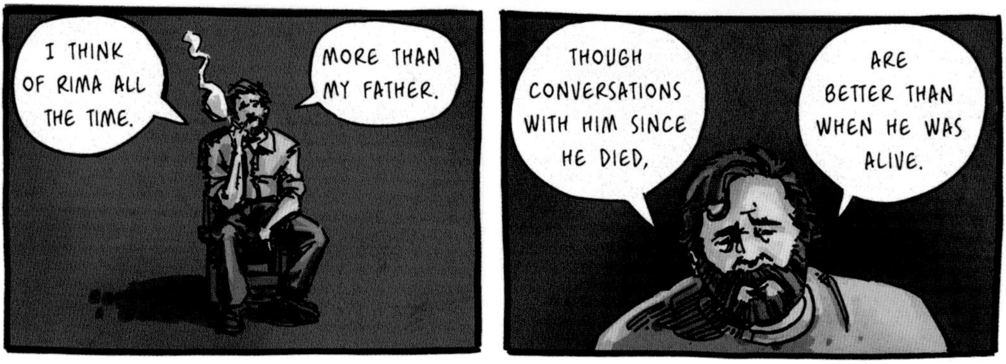
I THINK OF RIMA ALL THE TIME.
MORE THAN MY FATHER.
THOUGH CONVERSATIONS WITH HIM SINCE HE DIED,
ARE BETTER THAN WHEN HE WAS ALIVE.

"THE FIRST TIME I WAS INTRODUCED TO RIMA WAS AT AN AUNT'S HOUSE. SHE WAS ABSOLUTELY BEAUTIFUL! SHE HAD GIVEN UP JOSÉ LIMÓN BY THEN...

"I FELL VIOLENTLY IN LOVE WITH HER...I MADE HER ALL KINDS OF WEIRD PROMISES."

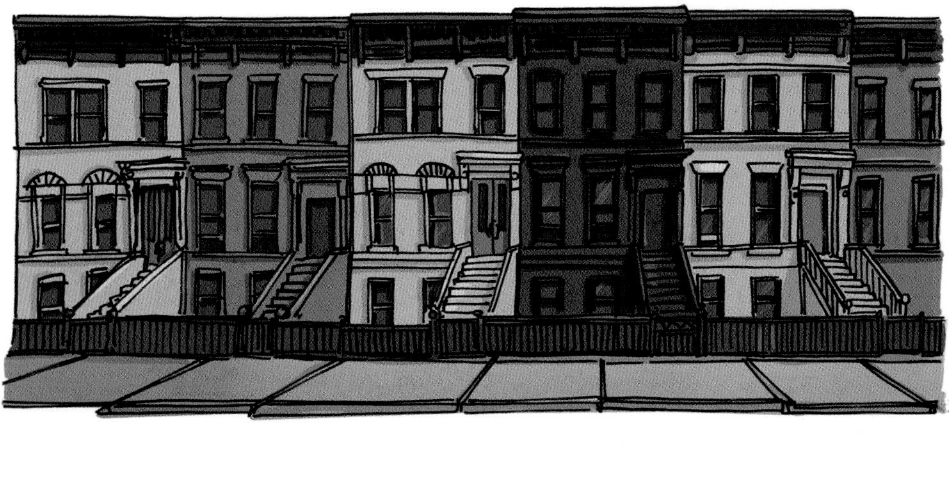

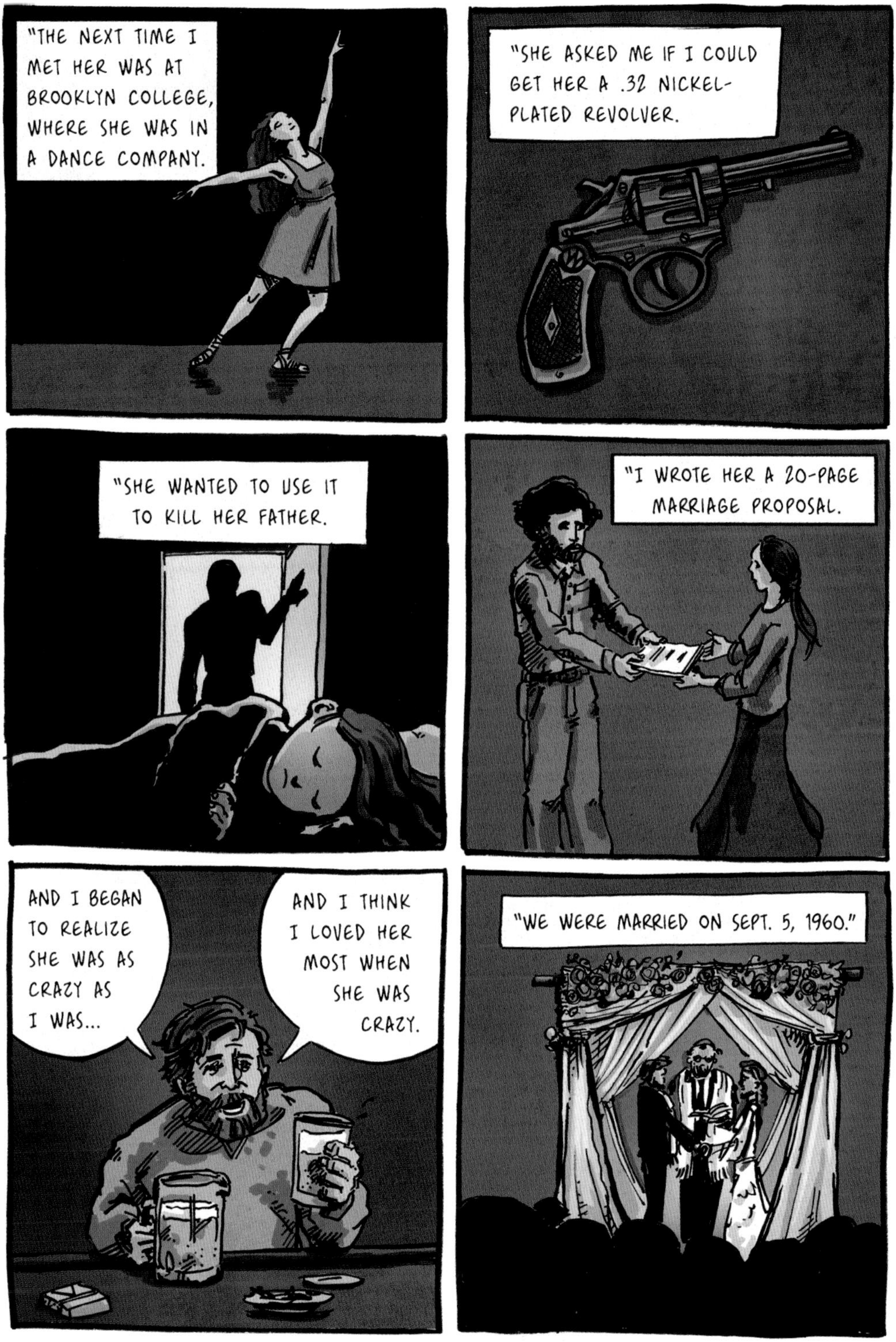
"THE NEXT TIME I MET HER WAS AT BROOKLYN COLLEGE, WHERE SHE WAS IN A DANCE COMPANY.
"SHE ASKED ME IF I COULD GET HER A .32 NICKEL-PLATED REVOLVER.
"SHE WANTED TO USE IT TO KILL HER FATHER.
"I WROTE HER A 20-PAGE MARRIAGE PROPOSAL.
AND I BEGAN TO REALIZE SHE WAS AS CRAZY AS I WAS...
AND I THINK I LOVED HER MOST WHEN SHE WAS CRAZY.
"WE WERE MARRIED ON SEPT. 5, 1960."

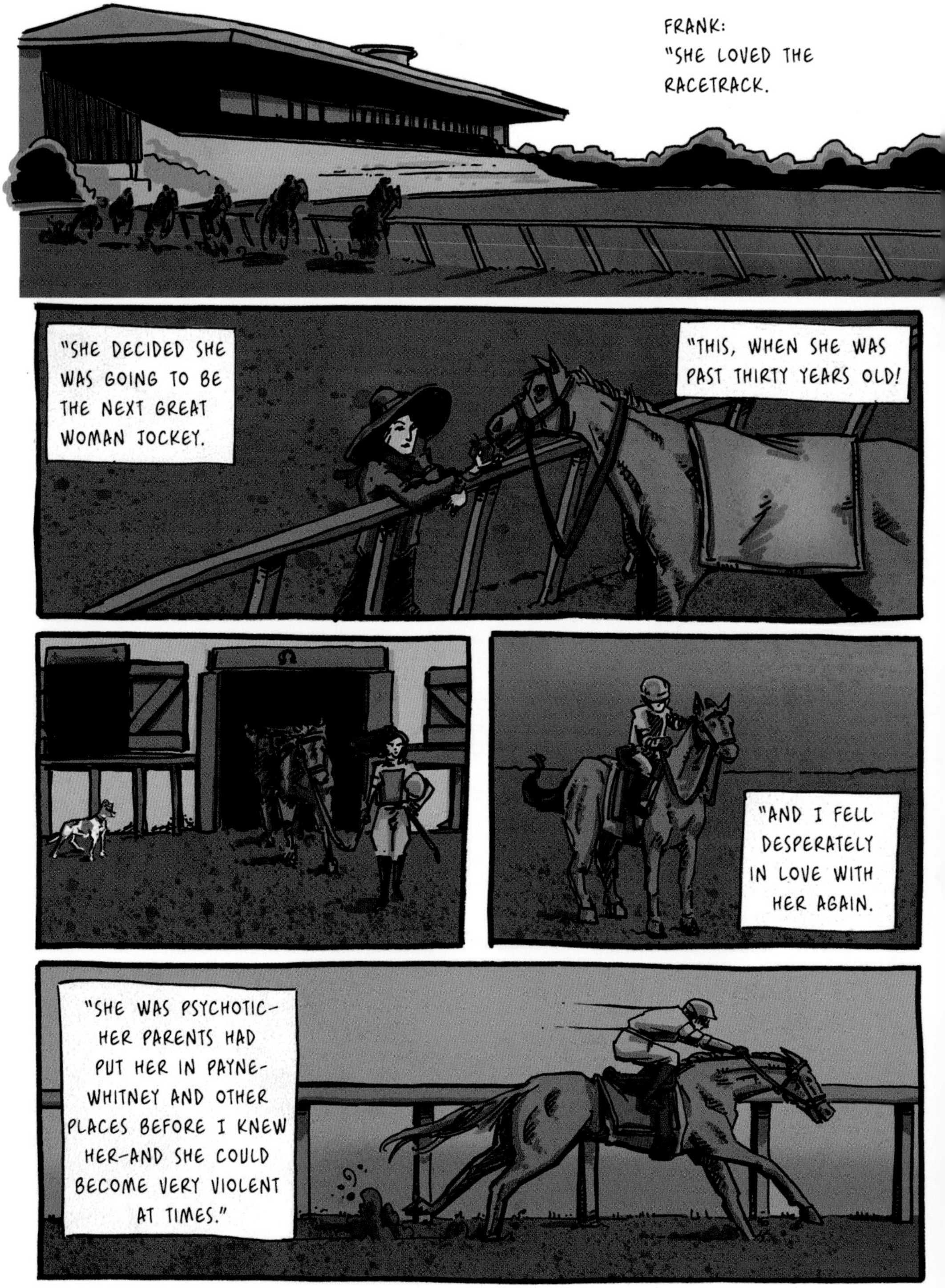
FRANK:
"SHE LOVED THE RACETRACK.
"SHE DECIDED SHE WAS GOING TO BE THE NEXT GREAT WOMAN JOCKEY.
"THIS, WHEN SHE WAS PAST THIRTY YEARS OLD!
"AND I FELL DESPERATELY IN LOVE WITH HER AGAIN.
"SHE WAS PSYCHOTIC-HER PARENTS HAD PUT HER IN PAYNE-WHITNEY AND OTHER PLACES BEFORE I KNEW HER-AND SHE COULD BECOME VERY VIOLENT AT TIMES."

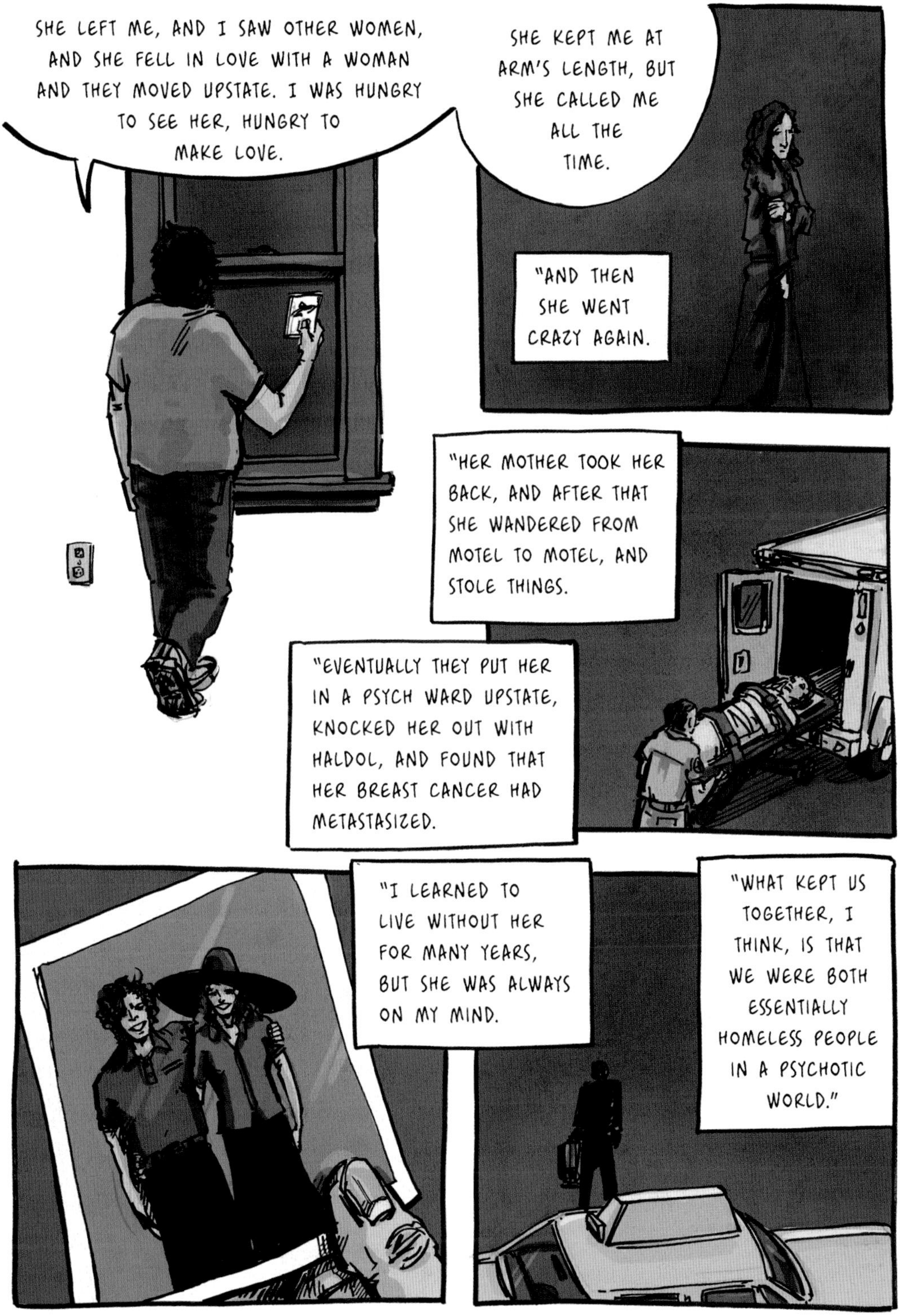
SHE LEFT ME, AND I SAW OTHER WOMEN, AND SHE FELL IN LOVE WITH A WOMAN AND THEY MOVED UPSTATE. I WAS HUNGRY TO SEE HER, HUNGRY TO MAKE LOVE.
SHE KEPT ME AT ARM'S LENGTH, BUT SHE CALLED ME ALL THE TIME.
"AND THEN SHE WENT CRAZY AGAIN.
"HER MOTHER TOOK HER BACK, AND AFTER THAT SHE WANDERED FROM MOTEL TO MOTEL, AND STOLE THINGS.
"EVENTUALLY THEY PUT HER IN A PSYCH WARD UPSTATE, KNOCKED HER OUT WITH HALDOL, AND FOUND THAT HER BREAST CANCER HAD METASTASIZED.
"I LEARNED TO LIVE WITHOUT HER FOR MANY YEARS, BUT SHE WAS ALWAYS ON MY MIND.
"WHAT KEPT US TOGETHER, I THINK, IS THAT WE WERE BOTH ESSENTIALLY HOMELESS PEOPLE IN A PSYCHOTIC WORLD."

"ONE TIME SHE TOOK 20 NEMBUTAL AND ASKED ME NOT TO INTERFERE WITH HER SUICIDE.

"BUT I WENT AGAINST MY PROMISE AND GOT THERE WITH HER MOTHER AND SHE WAS STILL BREATHING.

"SHE HAD LEFT NOTES FOR EVERYONE AND PUT EVERY SHARP INSTRUMENT INTO THE TOILET.

"AND THEN, LATER, WHEN SHE WAS DYING OF CANCER, I DECIDED I HAD TO KILL HER.

PLEASE ...please...

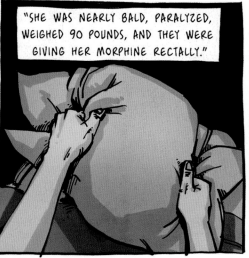

"SHE WAS NEARLY BALD, PARALYZED, WEIGHED 90 POUNDS, AND THEY WERE GIVING HER MORPHINE RECTALLY."

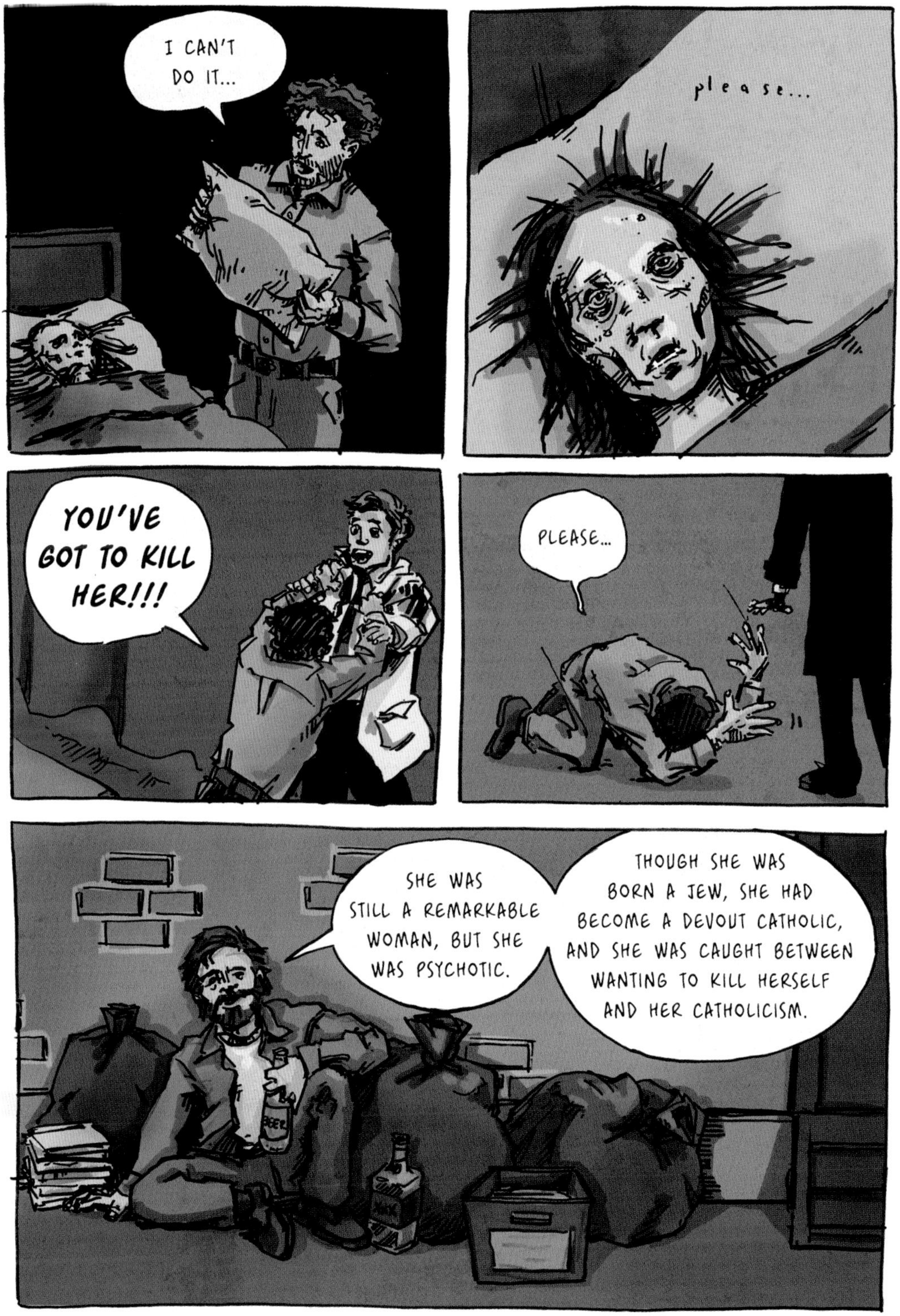
I CAN'T DO IT...
please...
YOU'VE GOT TO KILL HER!!!
PLEASE...
SHE WAS STILL A REMARKABLE WOMAN, BUT SHE WAS PSYCHOTIC.
THOUGH SHE WAS BORN A JEW, SHE HAD BECOME A DEVOUT CATHOLIC, AND SHE WAS CAUGHT BETWEEN WANTING TO KILL HERSELF AND HER CATHOLICISM.
BEER

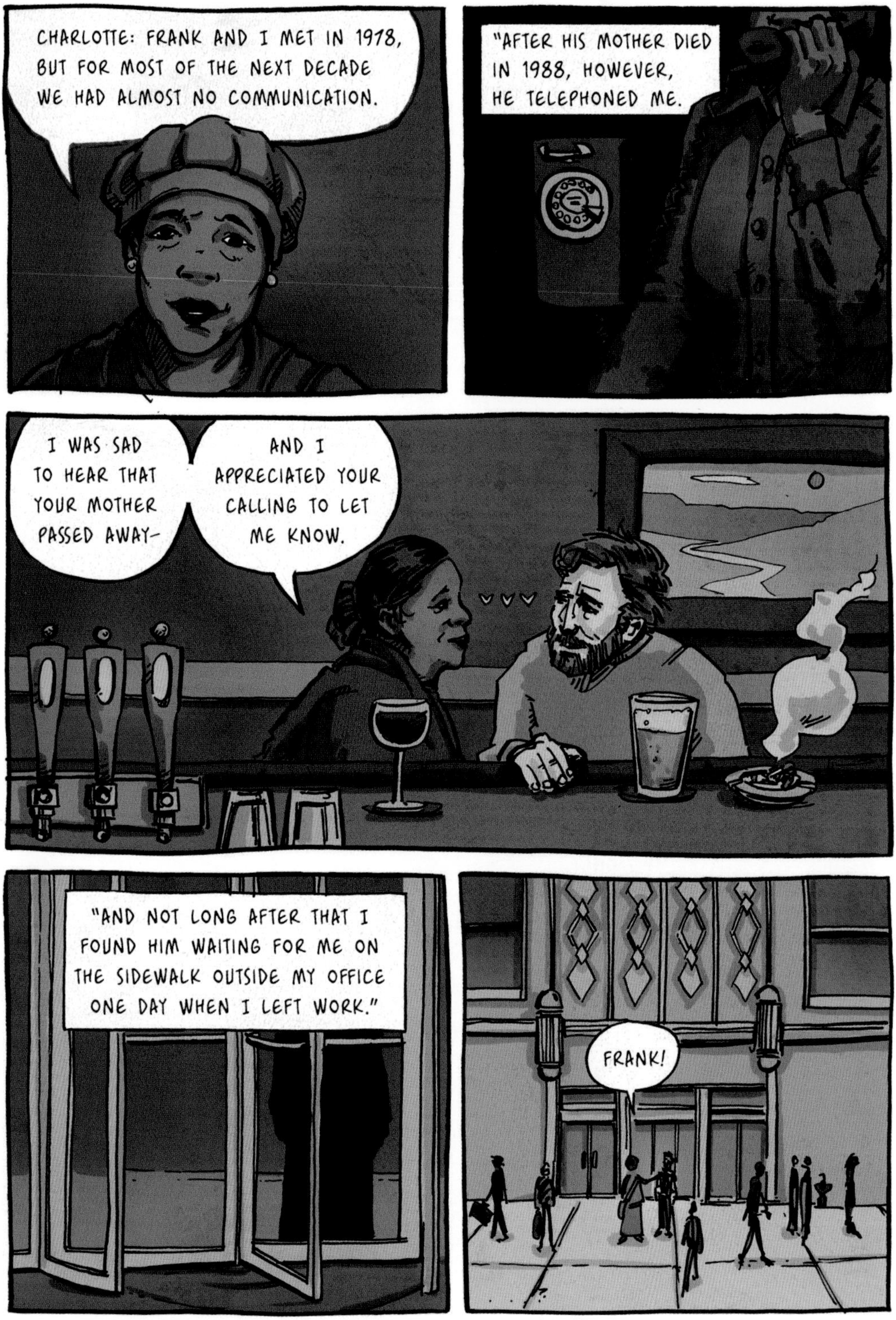
CHARLOTTE: FRANK AND I MET IN 1978, BUT FOR MOST OF THE NEXT DECADE WE HAD ALMOST NO COMMUNICATION.
"AFTER HIS MOTHER DIED IN 1988, HOWEVER, HE TELEPHONED ME.
I WAS SAD TO HEAR THAT YOUR MOTHER PASSED AWAY-
AND I APPRECIATED YOUR CALLING TO LET ME KNOW.
"AND NOT LONG AFTER THAT I FOUND HIM WAITING FOR ME ON THE SIDEWALK OUTSIDE MY OFFICE ONE DAY WHEN I LEFT WORK."
FRANK!

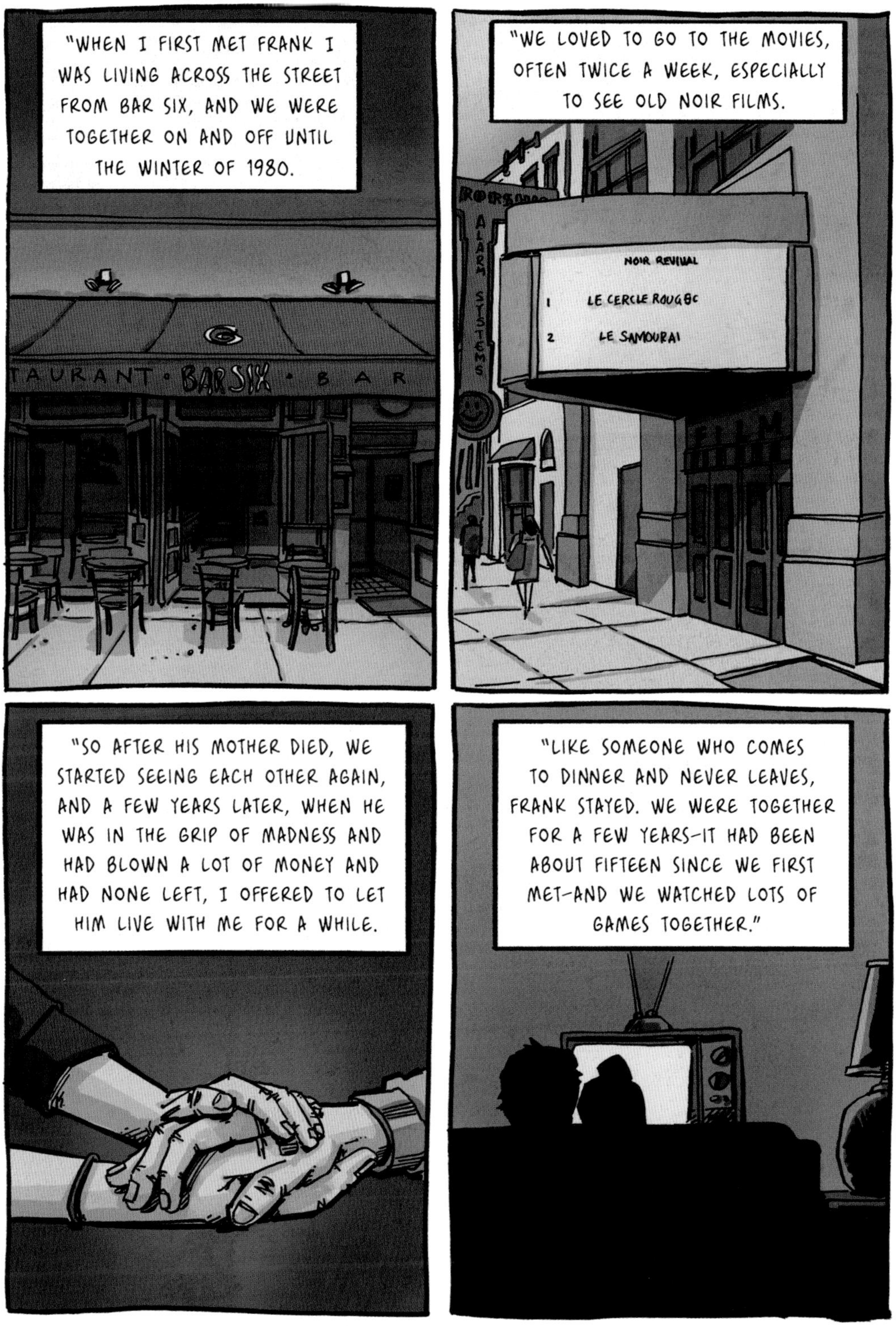
"WHEN I FIRST MET FRANK I WAS LIVING ACROSS THE STREET FROM BAR SIX, AND WE WERE TOGETHER ON AND OFF UNTIL THE WINTER OF 1980.
TAURANT • BAR SIX • BAR
"WE LOVED TO GO TO THE MOVIES, OFTEN TWICE A WEEK, ESPECIALLY TO SEE OLD NOIR FILMS.
ALARM SYSTEMS
NOIR REVIVAL
1 LE CERCLE ROUGE
2 LE SAMOURAI
"SO AFTER HIS MOTHER DIED, WE STARTED SEEING EACH OTHER AGAIN, AND A FEW YEARS LATER, WHEN HE WAS IN THE GRIP OF MADNESS AND HAD BLOWN A LOT OF MONEY AND HAD NONE LEFT, I OFFERED TO LET HIM LIVE WITH ME FOR A WHILE.
"LIKE SOMEONE WHO COMES TO DINNER AND NEVER LEAVES, FRANK STAYED. WE WERE TOGETHER FOR A FEW YEARS–IT HAD BEEN ABOUT FIFTEEN SINCE WE FIRST MET–AND WE WATCHED LOTS OF GAMES TOGETHER."

"IT WAS ONLY WHEN SOMEONE RECOGNIZED HIM ON THE STREET ONE DAY AND STARTED REMINISCING ABOUT WHAT A GREAT BALLPLAYER FRANK WAS THAT I LEARNED HE'D EVER EVEN PLAYED BASKETBALL.

FRANK!

FRANKIE KING!!!

MAN, YOU WERE THE GREATEST BALLPLAYER I EVER SAW, FRANK! REMEMBER THAT GAME FOR THE DIVISION CHAMPIONSHIP AGAINST ERASMUS AND JOHNNY LEE? YOU WERE INCREDIBLE! BUT HOW COME THINGS DIDN'T WORK OUT AT NORTH CAROLINA?

HEY MAN, WHAT GIVES?!?

"WE WERE MARRIED IN 1999...

"AND STAYED TOGETHER UNTIL HE DIED."

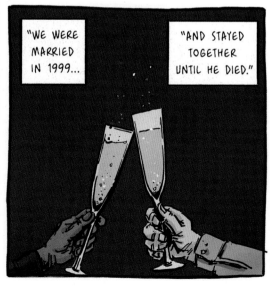

"FRANK WAS NOT A CAREFUL WRITER, BUT HE WAS INTREPID AND WOULD TURN OUT COPY WITHOUT HAVING TO REVISE—HE WAS AN AMAZINGLY FACILE WRITER—AND HE GOT ME STARTED AS A WRITER.

"RIMA WAS A TOTAL WHACK-JOB. SHE WAS VERY BAD FOR FRANK.

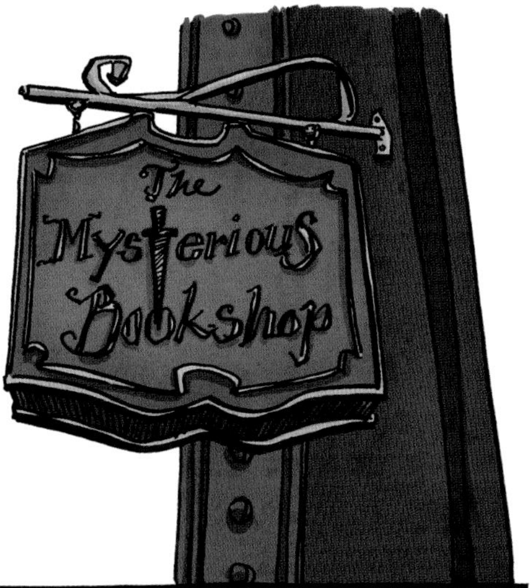
The Mysterious Bookshop

"HE ENCOURAGED ME TO WRITE NOVELS, AND HE WORKED WITH ME ON THEM. I'D WRITTEN BEFORE—POEMS, STORIES, ESSAYS—AND I'D EARNED MY LIVING AS AN EDITOR.

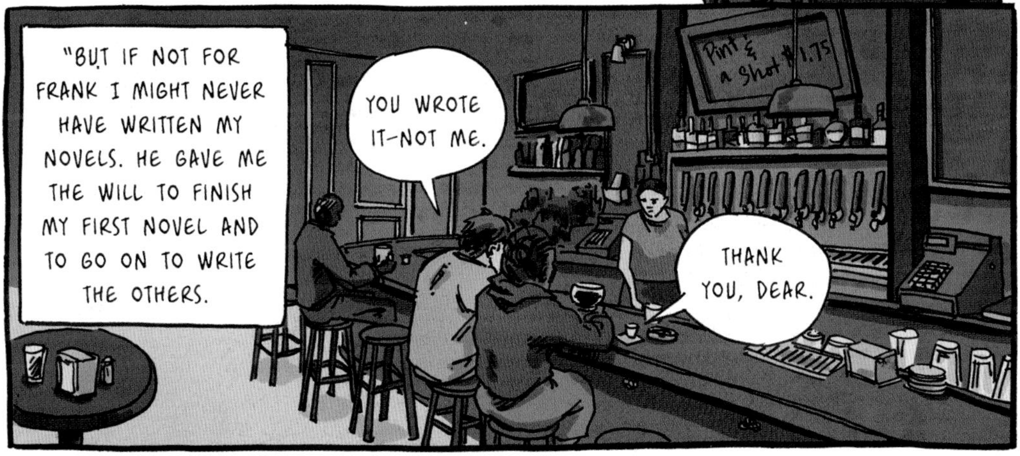
"BUT IF NOT FOR FRANK I MIGHT NEVER HAVE WRITTEN MY NOVELS. HE GAVE ME THE WILL TO FINISH MY FIRST NOVEL AND TO GO ON TO WRITE THE OTHERS.
Pint & a Shot $1.75
YOU WROTE IT—NOT ME.
THANK YOU, DEAR.

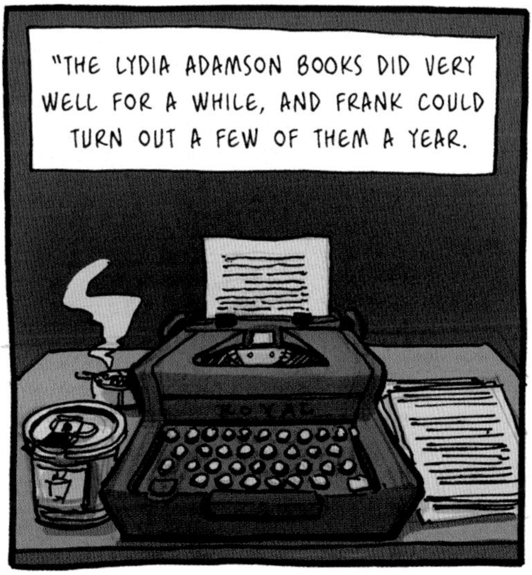
"THE LYDIA ADAMSON BOOKS DID VERY WELL FOR A WHILE, AND FRANK COULD TURN OUT A FEW OF THEM A YEAR.
ROYAL

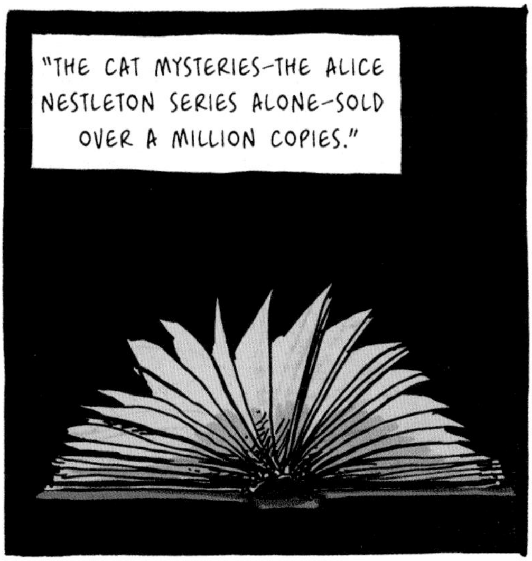
"THE CAT MYSTERIES—THE ALICE NESTLETON SERIES ALONE—SOLD OVER A MILLION COPIES."

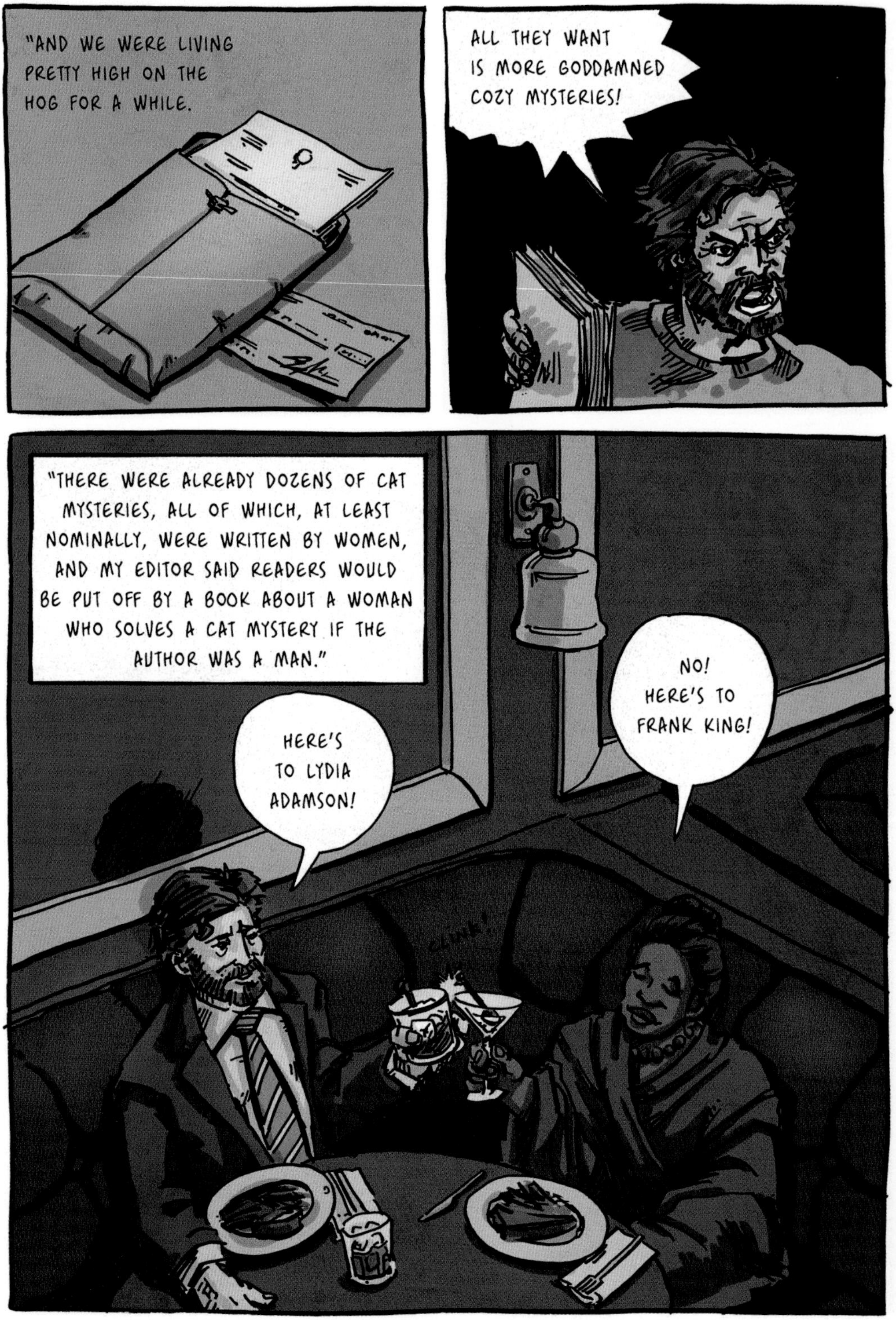
"AND WE WERE LIVING PRETTY HIGH ON THE HOG FOR A WHILE.
ALL THEY WANT IS MORE GODDAMNED COZY MYSTERIES!
"THERE WERE ALREADY DOZENS OF CAT MYSTERIES, ALL OF WHICH, AT LEAST NOMINALLY, WERE WRITTEN BY WOMEN, AND MY EDITOR SAID READERS WOULD BE PUT OFF BY A BOOK ABOUT A WOMAN WHO SOLVES A CAT MYSTERY IF THE AUTHOR WAS A MAN."
HERE'S TO LYDIA ADAMSON!
NO! HERE'S TO FRANK KING!

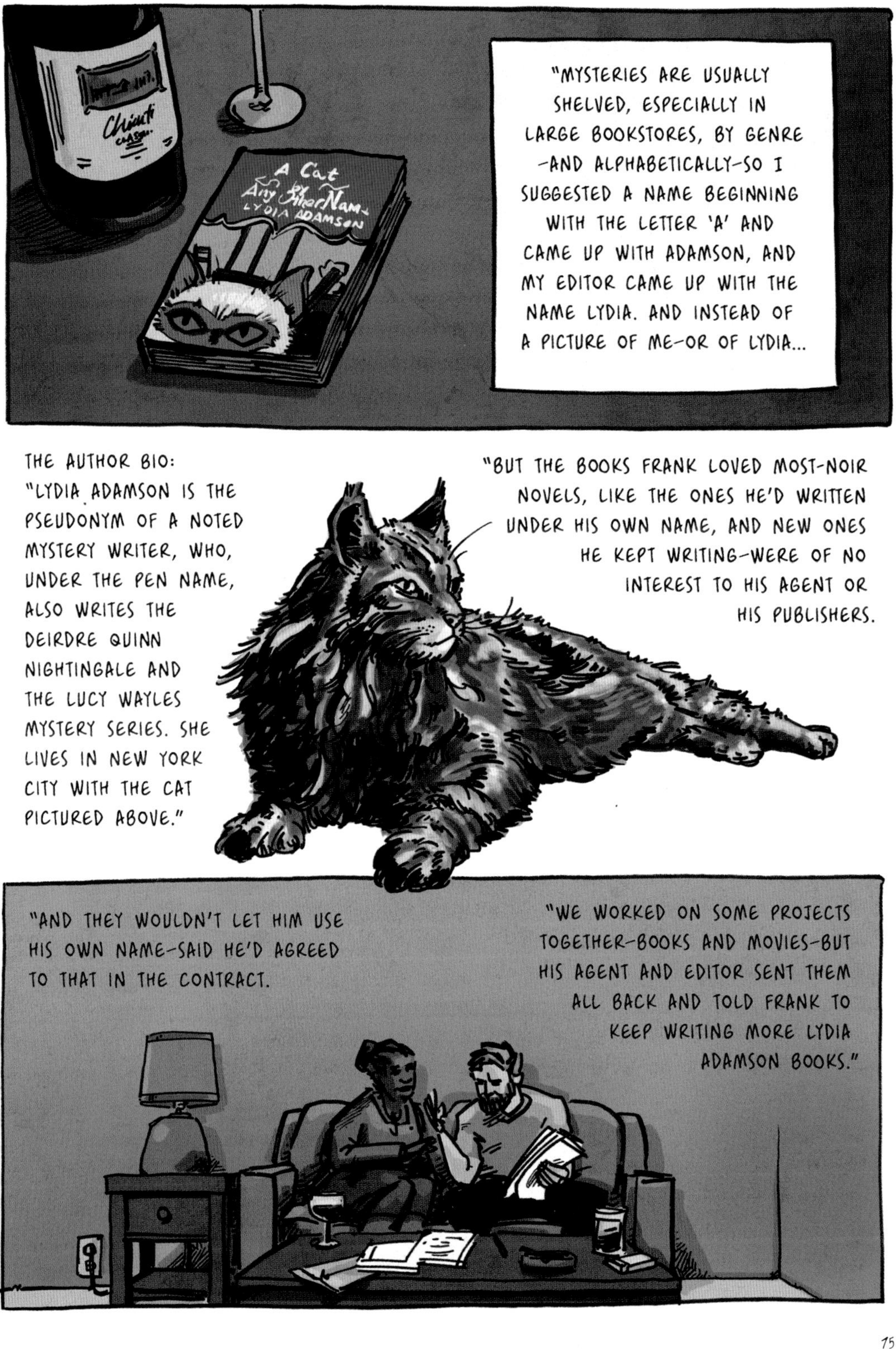
"MYSTERIES ARE USUALLY SHELVED, ESPECIALLY IN LARGE BOOKSTORES, BY GENRE —AND ALPHABETICALLY—SO I SUGGESTED A NAME BEGINNING WITH THE LETTER 'A' AND CAME UP WITH ADAMSON, AND MY EDITOR CAME UP WITH THE NAME LYDIA. AND INSTEAD OF A PICTURE OF ME—OR OF LYDIA...
LYDIA ADAMSON
THE AUTHOR BIO: "LYDIA ADAMSON IS THE PSEUDONYM OF A NOTED MYSTERY WRITER, WHO, UNDER THE PEN NAME, ALSO WRITES THE DEIRDRE QUINN NIGHTINGALE AND THE LUCY WAYLES MYSTERY SERIES. SHE LIVES IN NEW YORK CITY WITH THE CAT PICTURED ABOVE."
"BUT THE BOOKS FRANK LOVED MOST-NOIR NOVELS, LIKE THE ONES HE'D WRITTEN UNDER HIS OWN NAME, AND NEW ONES HE KEPT WRITING—WERE OF NO INTEREST TO HIS AGENT OR HIS PUBLISHERS.
"AND THEY WOULDN'T LET HIM USE HIS OWN NAME—SAID HE'D AGREED TO THAT IN THE CONTRACT.
"WE WORKED ON SOME PROJECTS TOGETHER—BOOKS AND MOVIES—BUT HIS AGENT AND EDITOR SENT THEM ALL BACK AND TOLD FRANK TO KEEP WRITING MORE LYDIA ADAMSON BOOKS."

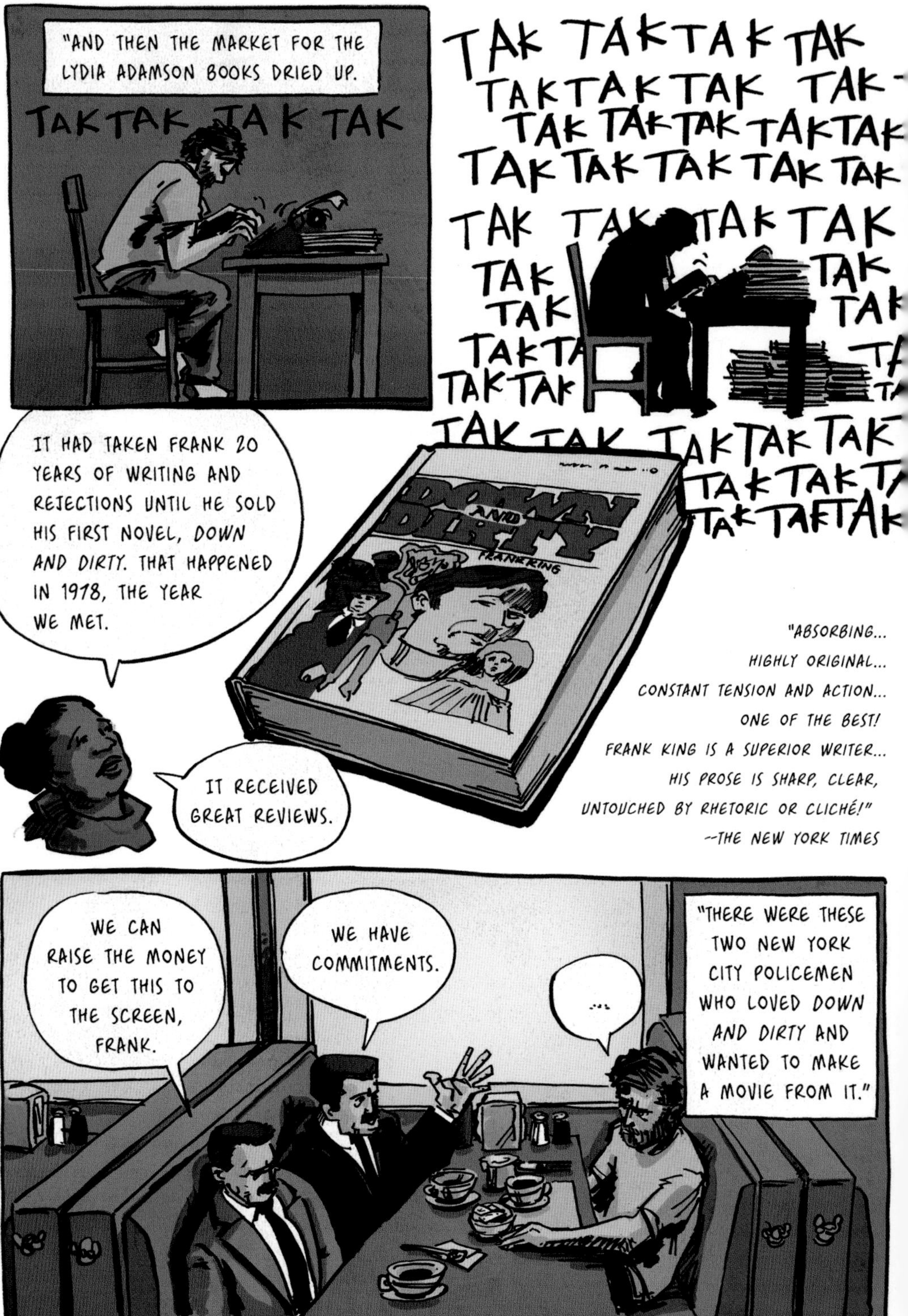
"AND THEN THE MARKET FOR THE LYDIA ADAMSON BOOKS DRIED UP.
TAKTAK TAK TAK
TAK TAKTAK TAK
TAKTAKTAK TAK
TAK TAKTAK TAKTAK
TAK TAK TAK TAK TAK
TAK TAK TAK
TAK TAK
TAK TAK
TAKTA
TAKTAK
TAK TAK TAKTAK TAK
TAKTAKTA
TAKTAKTAK
IT HAD TAKEN FRANK 20 YEARS OF WRITING AND REJECTIONS UNTIL HE SOLD HIS FIRST NOVEL, DOWN AND DIRTY. THAT HAPPENED IN 1978, THE YEAR WE MET.
DOWN AND DIRTY
FRANK KING
IT RECEIVED GREAT REVIEWS.
"ABSORBING... HIGHLY ORIGINAL... CONSTANT TENSION AND ACTION... ONE OF THE BEST! FRANK KING IS A SUPERIOR WRITER... HIS PROSE IS SHARP, CLEAR, UNTOUCHED BY RHETORIC OR CLICHÉ!" --THE NEW YORK TIMES
WE CAN RAISE THE MONEY TO GET THIS TO THE SCREEN, FRANK.
WE HAVE COMMITMENTS.
...
"THERE WERE THESE TWO NEW YORK CITY POLICEMEN WHO LOVED DOWN AND DIRTY AND WANTED TO MAKE A MOVIE FROM IT."

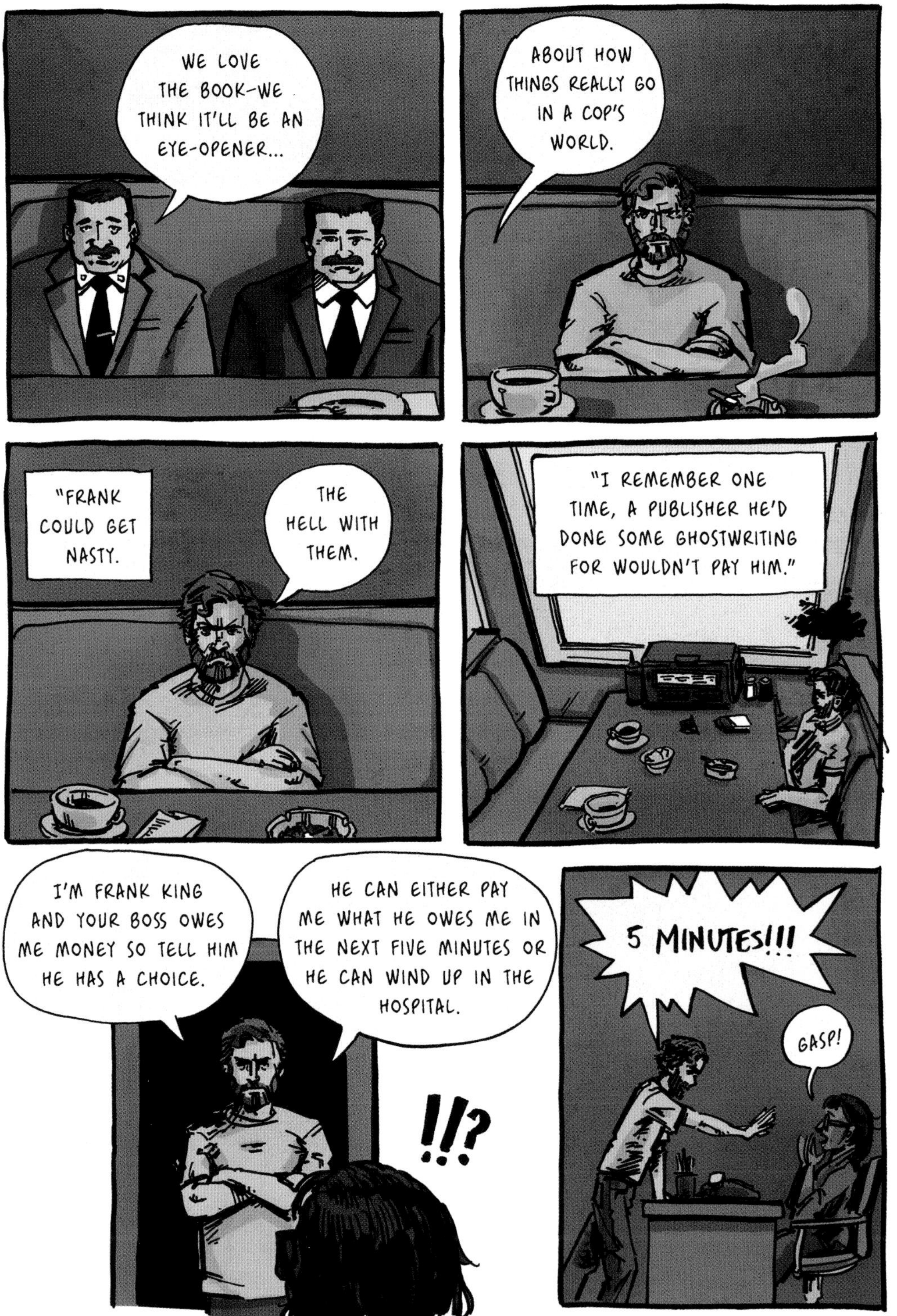
WE LOVE THE BOOK—WE THINK IT'LL BE AN EYE-OPENER...
ABOUT HOW THINGS REALLY GO IN A COP'S WORLD.
"FRANK COULD GET NASTY.
THE HELL WITH THEM.
"I REMEMBER ONE TIME, A PUBLISHER HE'D DONE SOME GHOSTWRITING FOR WOULDN'T PAY HIM."
I'M FRANK KING AND YOUR BOSS OWES ME MONEY SO TELL HIM HE HAS A CHOICE.
HE CAN EITHER PAY ME WHAT HE OWES ME IN THE NEXT FIVE MINUTES OR HE CAN WIND UP IN THE HOSPITAL.
!!?
5 MINUTES!!!
GASP!

tic toc tic toc tic toc tic toc tic toc tic toc

FIVE MINUTES LATER...

H-H-HERE YOU GO!

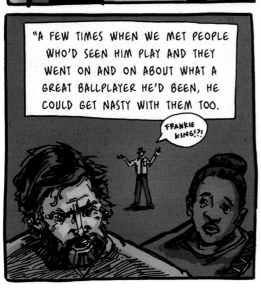

"A FEW TIMES WHEN WE MET PEOPLE WHO'D SEEN HIM PLAY AND THEY WENT ON AND ON ABOUT WHAT A GREAT BALLPLAYER HE'D BEEN, HE COULD GET NASTY WITH THEM TOO.

FRANKIE KING!?!

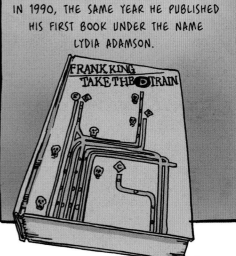

"THE LAST NOVEL HE EVER PUBLISHED UNDER HIS OWN NAME APPEARED IN 1990, THE SAME YEAR HE PUBLISHED HIS FIRST BOOK UNDER THE NAME LYDIA ADAMSON.

FRANK KING
TAKE THE D TRAIN

"IN ALL HE PUBLISHED 43 NOVELS... THAT WE KNOW OF!

A CAT BY ANY OTHER NAME

"FROM THE TIME OF THE PUBLICATION OF *A CAT ON THE BUS* IN 2002 UNTIL FRANK'S DEATH IN 2015, HE KEPT WRITING EVERY DAY—BOOK AFTER BOOK AND PROPOSAL AFTER PROPOSAL—AND WAS RELENTLESS ABOUT SENDING OUT HIS WORK."

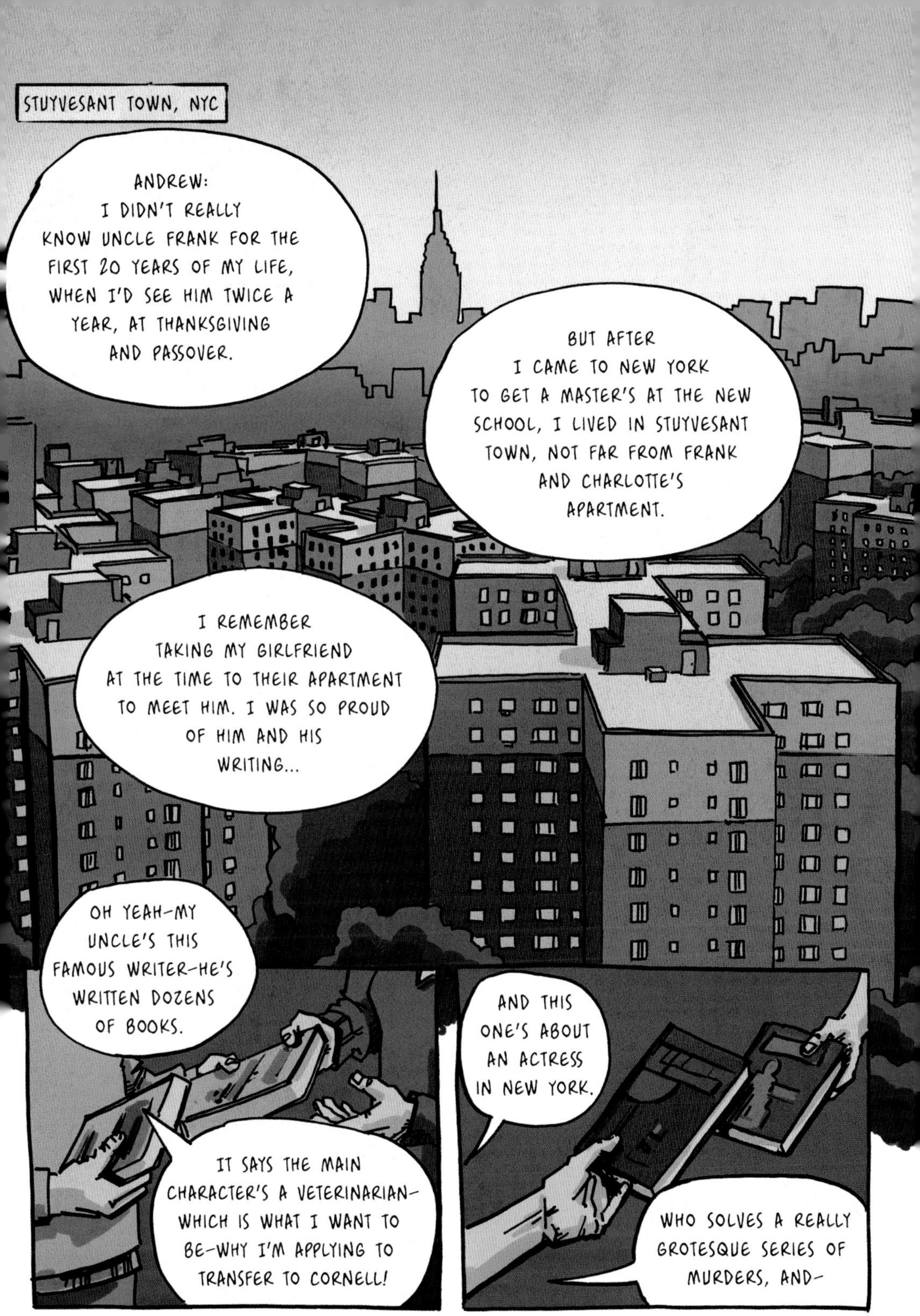
STUYVESANT TOWN, NYC
ANDREW: I DIDN'T REALLY KNOW UNCLE FRANK FOR THE FIRST 20 YEARS OF MY LIFE, WHEN I'D SEE HIM TWICE A YEAR, AT THANKSGIVING AND PASSOVER.
BUT AFTER I CAME TO NEW YORK TO GET A MASTER'S AT THE NEW SCHOOL, I LIVED IN STUYVESANT TOWN, NOT FAR FROM FRANK AND CHARLOTTE'S APARTMENT.
I REMEMBER TAKING MY GIRLFRIEND AT THE TIME TO THEIR APARTMENT TO MEET HIM. I WAS SO PROUD OF HIM AND HIS WRITING...
OH YEAH–MY UNCLE'S THIS FAMOUS WRITER–HE'S WRITTEN DOZENS OF BOOKS.
IT SAYS THE MAIN CHARACTER'S A VETERINARIAN–WHICH IS WHAT I WANT TO BE–WHY I'M APPLYING TO TRANSFER TO CORNELL!
AND THIS ONE'S ABOUT AN ACTRESS IN NEW YORK.
WHO SOLVES A REALLY GROTESQUE SERIES OF MURDERS, AND–

I TOLD YOU BEFORE NOT TO WASTE YOUR TIME READING MY BOOKS—

SNATCH

THOSE BOOKS WERE JUST SILLY STUFF I TURNED OUT TO EARN A BUCK.

BUT UNCLE FRANK!!!

HERE, LET ME GIVE YOU SOMETHING GOOD.

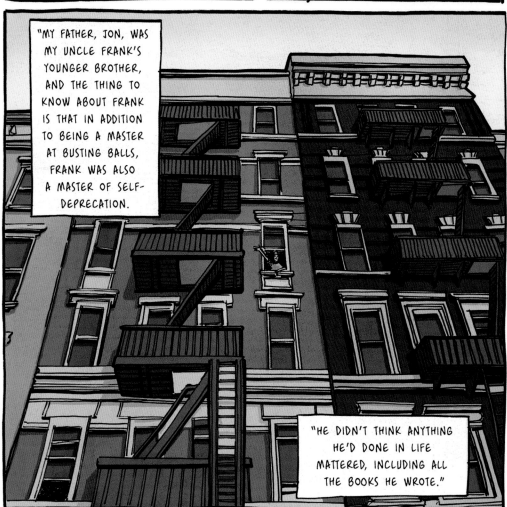

"MY FATHER, JON, WAS MY UNCLE FRANK'S YOUNGER BROTHER, AND THE THING TO KNOW ABOUT FRANK IS THAT IN ADDITION TO BEING A MASTER AT BUSTING BALLS, FRANK WAS ALSO A MASTER OF SELF-DEPRECATION.

"HE DIDN'T THINK ANYTHING HE'D DONE IN LIFE MATTERED, INCLUDING ALL THE BOOKS HE WROTE."

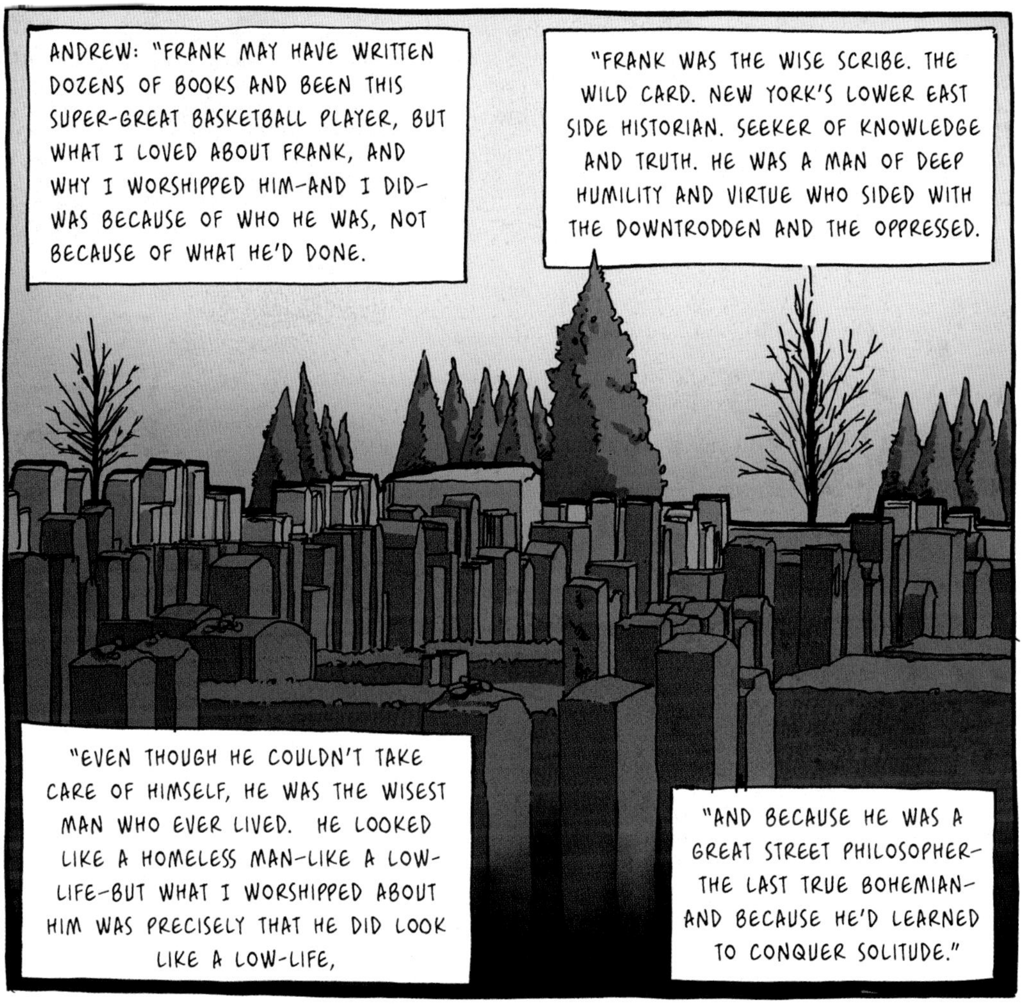
ANDREW: "FRANK MAY HAVE WRITTEN DOZENS OF BOOKS AND BEEN THIS SUPER-GREAT BASKETBALL PLAYER, BUT WHAT I LOVED ABOUT FRANK, AND WHY I WORSHIPPED HIM–AND I DID–WAS BECAUSE OF WHO HE WAS, NOT BECAUSE OF WHAT HE'D DONE.
"FRANK WAS THE WISE SCRIBE. THE WILD CARD. NEW YORK'S LOWER EAST SIDE HISTORIAN. SEEKER OF KNOWLEDGE AND TRUTH. HE WAS A MAN OF DEEP HUMILITY AND VIRTUE WHO SIDED WITH THE DOWNTRODDEN AND THE OPPRESSED.
"EVEN THOUGH HE COULDN'T TAKE CARE OF HIMSELF, HE WAS THE WISEST MAN WHO EVER LIVED. HE LOOKED LIKE A HOMELESS MAN–LIKE A LOW-LIFE–BUT WHAT I WORSHIPPED ABOUT HIM WAS PRECISELY THAT HE DID LOOK LIKE A LOW-LIFE,
"AND BECAUSE HE WAS A GREAT STREET PHILOSOPHER–THE LAST TRUE BOHEMIAN–AND BECAUSE HE'D LEARNED TO CONQUER SOLITUDE."

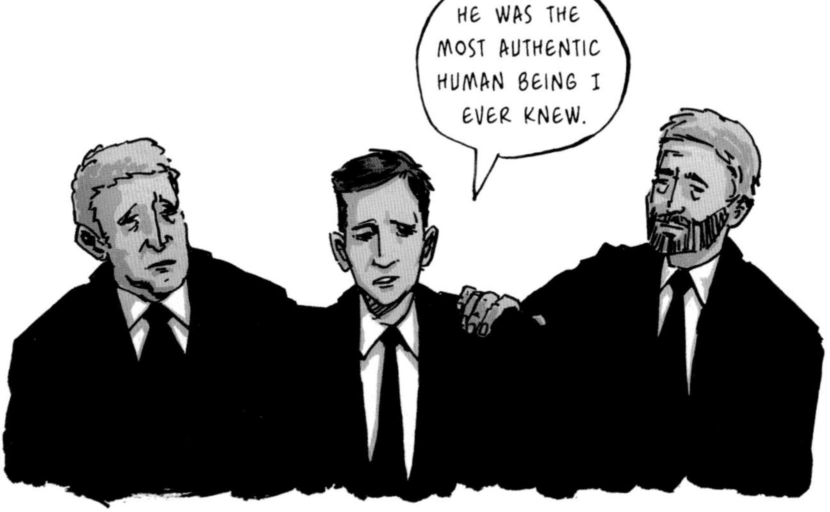
HE WAS THE MOST AUTHENTIC HUMAN BEING I EVER KNEW.

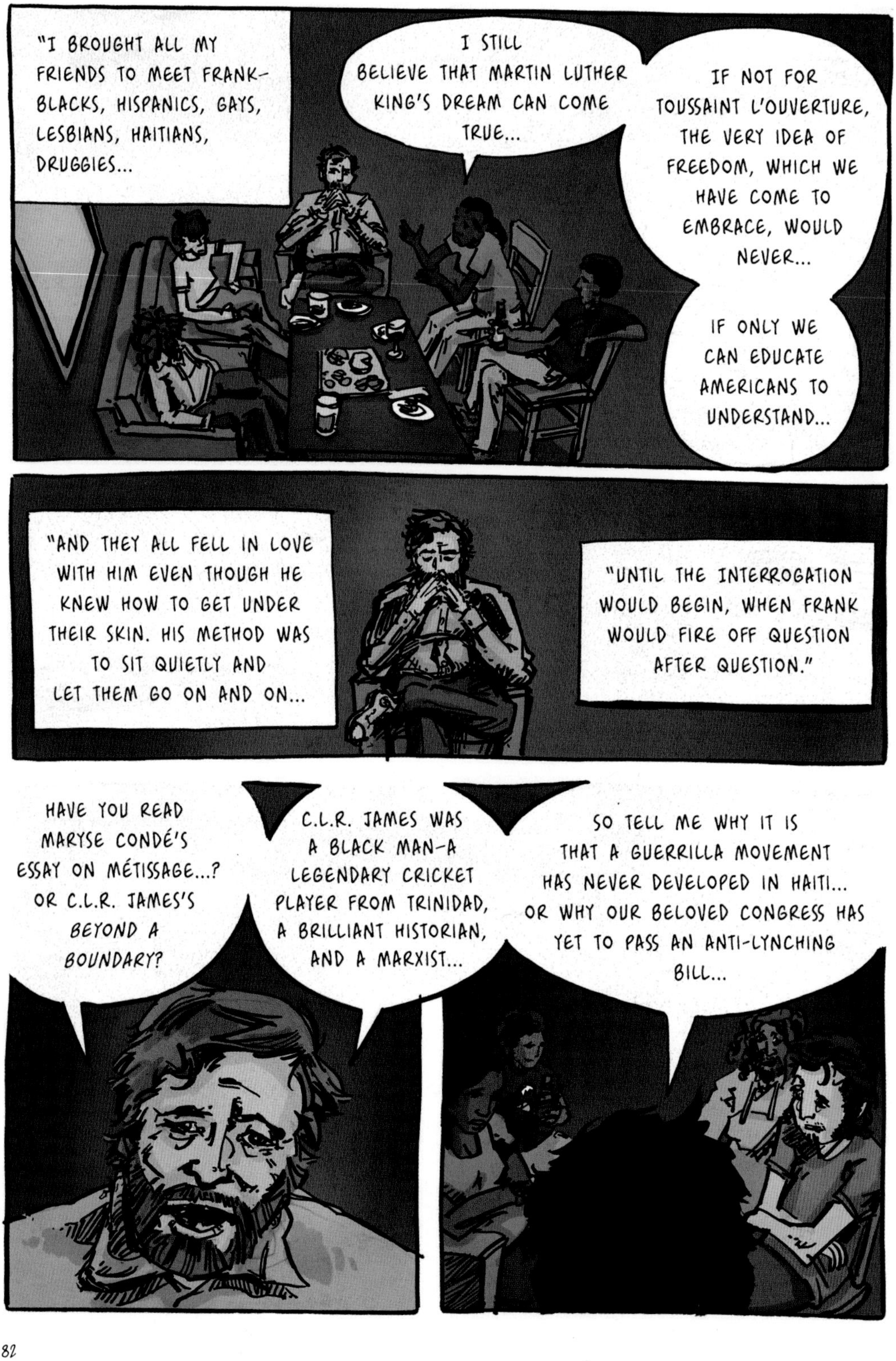
"I BROUGHT ALL MY FRIENDS TO MEET FRANK-BLACKS, HISPANICS, GAYS, LESBIANS, HAITIANS, DRUGGIES...
I STILL BELIEVE THAT MARTIN LUTHER KING'S DREAM CAN COME TRUE...
IF NOT FOR TOUSSAINT L'OUVERTURE, THE VERY IDEA OF FREEDOM, WHICH WE HAVE COME TO EMBRACE, WOULD NEVER...
IF ONLY WE CAN EDUCATE AMERICANS TO UNDERSTAND...
"AND THEY ALL FELL IN LOVE WITH HIM EVEN THOUGH HE KNEW HOW TO GET UNDER THEIR SKIN. HIS METHOD WAS TO SIT QUIETLY AND LET THEM GO ON AND ON...
"UNTIL THE INTERROGATION WOULD BEGIN, WHEN FRANK WOULD FIRE OFF QUESTION AFTER QUESTION."
HAVE YOU READ MARYSE CONDÉ'S ESSAY ON MÉTISSAGE...? OR C.L.R. JAMES'S *BEYOND A BOUNDARY*?
C.L.R. JAMES WAS A BLACK MAN-A LEGENDARY CRICKET PLAYER FROM TRINIDAD, A BRILLIANT HISTORIAN, AND A MARXIST...
SO TELL ME WHY IT IS THAT A GUERRILLA MOVEMENT HAS NEVER DEVELOPED IN HAITI... OR WHY OUR BELOVED CONGRESS HAS YET TO PASS AN ANTI-LYNCHING BILL...

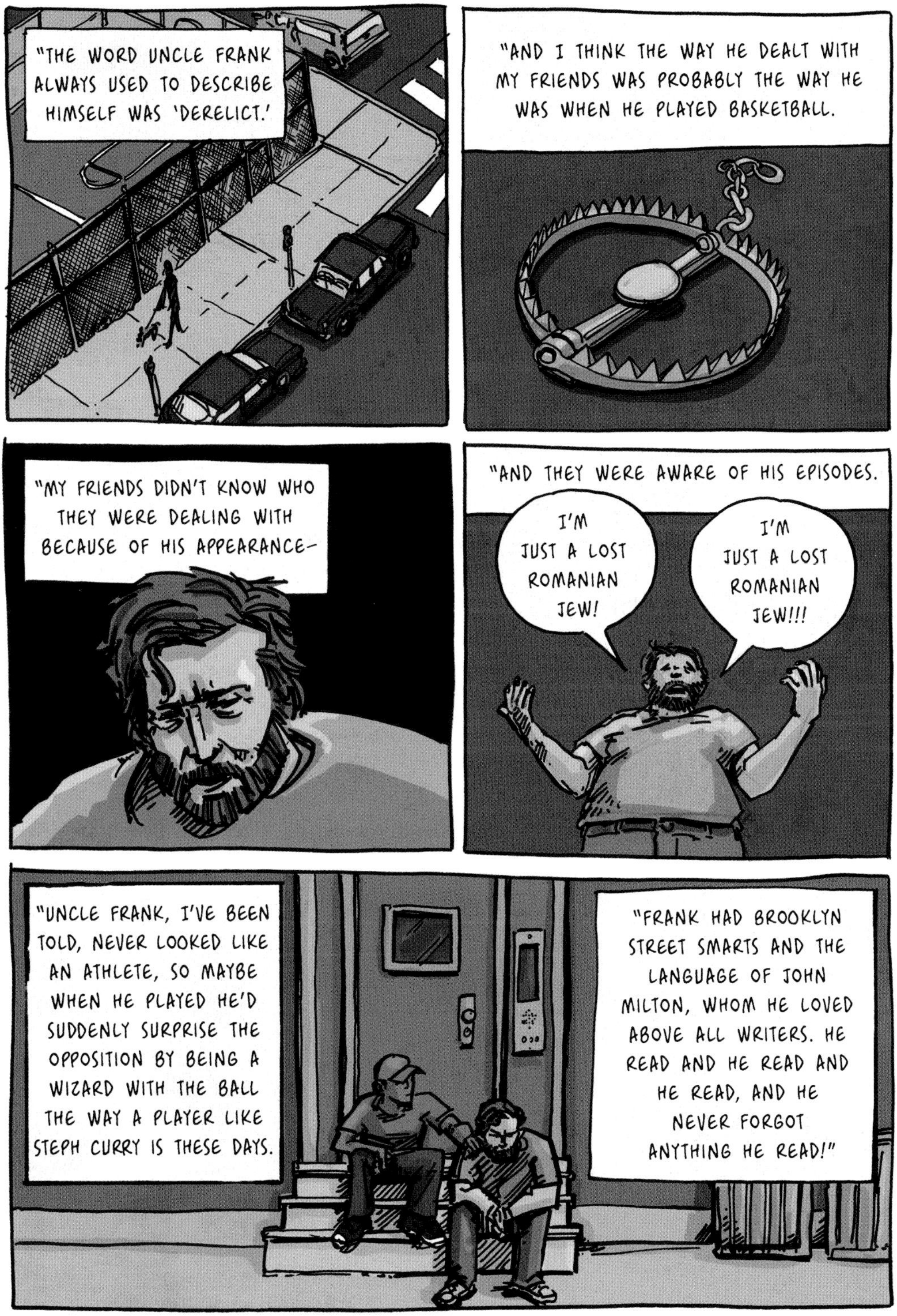
"THE WORD UNCLE FRANK ALWAYS USED TO DESCRIBE HIMSELF WAS 'DERELICT.'
"AND I THINK THE WAY HE DEALT WITH MY FRIENDS WAS PROBABLY THE WAY HE WAS WHEN HE PLAYED BASKETBALL.
"MY FRIENDS DIDN'T KNOW WHO THEY WERE DEALING WITH BECAUSE OF HIS APPEARANCE-
"AND THEY WERE AWARE OF HIS EPISODES.
I'M JUST A LOST ROMANIAN JEW!
I'M JUST A LOST ROMANIAN JEW!!!
"UNCLE FRANK, I'VE BEEN TOLD, NEVER LOOKED LIKE AN ATHLETE, SO MAYBE WHEN HE PLAYED HE'D SUDDENLY SURPRISE THE OPPOSITION BY BEING A WIZARD WITH THE BALL THE WAY A PLAYER LIKE STEPH CURRY IS THESE DAYS.
"FRANK HAD BROOKLYN STREET SMARTS AND THE LANGUAGE OF JOHN MILTON, WHOM HE LOVED ABOVE ALL WRITERS. HE READ AND HE READ AND HE READ, AND HE NEVER FORGOT ANYTHING HE READ!"

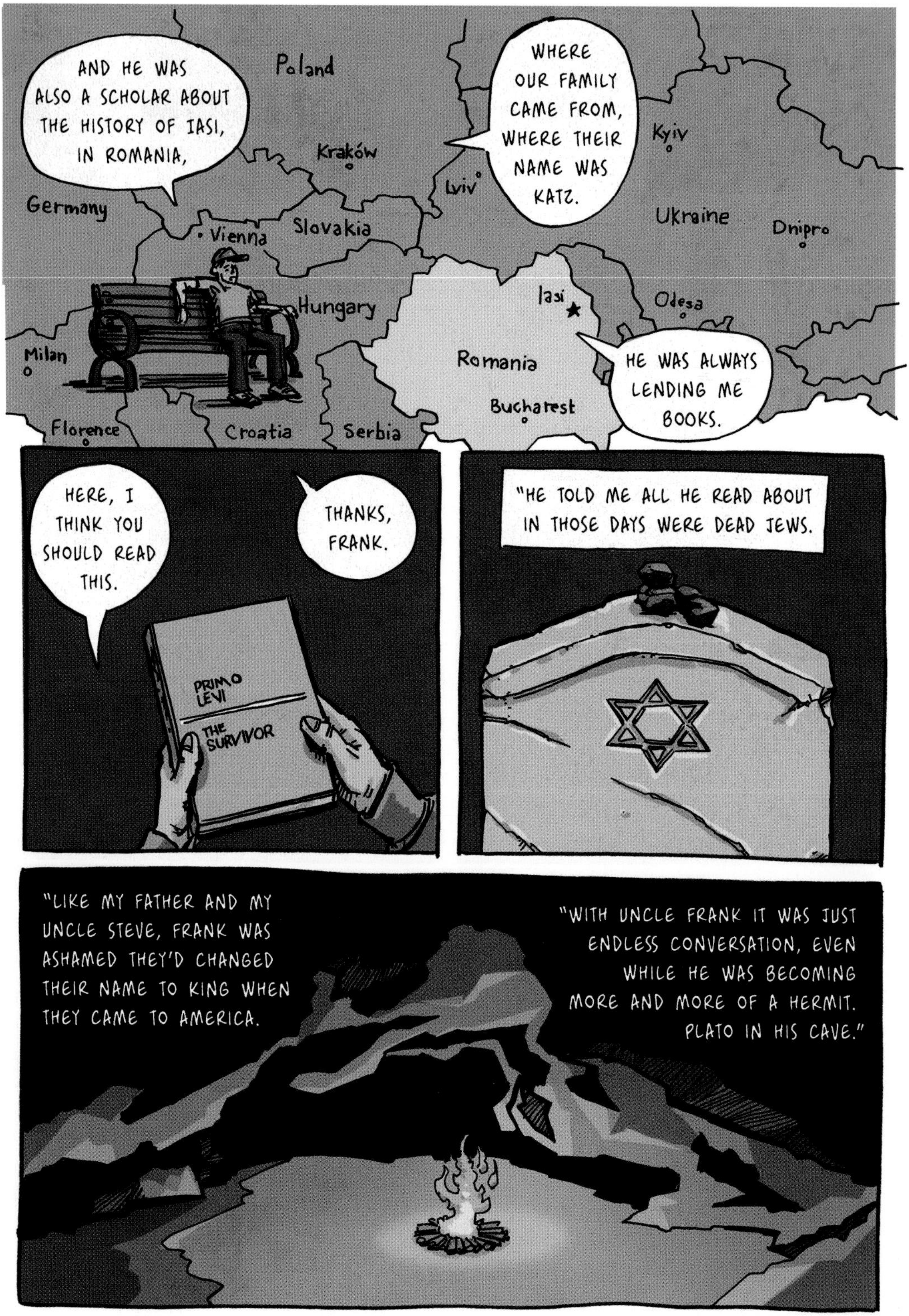
AND HE WAS ALSO A SCHOLAR ABOUT THE HISTORY OF IASI, IN ROMANIA,
Poland
Germany
Kraków
Vienna
Slovakia
Lviv
WHERE OUR FAMILY CAME FROM, WHERE THEIR NAME WAS KATZ.
Kyiv
Ukraine
Dnipro
Hungary
Iasi
Odesa
Milan
Romania
Bucharest
Florence
Croatia
Serbia
HE WAS ALWAYS LENDING ME BOOKS.
HERE, I THINK YOU SHOULD READ THIS.
THANKS, FRANK.
PRIMO LEVI
THE SURVIVOR
"HE TOLD ME ALL HE READ ABOUT IN THOSE DAYS WERE DEAD JEWS.
"LIKE MY FATHER AND MY UNCLE STEVE, FRANK WAS ASHAMED THEY'D CHANGED THEIR NAME TO KING WHEN THEY CAME TO AMERICA.
"WITH UNCLE FRANK IT WAS JUST ENDLESS CONVERSATION, EVEN WHILE HE WAS BECOMING MORE AND MORE OF A HERMIT. PLATO IN HIS CAVE."

JON KING: "POLIO AFFECTED MY KNEES. STARTING WHEN I WAS THREE YEARS OLD, AND FOR THREE YEARS, I HAD TO GO BACK AND FORTH FROM BROOKLYN TO MOUNT SINAI HOSPITAL IN MANHATTAN TWO TIMES A WEEK.

Jonathan A. King
Professor of
Molecular Biology

"I HAD SPECIAL SHOES, AND BRACES, AND KIDS IN THE STREET MADE FUN OF ME A LOT.

I WAS ALWAYS THE LAST TAKEN FOR TEAMS WHEN WE CHOSE UP SIDES. AND BEING CALLED NAMES, AND HUMILIATED,

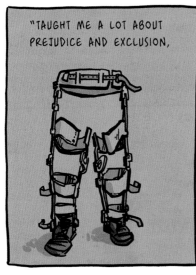

"TAUGHT ME A LOT ABOUT PREJUDICE AND EXCLUSION,

"AND MY POLITICS PROBABLY COME FROM THIS PERIOD OF MY LIFE. I WAS THE MOST POLITICALLY ACTIVE OF THE THREE KING BROTHERS."

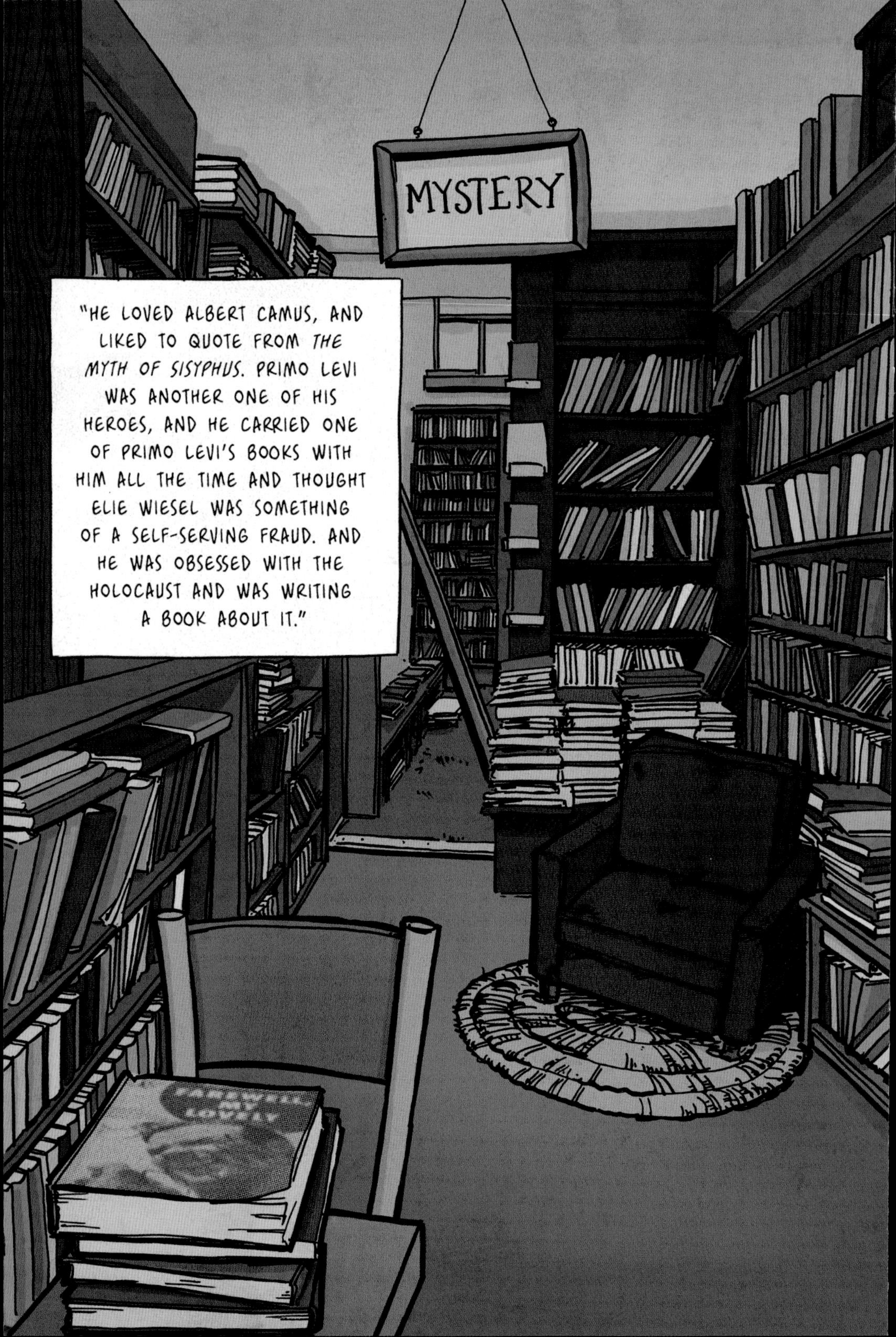
MYSTERY
"HE LOVED ALBERT CAMUS, AND LIKED TO QUOTE FROM *THE MYTH OF SISYPHUS*. PRIMO LEVI WAS ANOTHER ONE OF HIS HEROES, AND HE CARRIED ONE OF PRIMO LEVI'S BOOKS WITH HIM ALL THE TIME AND THOUGHT ELIE WIESEL WAS SOMETHING OF A SELF-SERVING FRAUD. AND HE WAS OBSESSED WITH THE HOLOCAUST AND WAS WRITING A BOOK ABOUT IT."
FAREWELL MY LOVELY

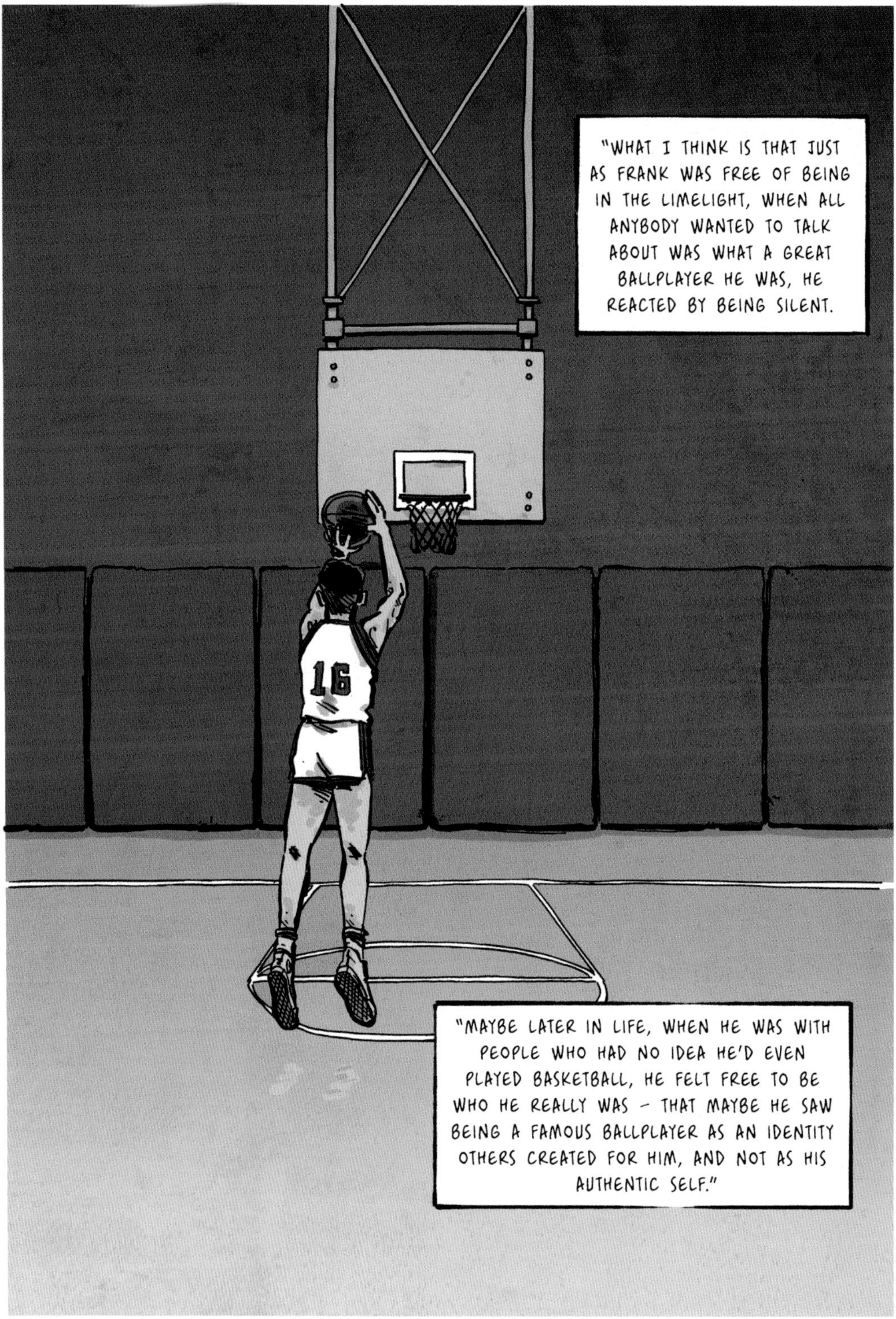
"WHAT I THINK IS THAT JUST AS FRANK WAS FREE OF BEING IN THE LIMELIGHT, WHEN ALL ANYBODY WANTED TO TALK ABOUT WAS WHAT A GREAT BALLPLAYER HE WAS, HE REACTED BY BEING SILENT.
16
"MAYBE LATER IN LIFE, WHEN HE WAS WITH PEOPLE WHO HAD NO IDEA HE'D EVEN PLAYED BASKETBALL, HE FELT FREE TO BE WHO HE REALLY WAS – THAT MAYBE HE SAW BEING A FAMOUS BALLPLAYER AS AN IDENTITY OTHERS CREATED FOR HIM, AND NOT AS HIS AUTHENTIC SELF."

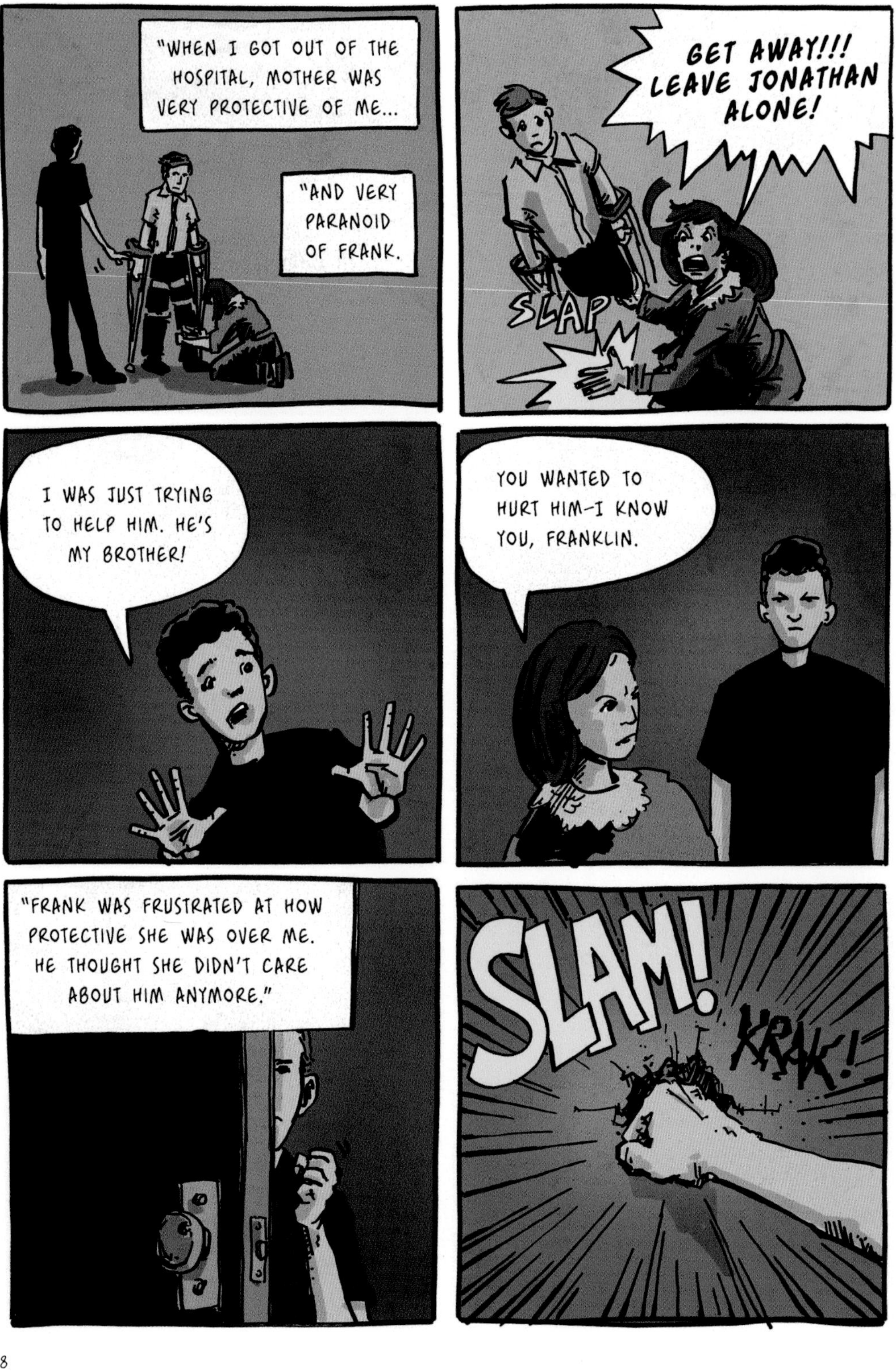
"WHEN I GOT OUT OF THE HOSPITAL, MOTHER WAS VERY PROTECTIVE OF ME...
"AND VERY PARANOID OF FRANK.
GET AWAY!!! LEAVE JONATHAN ALONE!
SLAP
I WAS JUST TRYING TO HELP HIM. HE'S MY BROTHER!
YOU WANTED TO HURT HIM—I KNOW YOU, FRANKLIN.
"FRANK WAS FRUSTRATED AT HOW PROTECTIVE SHE WAS OVER ME. HE THOUGHT SHE DIDN'T CARE ABOUT HIM ANYMORE."
SLAM!
KRAK!

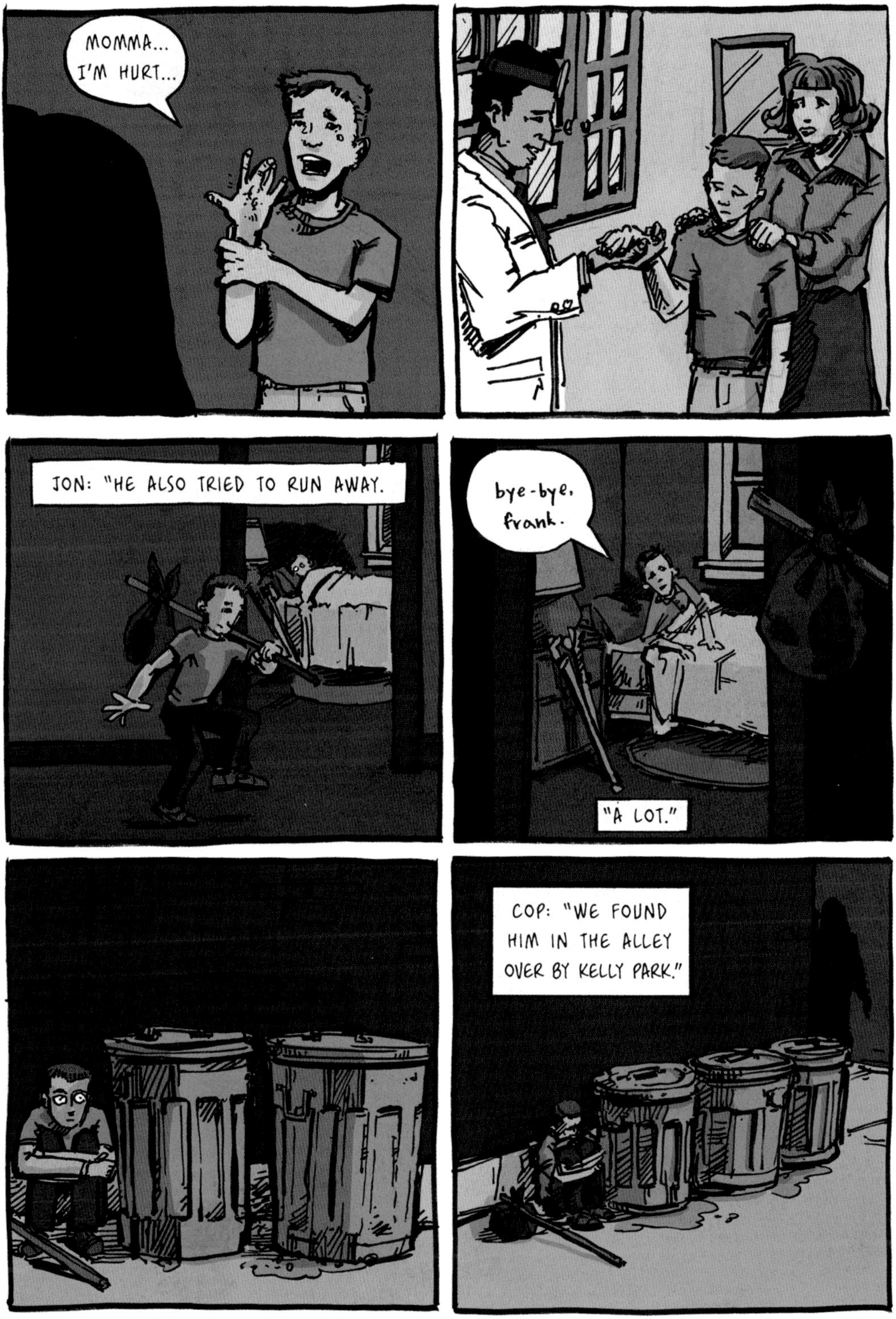

MOMMA...
I'M HURT...
JON: "HE ALSO TRIED TO RUN AWAY.
bye-bye, frank.
"A LOT."
COP: "WE FOUND HIM IN THE ALLEY OVER BY KELLY PARK."

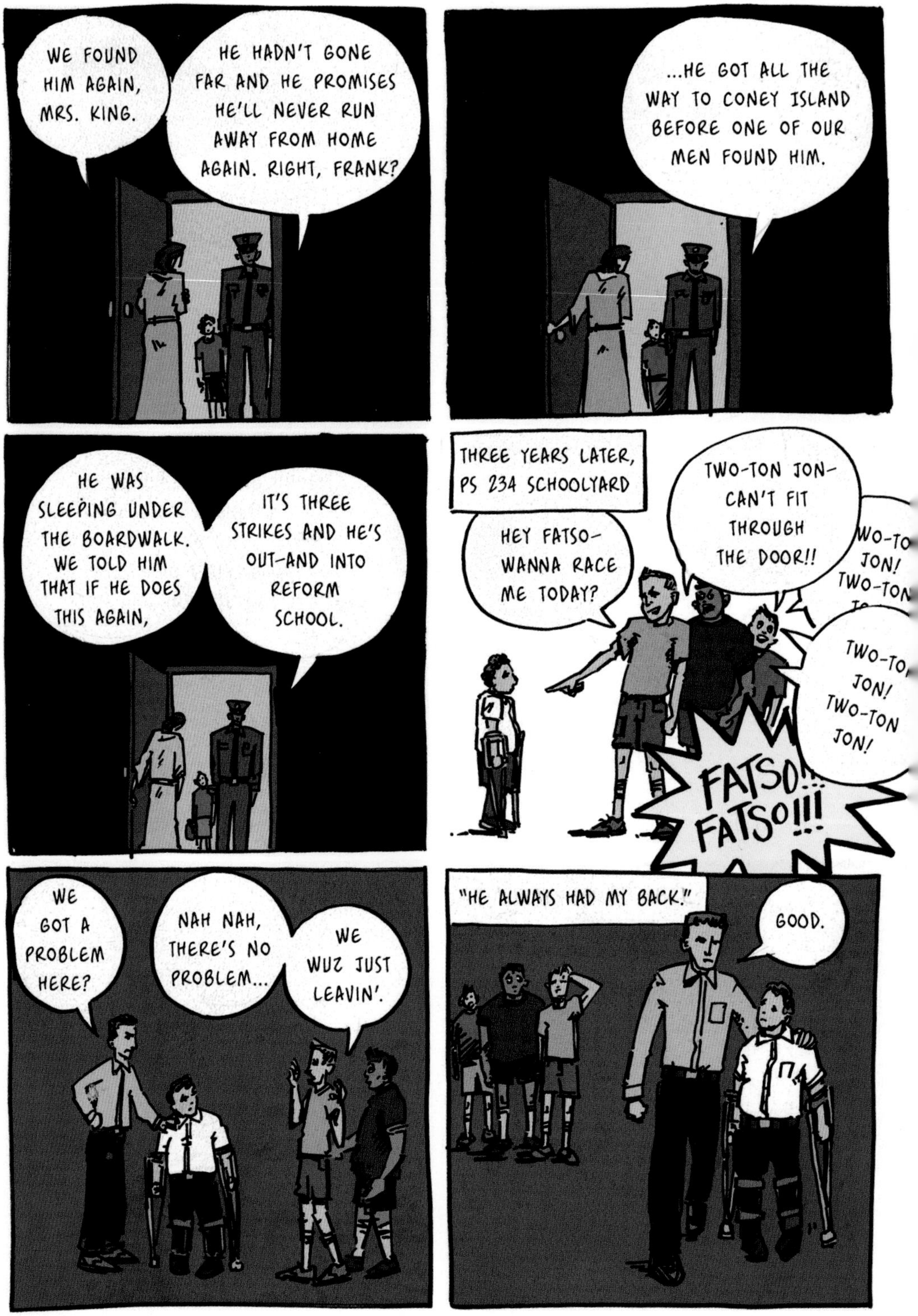
WE FOUND HIM AGAIN, MRS. KING.
HE HADN'T GONE FAR AND HE PROMISES HE'LL NEVER RUN AWAY FROM HOME AGAIN. RIGHT, FRANK?
...HE GOT ALL THE WAY TO CONEY ISLAND BEFORE ONE OF OUR MEN FOUND HIM.
HE WAS SLEEPING UNDER THE BOARDWALK. WE TOLD HIM THAT IF HE DOES THIS AGAIN,
IT'S THREE STRIKES AND HE'S OUT–AND INTO REFORM SCHOOL.
THREE YEARS LATER, PS 234 SCHOOLYARD
HEY FATSO– WANNA RACE ME TODAY?
TWO-TON JON– CAN'T FIT THROUGH THE DOOR!!
TWO-TON JON! TWO-TON JON! TWO-TON JON!
FATSO!!! FATSO!!!
WE GOT A PROBLEM HERE?
NAH NAH, THERE'S NO PROBLEM...
WE WUZ JUST LEAVIN'.
"HE ALWAYS HAD MY BACK."
GOOD.

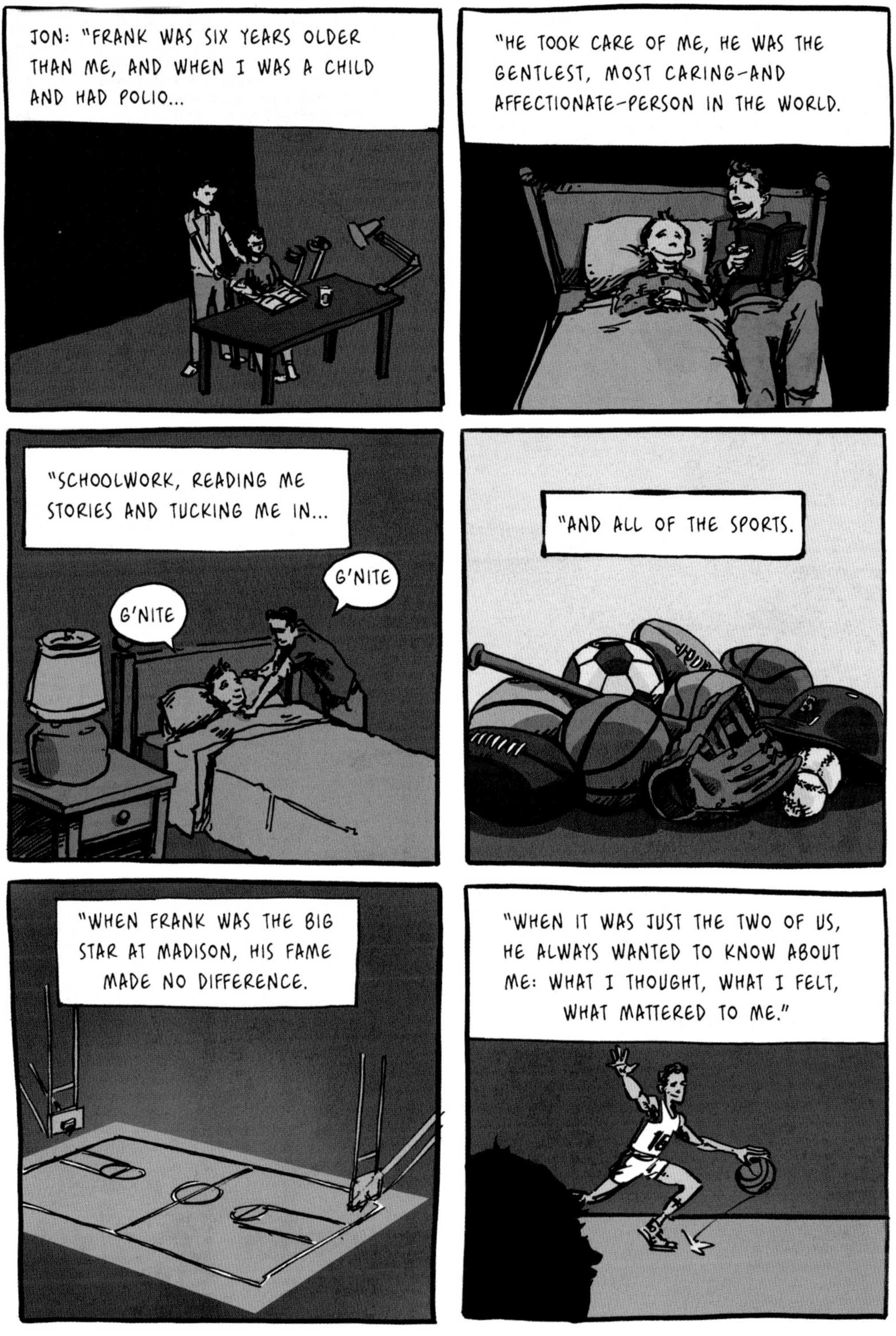
JON: "FRANK WAS SIX YEARS OLDER THAN ME, AND WHEN I WAS A CHILD AND HAD POLIO...
"HE TOOK CARE OF ME, HE WAS THE GENTLEST, MOST CARING—AND AFFECTIONATE—PERSON IN THE WORLD.
"SCHOOLWORK, READING ME STORIES AND TUCKING ME IN...
G'NITE
G'NITE
"AND ALL OF THE SPORTS.
"WHEN FRANK WAS THE BIG STAR AT MADISON, HIS FAME MADE NO DIFFERENCE.
"WHEN IT WAS JUST THE TWO OF US, HE ALWAYS WANTED TO KNOW ABOUT ME: WHAT I THOUGHT, WHAT I FELT, WHAT MATTERED TO ME."

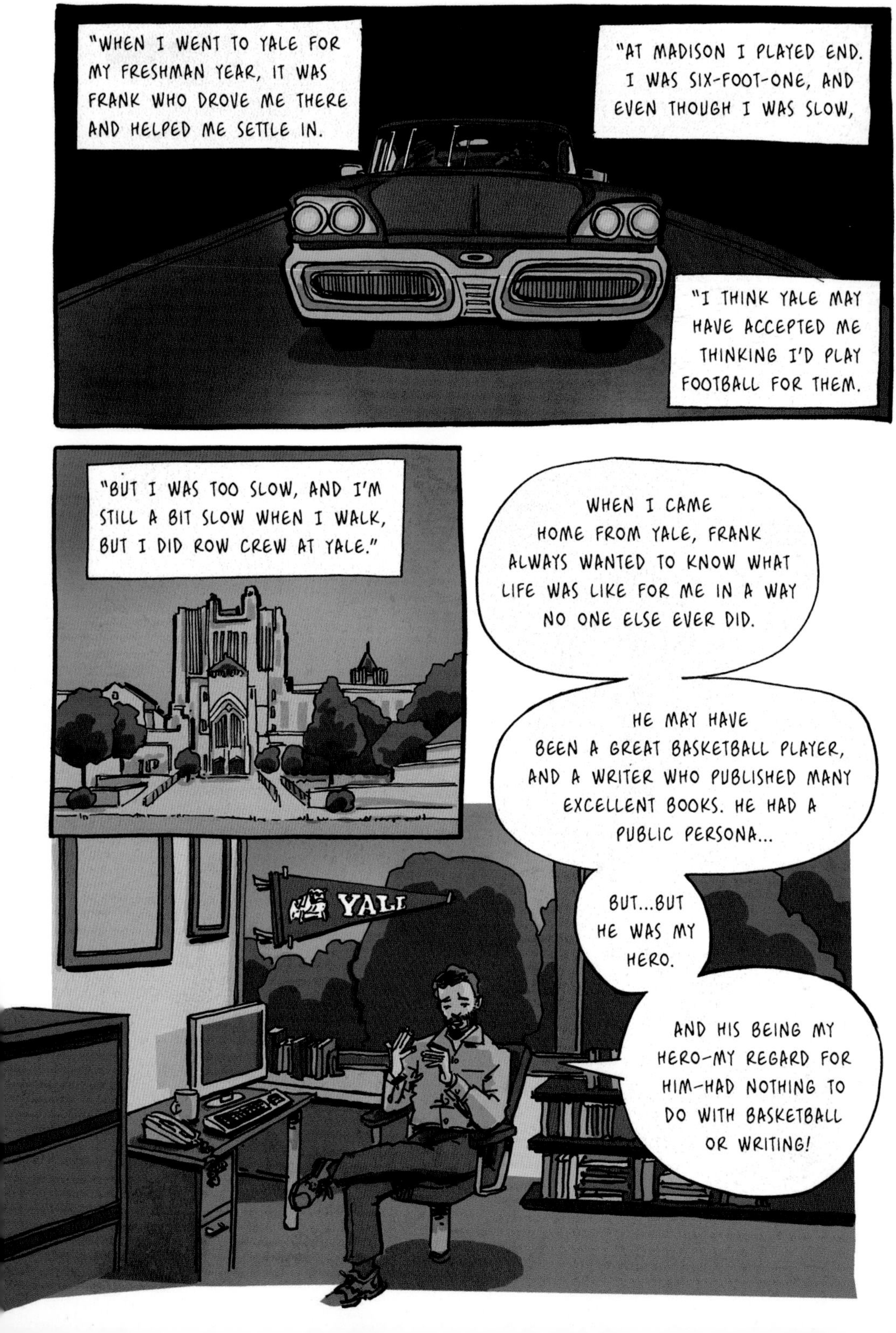
"WHEN I WENT TO YALE FOR MY FRESHMAN YEAR, IT WAS FRANK WHO DROVE ME THERE AND HELPED ME SETTLE IN.
"AT MADISON I PLAYED END. I WAS SIX-FOOT-ONE, AND EVEN THOUGH I WAS SLOW,
"I THINK YALE MAY HAVE ACCEPTED ME THINKING I'D PLAY FOOTBALL FOR THEM.
"BUT I WAS TOO SLOW, AND I'M STILL A BIT SLOW WHEN I WALK, BUT I DID ROW CREW AT YALE."
WHEN I CAME HOME FROM YALE, FRANK ALWAYS WANTED TO KNOW WHAT LIFE WAS LIKE FOR ME IN A WAY NO ONE ELSE EVER DID.
HE MAY HAVE BEEN A GREAT BASKETBALL PLAYER, AND A WRITER WHO PUBLISHED MANY EXCELLENT BOOKS. HE HAD A PUBLIC PERSONA...
BUT...BUT HE WAS MY HERO.
AND HIS BEING MY HERO—MY REGARD FOR HIM—HAD NOTHING TO DO WITH BASKETBALL OR WRITING!
YALE

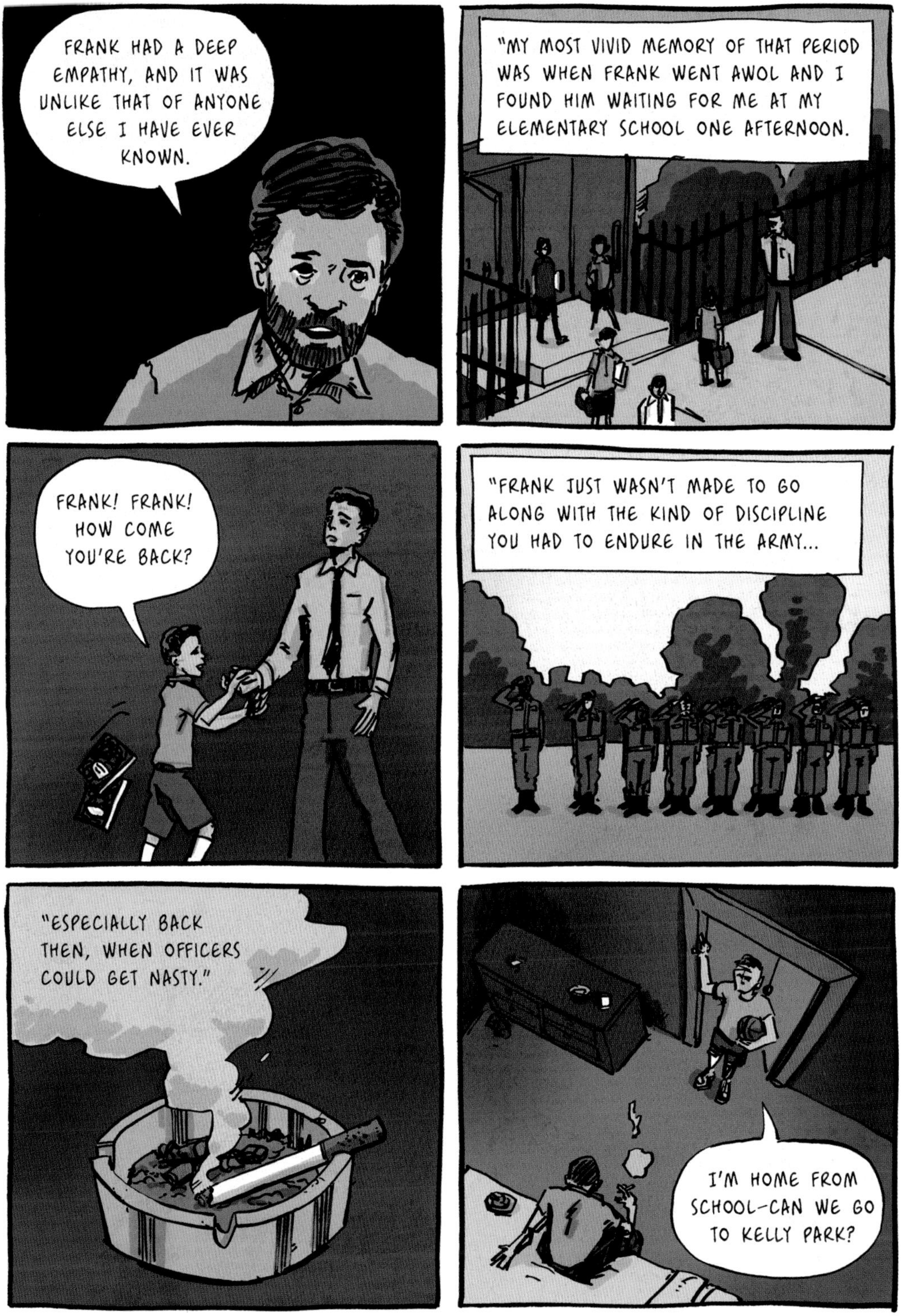
FRANK HAD A DEEP EMPATHY, AND IT WAS UNLIKE THAT OF ANYONE ELSE I HAVE EVER KNOWN.
"MY MOST VIVID MEMORY OF THAT PERIOD WAS WHEN FRANK WENT AWOL AND I FOUND HIM WAITING FOR ME AT MY ELEMENTARY SCHOOL ONE AFTERNOON.
FRANK! FRANK! HOW COME YOU'RE BACK?
"FRANK JUST WASN'T MADE TO GO ALONG WITH THE KIND OF DISCIPLINE YOU HAD TO ENDURE IN THE ARMY...
"ESPECIALLY BACK THEN, WHEN OFFICERS COULD GET NASTY."
I'M HOME FROM SCHOOL—CAN WE GO TO KELLY PARK?

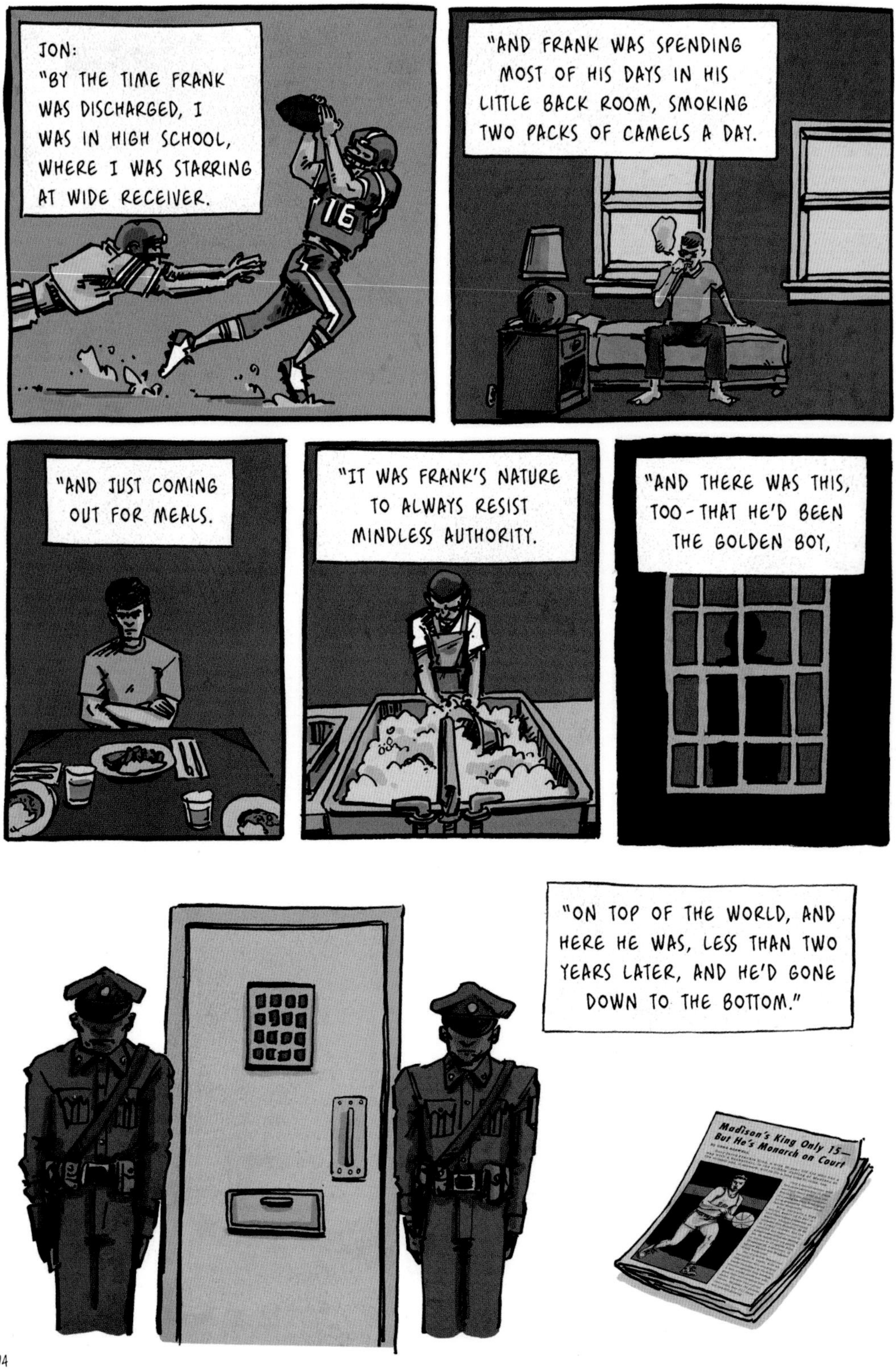
JON:
"BY THE TIME FRANK WAS DISCHARGED, I WAS IN HIGH SCHOOL, WHERE I WAS STARRING AT WIDE RECEIVER.
16
"AND FRANK WAS SPENDING MOST OF HIS DAYS IN HIS LITTLE BACK ROOM, SMOKING TWO PACKS OF CAMELS A DAY.
"AND JUST COMING OUT FOR MEALS.
"IT WAS FRANK'S NATURE TO ALWAYS RESIST MINDLESS AUTHORITY.
"AND THERE WAS THIS, TOO - THAT HE'D BEEN THE GOLDEN BOY,
"ON TOP OF THE WORLD, AND HERE HE WAS, LESS THAN TWO YEARS LATER, AND HE'D GONE DOWN TO THE BOTTOM."
Madison's King Only 15—
But He's Monarch on Court

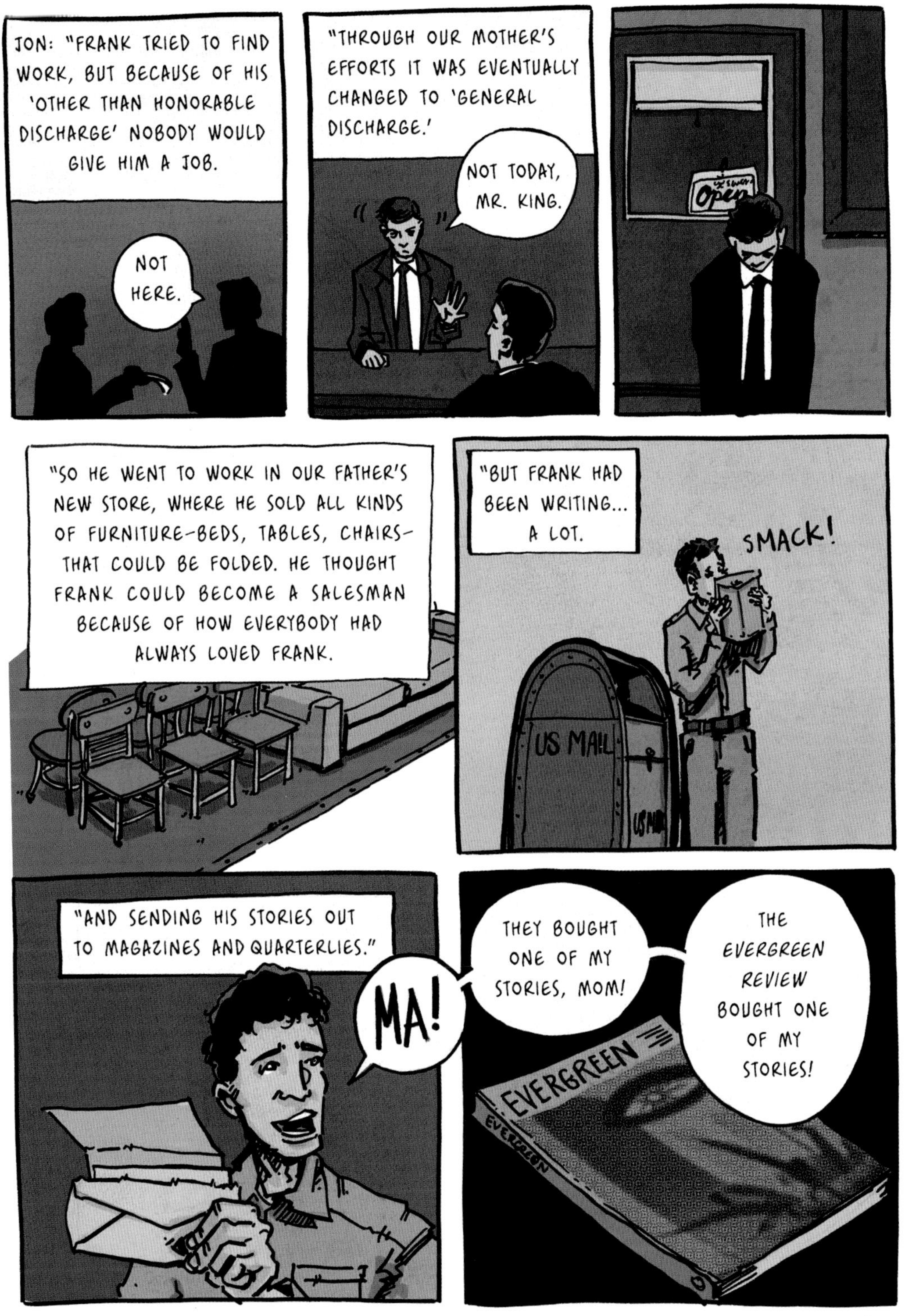
JON: "FRANK TRIED TO FIND WORK, BUT BECAUSE OF HIS 'OTHER THAN HONORABLE DISCHARGE' NOBODY WOULD GIVE HIM A JOB.
NOT HERE.
"THROUGH OUR MOTHER'S EFFORTS IT WAS EVENTUALLY CHANGED TO 'GENERAL DISCHARGE.'
NOT TODAY, MR. KING.
Open
"SO HE WENT TO WORK IN OUR FATHER'S NEW STORE, WHERE HE SOLD ALL KINDS OF FURNITURE—BEDS, TABLES, CHAIRS—THAT COULD BE FOLDED. HE THOUGHT FRANK COULD BECOME A SALESMAN BECAUSE OF HOW EVERYBODY HAD ALWAYS LOVED FRANK.
"BUT FRANK HAD BEEN WRITING... A LOT.
SMACK!
US MAIL
"AND SENDING HIS STORIES OUT TO MAGAZINES AND QUARTERLIES."
MA!
THEY BOUGHT ONE OF MY STORIES, MOM!
THE EVERGREEN REVIEW BOUGHT ONE OF MY STORIES!
EVERGREEN
EVERGREEN

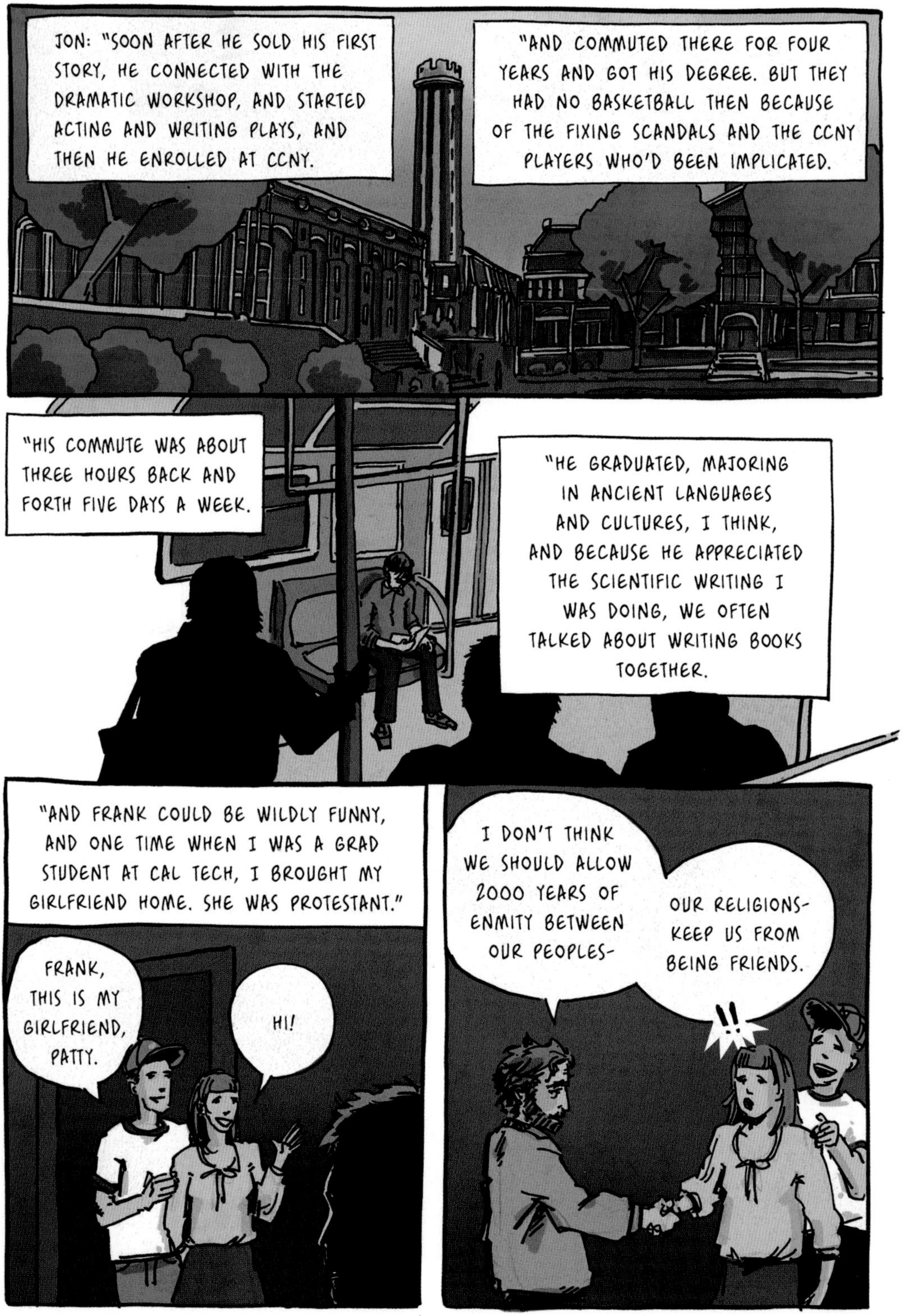

JON: "SOON AFTER HE SOLD HIS FIRST STORY, HE CONNECTED WITH THE DRAMATIC WORKSHOP, AND STARTED ACTING AND WRITING PLAYS, AND THEN HE ENROLLED AT CCNY.
"AND COMMUTED THERE FOR FOUR YEARS AND GOT HIS DEGREE. BUT THEY HAD NO BASKETBALL THEN BECAUSE OF THE FIXING SCANDALS AND THE CCNY PLAYERS WHO'D BEEN IMPLICATED.
"HIS COMMUTE WAS ABOUT THREE HOURS BACK AND FORTH FIVE DAYS A WEEK.
"HE GRADUATED, MAJORING IN ANCIENT LANGUAGES AND CULTURES, I THINK, AND BECAUSE HE APPRECIATED THE SCIENTIFIC WRITING I WAS DOING, WE OFTEN TALKED ABOUT WRITING BOOKS TOGETHER.
"AND FRANK COULD BE WILDLY FUNNY, AND ONE TIME WHEN I WAS A GRAD STUDENT AT CAL TECH, I BROUGHT MY GIRLFRIEND HOME. SHE WAS PROTESTANT."
FRANK, THIS IS MY GIRLFRIEND, PATTY.
HI!
I DON'T THINK WE SHOULD ALLOW 2000 YEARS OF ENMITY BETWEEN OUR PEOPLES-
OUR RELIGIONS- KEEP US FROM BEING FRIENDS.
!!

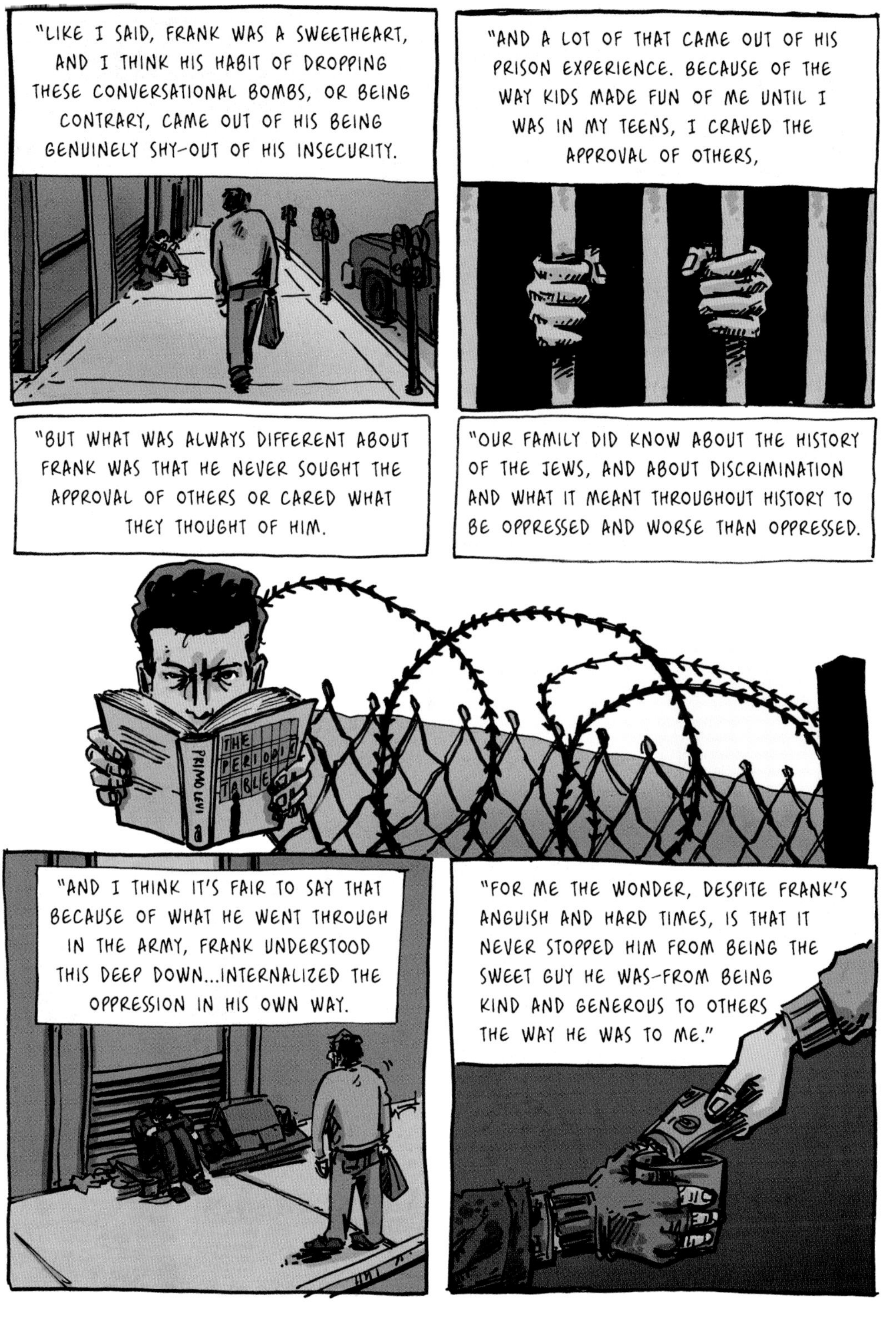
"LIKE I SAID, FRANK WAS A SWEETHEART, AND I THINK HIS HABIT OF DROPPING THESE CONVERSATIONAL BOMBS, OR BEING CONTRARY, CAME OUT OF HIS BEING GENUINELY SHY-OUT OF HIS INSECURITY.
"AND A LOT OF THAT CAME OUT OF HIS PRISON EXPERIENCE. BECAUSE OF THE WAY KIDS MADE FUN OF ME UNTIL I WAS IN MY TEENS, I CRAVED THE APPROVAL OF OTHERS,
"BUT WHAT WAS ALWAYS DIFFERENT ABOUT FRANK WAS THAT HE NEVER SOUGHT THE APPROVAL OF OTHERS OR CARED WHAT THEY THOUGHT OF HIM.
"OUR FAMILY DID KNOW ABOUT THE HISTORY OF THE JEWS, AND ABOUT DISCRIMINATION AND WHAT IT MEANT THROUGHOUT HISTORY TO BE OPPRESSED AND WORSE THAN OPPRESSED.
PRIMO LEVI
THE PERIODIC TABLE
"AND I THINK IT'S FAIR TO SAY THAT BECAUSE OF WHAT HE WENT THROUGH IN THE ARMY, FRANK UNDERSTOOD THIS DEEP DOWN...INTERNALIZED THE OPPRESSION IN HIS OWN WAY.
"FOR ME THE WONDER, DESPITE FRANK'S ANGUISH AND HARD TIMES, IS THAT IT NEVER STOPPED HIM FROM BEING THE SWEET GUY HE WAS-FROM BEING KIND AND GENEROUS TO OTHERS THE WAY HE WAS TO ME."

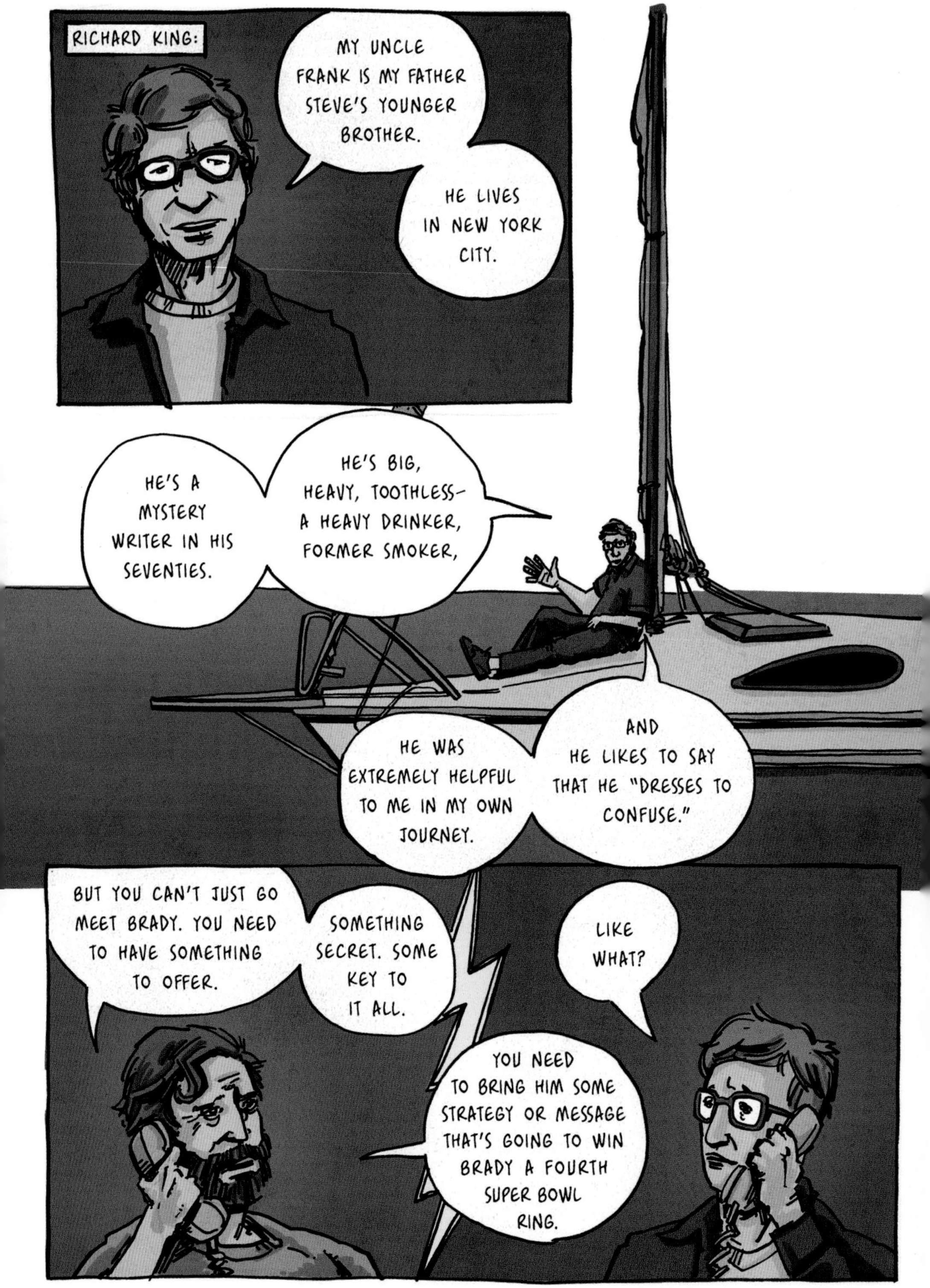
RICHARD KING:
MY UNCLE FRANK IS MY FATHER STEVE'S YOUNGER BROTHER.
HE LIVES IN NEW YORK CITY.
HE'S A MYSTERY WRITER IN HIS SEVENTIES.
HE'S BIG, HEAVY, TOOTHLESS— A HEAVY DRINKER, FORMER SMOKER,
HE WAS EXTREMELY HELPFUL TO ME IN MY OWN JOURNEY.
AND HE LIKES TO SAY THAT HE "DRESSES TO CONFUSE."
BUT YOU CAN'T JUST GO MEET BRADY. YOU NEED TO HAVE SOMETHING TO OFFER.
SOMETHING SECRET. SOME KEY TO IT ALL.
LIKE WHAT?
YOU NEED TO BRING HIM SOME STRATEGY OR MESSAGE THAT'S GOING TO WIN BRADY A FOURTH SUPER BOWL RING.

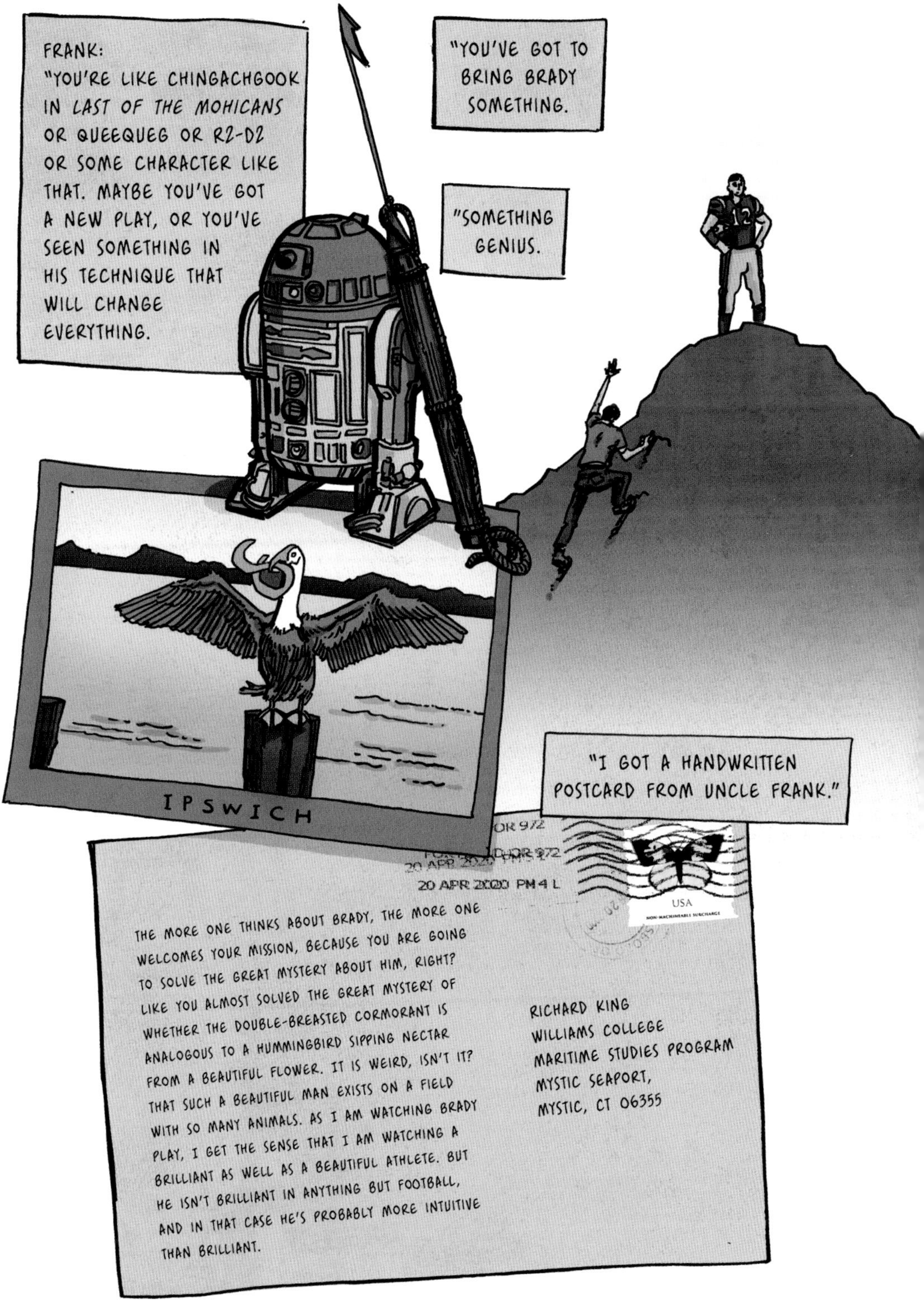
FRANK:
"YOU'RE LIKE CHINGACHGOOK IN *LAST OF THE MOHICANS* OR QUEEQUEG OR R2-D2 OR SOME CHARACTER LIKE THAT. MAYBE YOU'VE GOT A NEW PLAY, OR YOU'VE SEEN SOMETHING IN HIS TECHNIQUE THAT WILL CHANGE EVERYTHING.
"YOU'VE GOT TO BRING BRADY SOMETHING.
"SOMETHING GENIUS.
12
IPSWICH
"I GOT A HANDWRITTEN POSTCARD FROM UNCLE FRANK."
20 APR 2020 PM 4 L
USA
NON-MACHINEABLE SURCHARGE
THE MORE ONE THINKS ABOUT BRADY, THE MORE ONE WELCOMES YOUR MISSION, BECAUSE YOU ARE GOING TO SOLVE THE GREAT MYSTERY ABOUT HIM, RIGHT? LIKE YOU ALMOST SOLVED THE GREAT MYSTERY OF WHETHER THE DOUBLE-BREASTED CORMORANT IS ANALOGOUS TO A HUMMINGBIRD SIPPING NECTAR FROM A BEAUTIFUL FLOWER. IT IS WEIRD, ISN'T IT? THAT SUCH A BEAUTIFUL MAN EXISTS ON A FIELD WITH SO MANY ANIMALS. AS I AM WATCHING BRADY PLAY, I GET THE SENSE THAT I AM WATCHING A BRILLIANT AS WELL AS A BEAUTIFUL ATHLETE. BUT HE ISN'T BRILLIANT IN ANYTHING BUT FOOTBALL, AND IN THAT CASE HE'S PROBABLY MORE INTUITIVE THAN BRILLIANT.
RICHARD KING
WILLIAMS COLLEGE
MARITIME STUDIES PROGRAM
MYSTIC SEAPORT,
MYSTIC, CT 06355

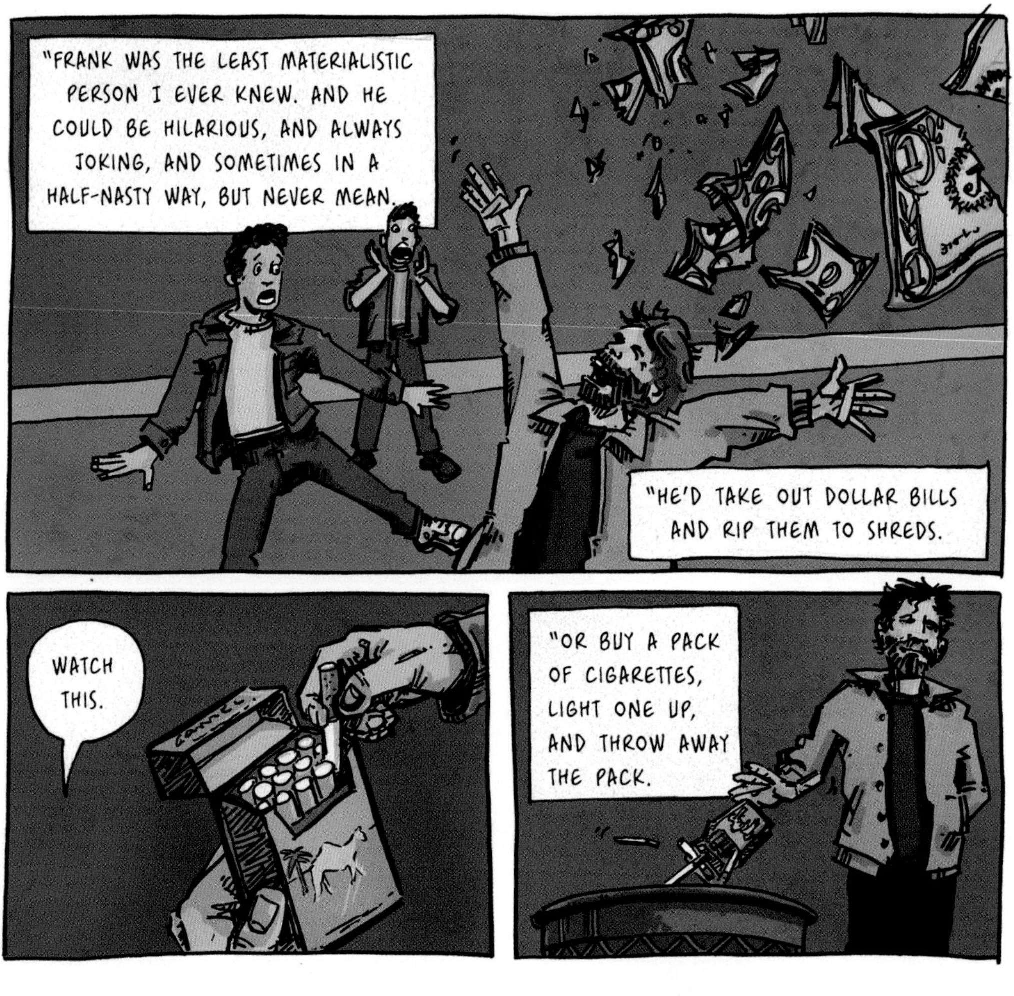
"FRANK WAS THE LEAST MATERIALISTIC PERSON I EVER KNEW. AND HE COULD BE HILARIOUS, AND ALWAYS JOKING, AND SOMETIMES IN A HALF-NASTY WAY, BUT NEVER MEAN.
"HE'D TAKE OUT DOLLAR BILLS AND RIP THEM TO SHREDS.
WATCH THIS.
"OR BUY A PACK OF CIGARETTES, LIGHT ONE UP, AND THROW AWAY THE PACK.

"I REMEMBER WHEN I WAS STRUGGLING WITH MY WRITING HE TOLD ME, 'SO HERE'S WHAT WE'RE GONNA DO, YOU AND ME—WE'RE GONNA WRITE A BOOK TOGETHER ABOUT THE REVOLUTIONARY WAR!'

HE EVEN SENT ME THE FIRST FORTY PAGES AS A MANUSCRIPT!"

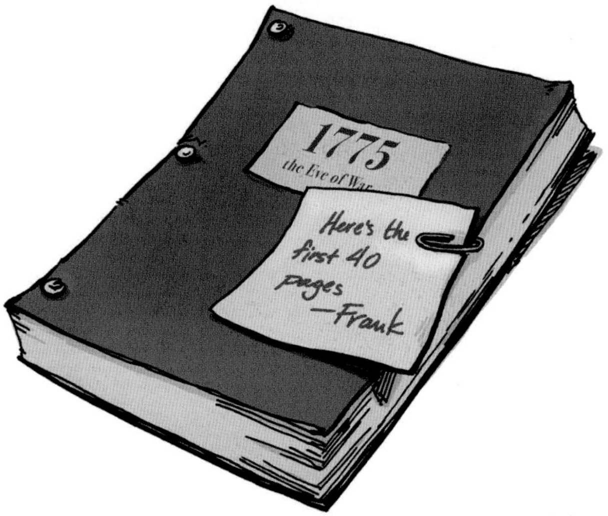
1775
the Eve of War
Here's the first 40 pages
—Frank

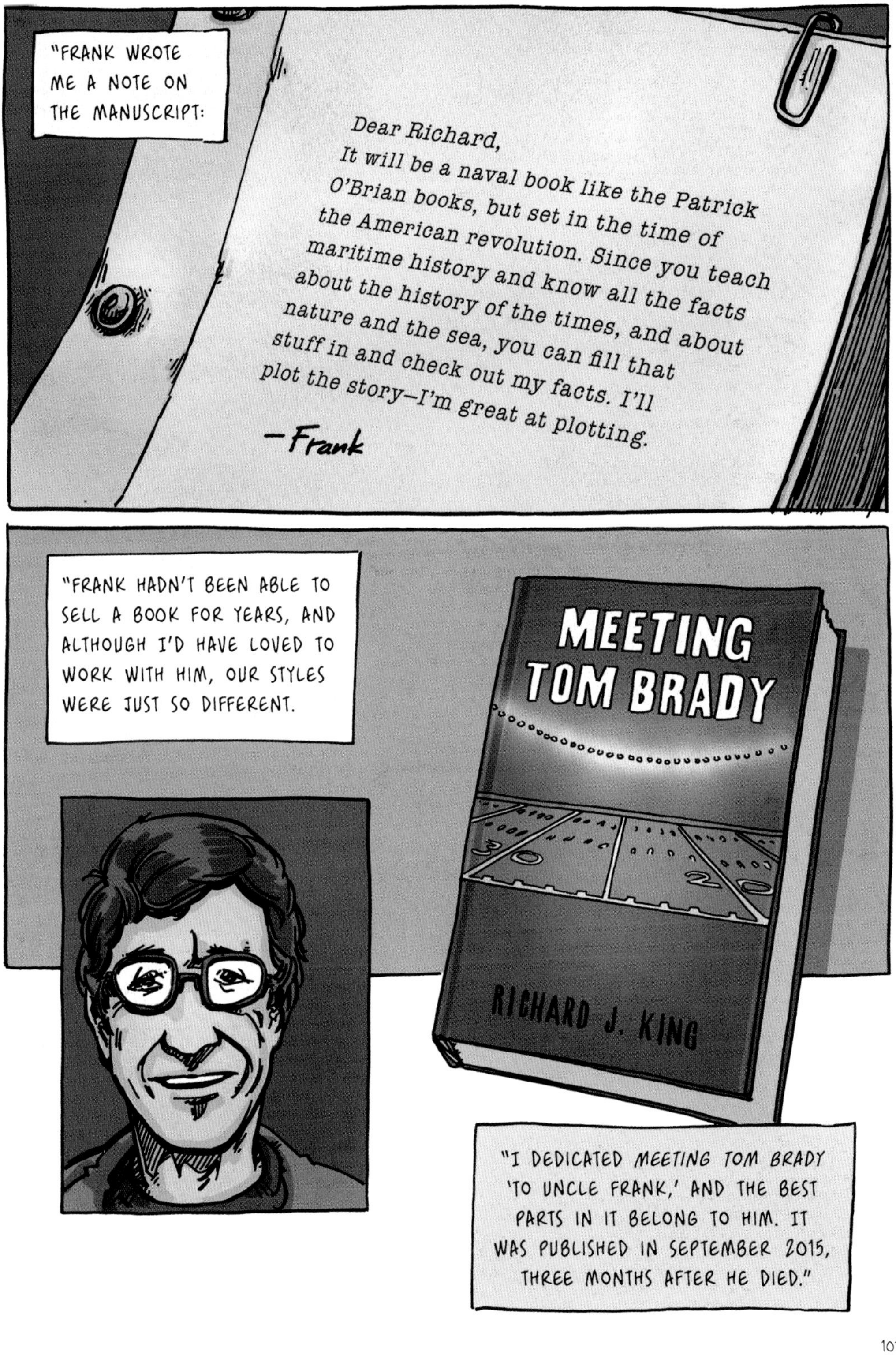
"FRANK WROTE ME A NOTE ON THE MANUSCRIPT:
Dear Richard,
It will be a naval book like the Patrick O'Brian books, but set in the time of the American revolution. Since you teach maritime history and know all the facts about the history of the times, and about nature and the sea, you can fill that stuff in and check out my facts. I'll plot the story—I'm great at plotting.
—Frank
"FRANK HADN'T BEEN ABLE TO SELL A BOOK FOR YEARS, AND ALTHOUGH I'D HAVE LOVED TO WORK WITH HIM, OUR STYLES WERE JUST SO DIFFERENT.
MEETING TOM BRADY
RICHARD J. KING
"I DEDICATED MEETING TOM BRADY 'TO UNCLE FRANK,' AND THE BEST PARTS IN IT BELONG TO HIM. IT WAS PUBLISHED IN SEPTEMBER 2015, THREE MONTHS AFTER HE DIED."

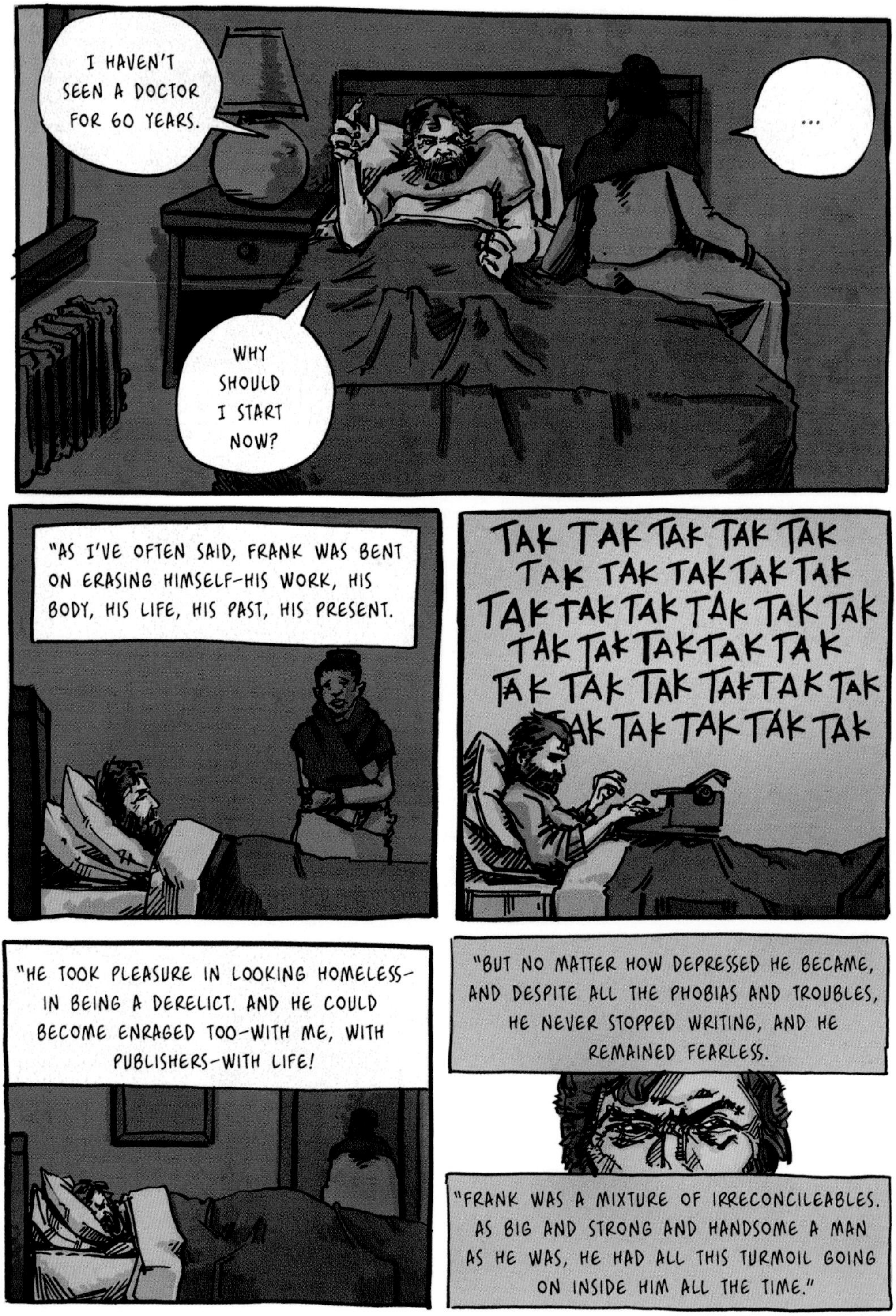
I HAVEN'T SEEN A DOCTOR FOR 60 YEARS.
...
WHY SHOULD I START NOW?
"AS I'VE OFTEN SAID, FRANK WAS BENT ON ERASING HIMSELF–HIS WORK, HIS BODY, HIS LIFE, HIS PAST, HIS PRESENT.
TAK TAK TAK TAK TAK
TAK TAK TAK TAK TAK
TAK TAK TAK TAK TAK TAK
TAK TAK TAK TAK TAK
TAK TAK TAK TAK TAK TAK
AK TAK TAK TAK TAK
"HE TOOK PLEASURE IN LOOKING HOMELESS–IN BEING A DERELICT. AND HE COULD BECOME ENRAGED TOO–WITH ME, WITH PUBLISHERS–WITH LIFE!
"BUT NO MATTER HOW DEPRESSED HE BECAME, AND DESPITE ALL THE PHOBIAS AND TROUBLES, HE NEVER STOPPED WRITING, AND HE REMAINED FEARLESS.
"FRANK WAS A MIXTURE OF IRRECONCILEABLES. AS BIG AND STRONG AND HANDSOME A MAN AS HE WAS, HE HAD ALL THIS TURMOIL GOING ON INSIDE HIM ALL THE TIME."

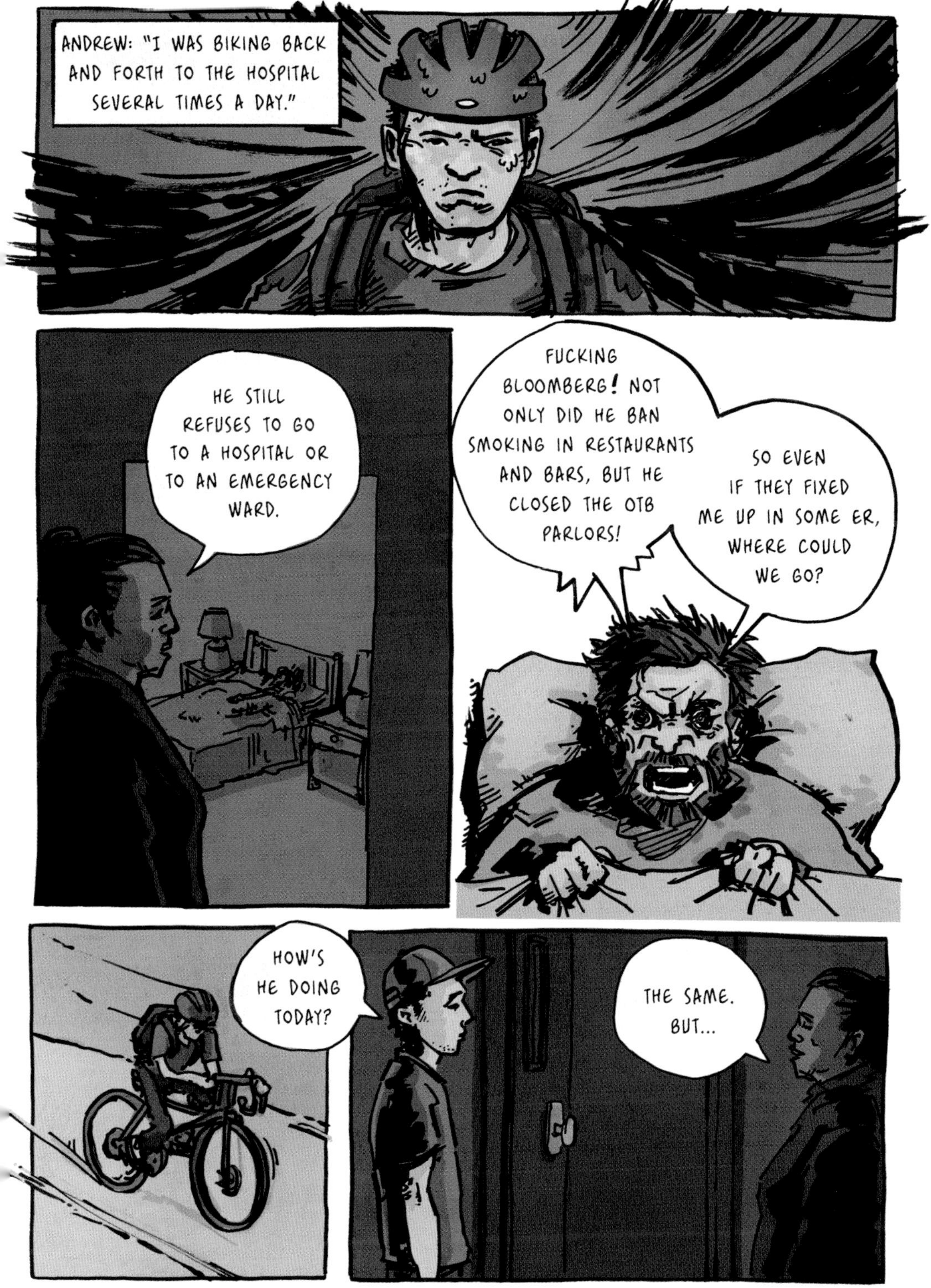
ANDREW: "I WAS BIKING BACK AND FORTH TO THE HOSPITAL SEVERAL TIMES A DAY."
HE STILL REFUSES TO GO TO A HOSPITAL OR TO AN EMERGENCY WARD.
FUCKING BLOOMBERG! NOT ONLY DID HE BAN SMOKING IN RESTAURANTS AND BARS, BUT HE CLOSED THE OTB PARLORS!
SO EVEN IF THEY FIXED ME UP IN SOME ER, WHERE COULD WE GO?
HOW'S HE DOING TODAY?
THE SAME. BUT...

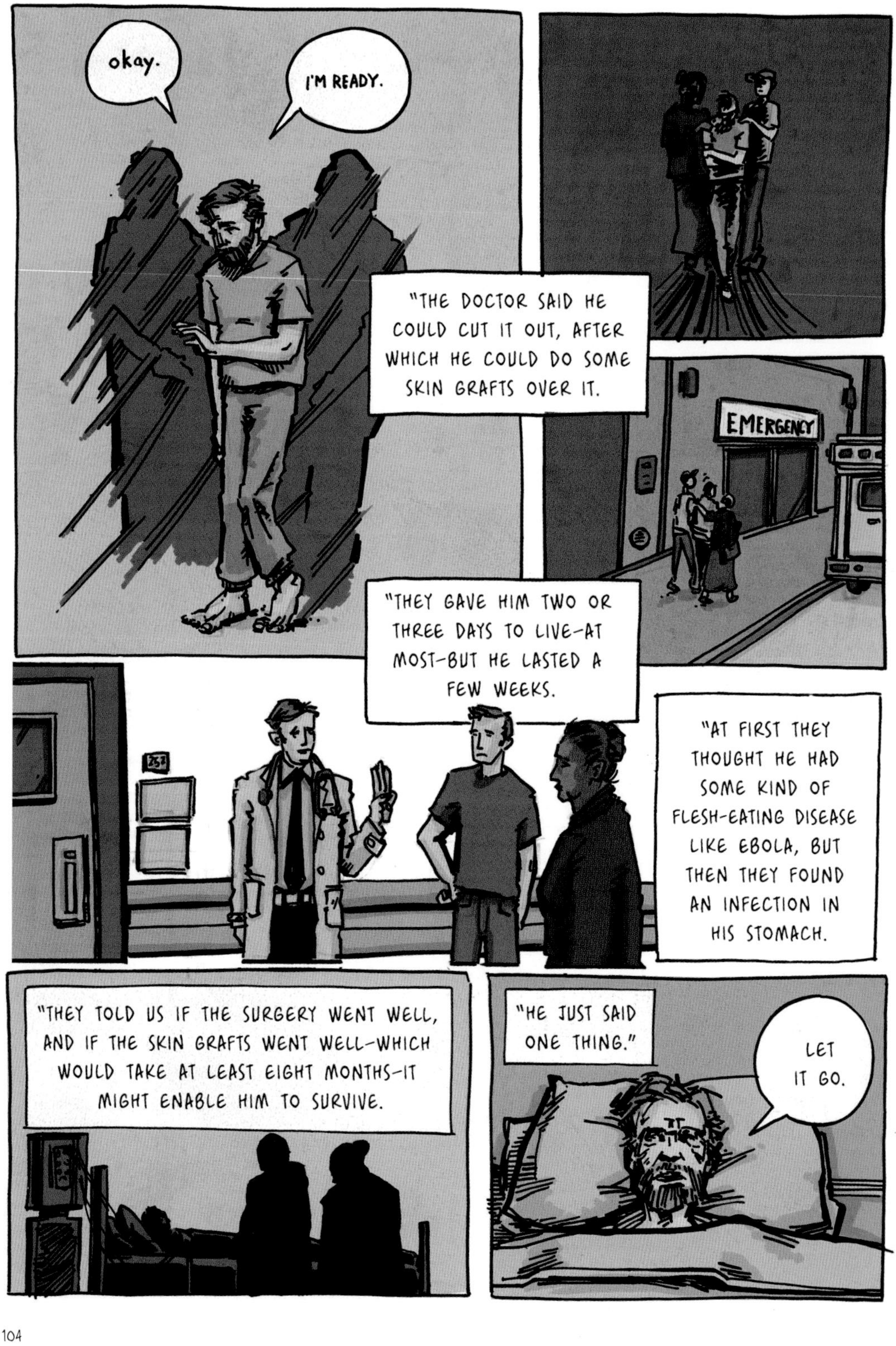
okay.
I'M READY.
"THE DOCTOR SAID HE COULD CUT IT OUT, AFTER WHICH HE COULD DO SOME SKIN GRAFTS OVER IT.
EMERGENCY
"THEY GAVE HIM TWO OR THREE DAYS TO LIVE—AT MOST—BUT HE LASTED A FEW WEEKS.
"AT FIRST THEY THOUGHT HE HAD SOME KIND OF FLESH-EATING DISEASE LIKE EBOLA, BUT THEN THEY FOUND AN INFECTION IN HIS STOMACH.
"THEY TOLD US IF THE SURGERY WENT WELL, AND IF THE SKIN GRAFTS WENT WELL—WHICH WOULD TAKE AT LEAST EIGHT MONTHS—IT MIGHT ENABLE HIM TO SURVIVE.
"HE JUST SAID ONE THING."
LET IT GO.

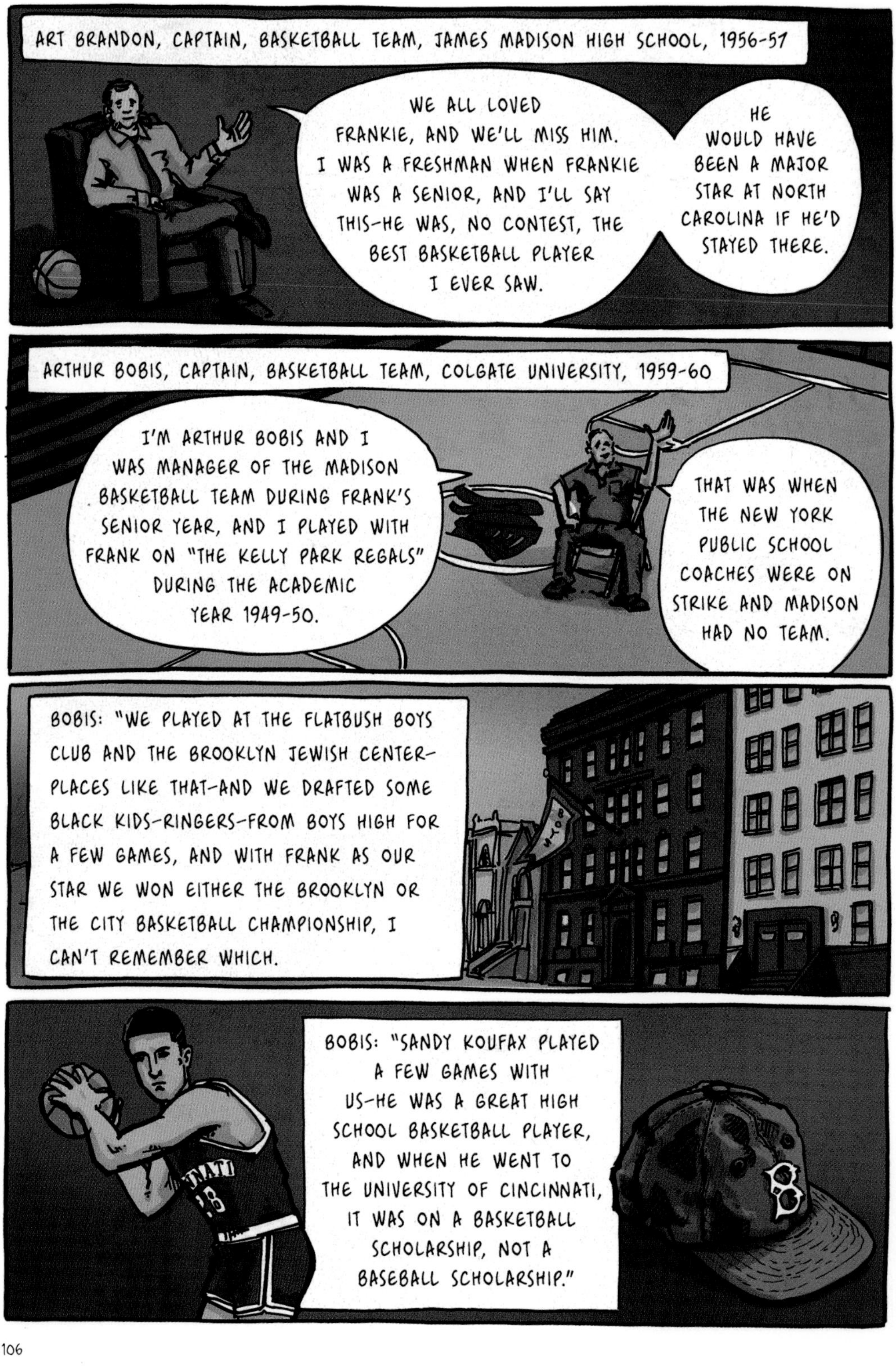
ART BRANDON, CAPTAIN, BASKETBALL TEAM, JAMES MADISON HIGH SCHOOL, 1956-57
WE ALL LOVED FRANKIE, AND WE'LL MISS HIM. I WAS A FRESHMAN WHEN FRANKIE WAS A SENIOR, AND I'LL SAY THIS—HE WAS, NO CONTEST, THE BEST BASKETBALL PLAYER I EVER SAW.
HE WOULD HAVE BEEN A MAJOR STAR AT NORTH CAROLINA IF HE'D STAYED THERE.
ARTHUR BOBIS, CAPTAIN, BASKETBALL TEAM, COLGATE UNIVERSITY, 1959-60
I'M ARTHUR BOBIS AND I WAS MANAGER OF THE MADISON BASKETBALL TEAM DURING FRANK'S SENIOR YEAR, AND I PLAYED WITH FRANK ON "THE KELLY PARK REGALS" DURING THE ACADEMIC YEAR 1949-50.
THAT WAS WHEN THE NEW YORK PUBLIC SCHOOL COACHES WERE ON STRIKE AND MADISON HAD NO TEAM.
BOBIS: "WE PLAYED AT THE FLATBUSH BOYS CLUB AND THE BROOKLYN JEWISH CENTER—PLACES LIKE THAT—AND WE DRAFTED SOME BLACK KIDS—RINGERS—FROM BOYS HIGH FOR A FEW GAMES, AND WITH FRANK AS OUR STAR WE WON EITHER THE BROOKLYN OR THE CITY BASKETBALL CHAMPIONSHIP, I CAN'T REMEMBER WHICH.
BOBIS: "SANDY KOUFAX PLAYED A FEW GAMES WITH US—HE WAS A GREAT HIGH SCHOOL BASKETBALL PLAYER, AND WHEN HE WENT TO THE UNIVERSITY OF CINCINNATI, IT WAS ON A BASKETBALL SCHOLARSHIP, NOT A BASEBALL SCHOLARSHIP."

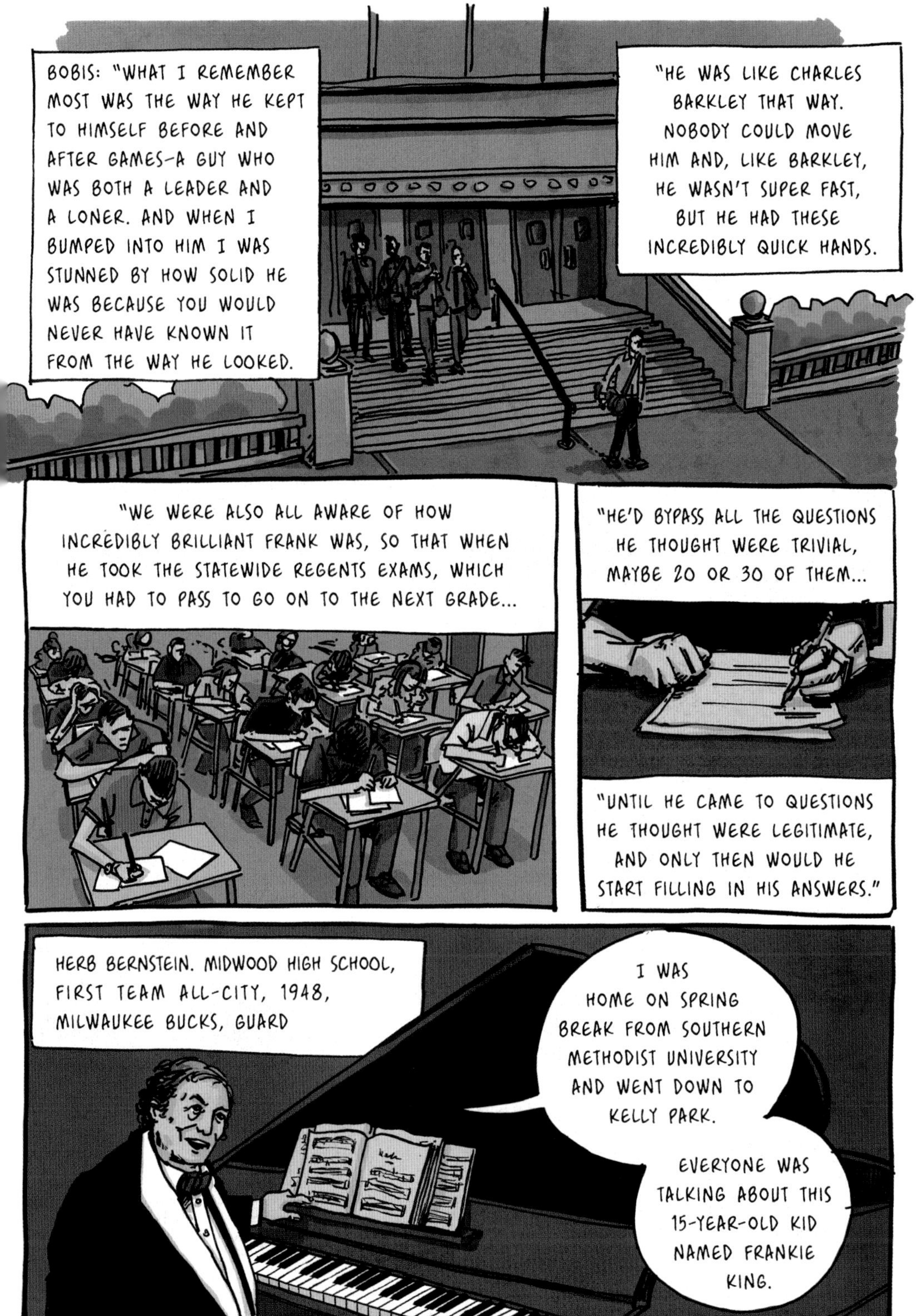
BOBIS: "WHAT I REMEMBER MOST WAS THE WAY HE KEPT TO HIMSELF BEFORE AND AFTER GAMES—A GUY WHO WAS BOTH A LEADER AND A LONER. AND WHEN I BUMPED INTO HIM I WAS STUNNED BY HOW SOLID HE WAS BECAUSE YOU WOULD NEVER HAVE KNOWN IT FROM THE WAY HE LOOKED.
"HE WAS LIKE CHARLES BARKLEY THAT WAY. NOBODY COULD MOVE HIM AND, LIKE BARKLEY, HE WASN'T SUPER FAST, BUT HE HAD THESE INCREDIBLY QUICK HANDS.
"WE WERE ALSO ALL AWARE OF HOW INCREDIBLY BRILLIANT FRANK WAS, SO THAT WHEN HE TOOK THE STATEWIDE REGENTS EXAMS, WHICH YOU HAD TO PASS TO GO ON TO THE NEXT GRADE...
"HE'D BYPASS ALL THE QUESTIONS HE THOUGHT WERE TRIVIAL, MAYBE 20 OR 30 OF THEM...
"UNTIL HE CAME TO QUESTIONS HE THOUGHT WERE LEGITIMATE, AND ONLY THEN WOULD HE START FILLING IN HIS ANSWERS."
HERB BERNSTEIN. MIDWOOD HIGH SCHOOL, FIRST TEAM ALL-CITY, 1948, MILWAUKEE BUCKS, GUARD
I WAS HOME ON SPRING BREAK FROM SOUTHERN METHODIST UNIVERSITY AND WENT DOWN TO KELLY PARK.
EVERYONE WAS TALKING ABOUT THIS 15-YEAR-OLD KID NAMED FRANKIE KING.

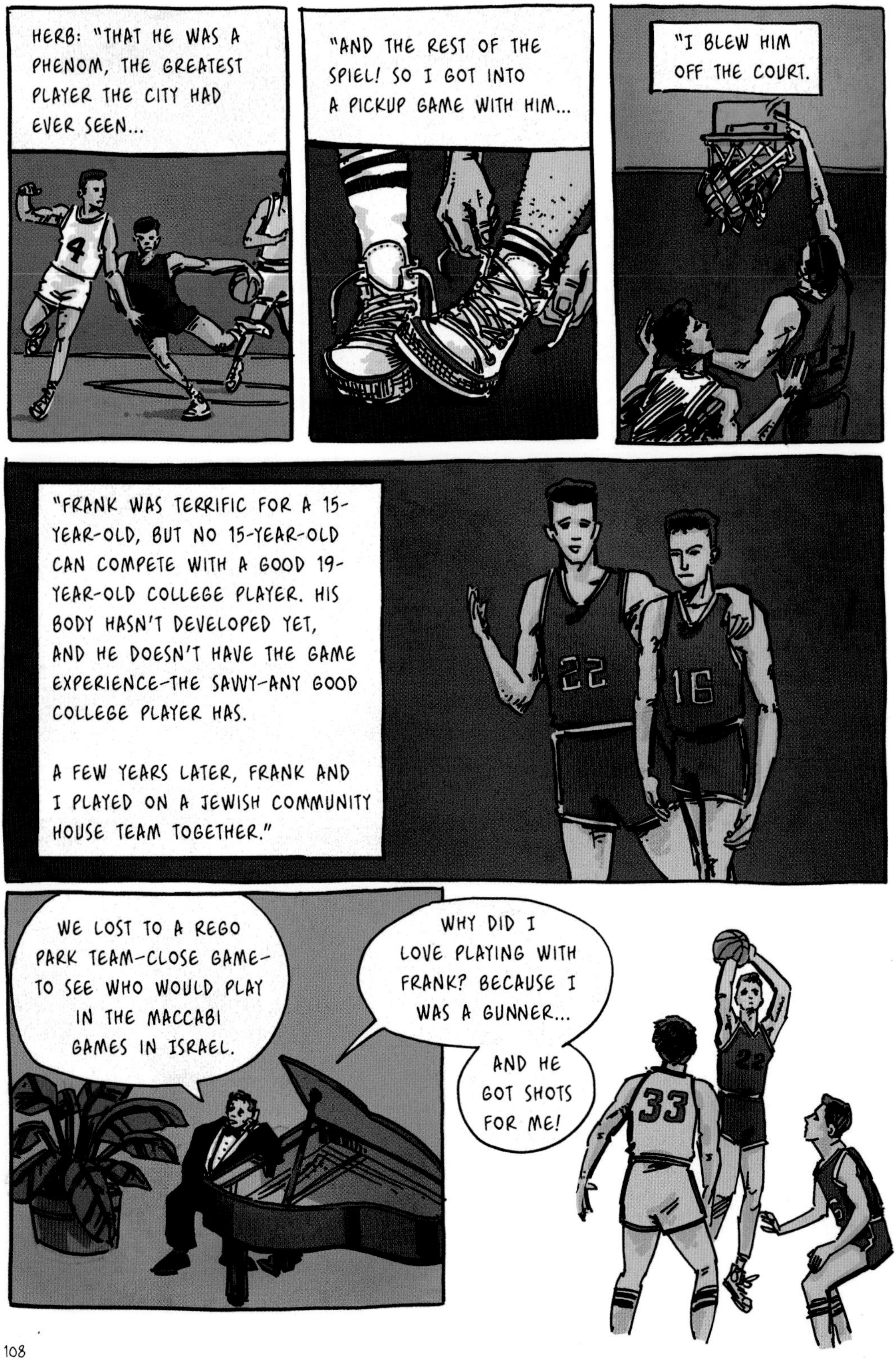
HERB: "THAT HE WAS A PHENOM, THE GREATEST PLAYER THE CITY HAD EVER SEEN...
"AND THE REST OF THE SPIEL! SO I GOT INTO A PICKUP GAME WITH HIM...
"I BLEW HIM OFF THE COURT.
"FRANK WAS TERRIFIC FOR A 15-YEAR-OLD, BUT NO 15-YEAR-OLD CAN COMPETE WITH A GOOD 19-YEAR-OLD COLLEGE PLAYER. HIS BODY HASN'T DEVELOPED YET, AND HE DOESN'T HAVE THE GAME EXPERIENCE–THE SAVVY–ANY GOOD COLLEGE PLAYER HAS.
A FEW YEARS LATER, FRANK AND I PLAYED ON A JEWISH COMMUNITY HOUSE TEAM TOGETHER."
22
16
WE LOST TO A REGO PARK TEAM–CLOSE GAME–TO SEE WHO WOULD PLAY IN THE MACCABI GAMES IN ISRAEL.
WHY DID I LOVE PLAYING WITH FRANK? BECAUSE I WAS A GUNNER...
AND HE GOT SHOTS FOR ME!
33
22

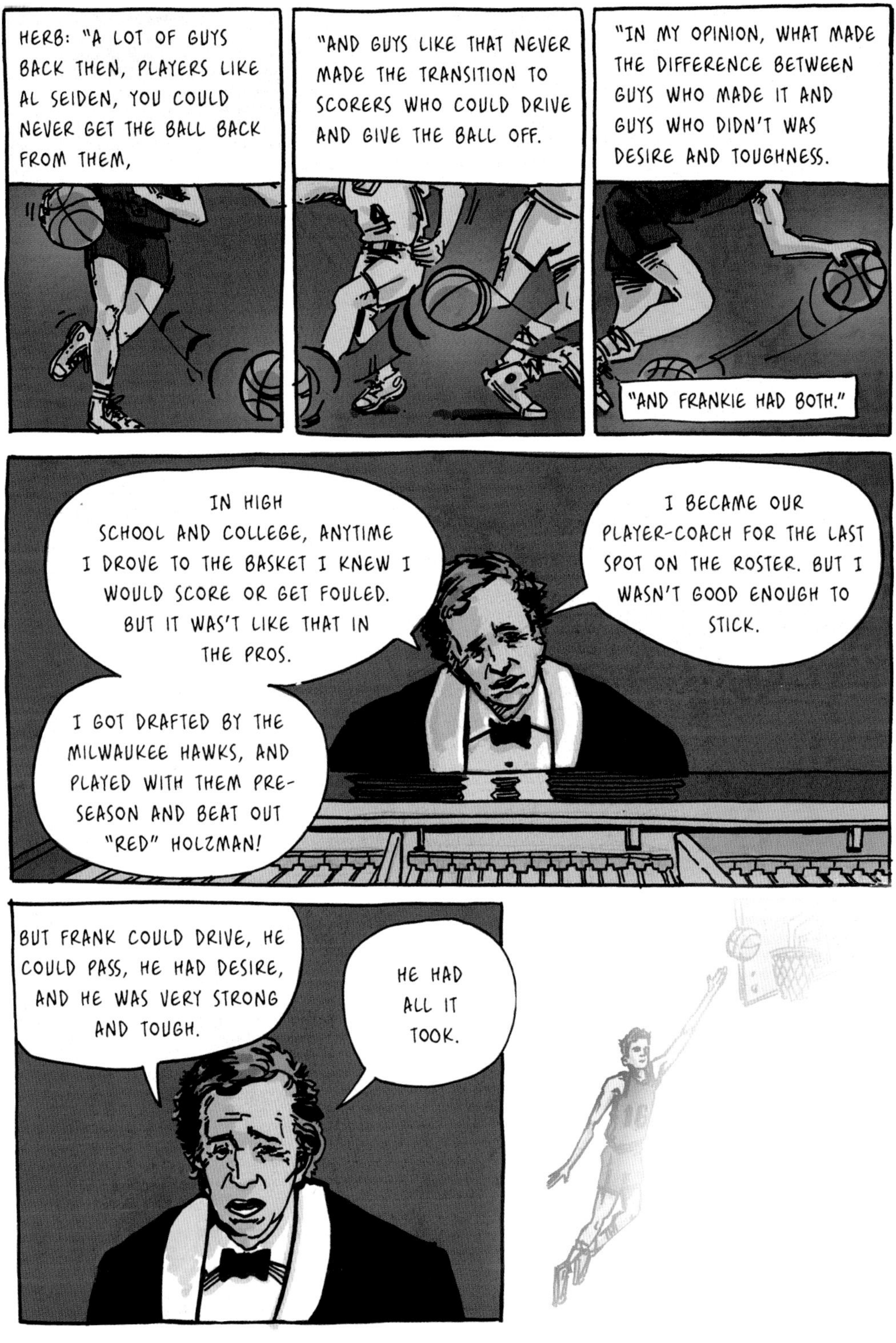
HERB: "A LOT OF GUYS BACK THEN, PLAYERS LIKE AL SEIDEN, YOU COULD NEVER GET THE BALL BACK FROM THEM,
"AND GUYS LIKE THAT NEVER MADE THE TRANSITION TO SCORERS WHO COULD DRIVE AND GIVE THE BALL OFF.
"IN MY OPINION, WHAT MADE THE DIFFERENCE BETWEEN GUYS WHO MADE IT AND GUYS WHO DIDN'T WAS DESIRE AND TOUGHNESS.
"AND FRANKIE HAD BOTH."
IN HIGH SCHOOL AND COLLEGE, ANYTIME I DROVE TO THE BASKET I KNEW I WOULD SCORE OR GET FOULED. BUT IT WASN'T LIKE THAT IN THE PROS.
I GOT DRAFTED BY THE MILWAUKEE HAWKS, AND PLAYED WITH THEM PRE-SEASON AND BEAT OUT "RED" HOLZMAN!
I BECAME OUR PLAYER-COACH FOR THE LAST SPOT ON THE ROSTER. BUT I WASN'T GOOD ENOUGH TO STICK.
BUT FRANK COULD DRIVE, HE COULD PASS, HE HAD DESIRE, AND HE WAS VERY STRONG AND TOUGH.
HE HAD ALL IT TOOK.

THE MONARCH OF MADISON-- 15 YEAR OLD FRANKIE KING!

By PHIL YARNELL

Baby-faced Frankie King, a 15-year old kid with a flair for dribbling is Madison's reigning king, and promises to be so for a long time to come!

A sophomore, with two more years to play for the Black and Gold, Frankie is the team's dauphin on a team that coach Jammy Moskowitz is more than mildly excited about.

King, normally a high scorer, scored only 6 points against previously unbeaten Fort Hamilton, 51-48 in a PSAL contest, yesterday but the wiry cager turned in a major rebounding and feeding job. And in three previous games, he scored 17 against Boys, 19 against St. Augustine's, 18 against Manual and 18 against Grady Vocational.

King's father is a former Haaren and Vermont U. cager, and he has an older brother who played varsity basketball for Vermont, so Frankie is bringing glory to a family tradition. He's steady as a rock, strong as a bull, and an excellent distributor, his eyes always alert to possibilities others might not see.

His future, local gym rats agree, is boundless. He has a fit, tight 5-11 frame, and his 171 pounds are all sinew and muscle. He's a baby-faced kid, for sure--and the sweetheart of Madison High.

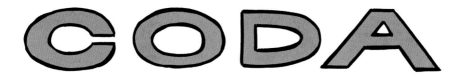

CODA

[WE JOIN FRANK'S CHARACTERS]

A CAT IN WOLF'S CLOTHING
A CAT, A MOUSE, AND TWO CORPSES EQUAL A MENAGERIE OF MURDER FOR A BEAUTIFUL SLEUTH
LYDIA ADAMSON
AN ALICE NESTLETON MYSTERY

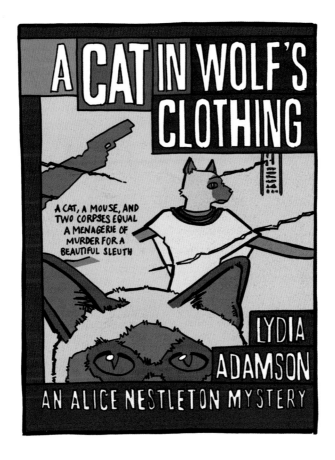

IN THE TWENTY-THREE CAT MYSTERIES FRANK KING WROTE, ALL TOLD IN THE FIRST-PERSON VOICE OF ALICE NESTLETON, AN ACTRESS WHO, WHEN OUT OF WORK, SUPPORTS HERSELF BY CAT-SITTING, THERE IS ONLY ONE PLAY, SOPHOCLES'S *PHILOCTETES,* THAT RECEIVES MORE THAN A PERFUNCTORY DESCRIPTION.

IN *A CAT IN WOLF'S CLOTHING,* ALICE EXPLAINS TO HER BOYFRIEND TONY WHY, IN AN ALL-FEMALE PRODUCTION, SHE'S CONSIDERING PLAYING THE PART OF ODYSSEUS...

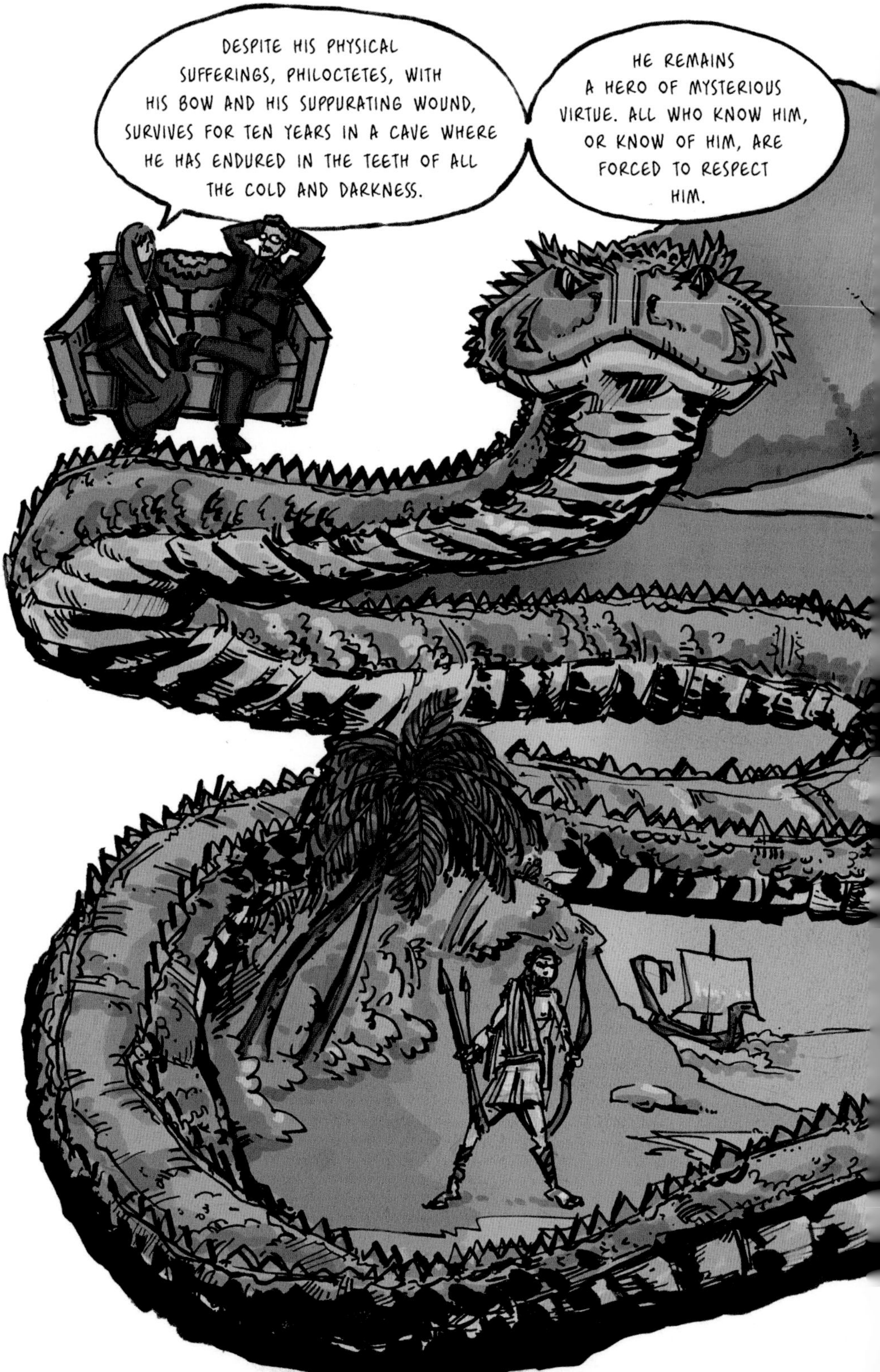
DESPITE HIS PHYSICAL SUFFERINGS, PHILOCTETES, WITH HIS BOW AND HIS SUPPURATING WOUND, SURVIVES FOR TEN YEARS IN A CAVE WHERE HE HAS ENDURED IN THE TEETH OF ALL THE COLD AND DARKNESS.
HE REMAINS A HERO OF MYSTERIOUS VIRTUE. ALL WHO KNOW HIM, OR KNOW OF HIM, ARE FORCED TO RESPECT HIM.

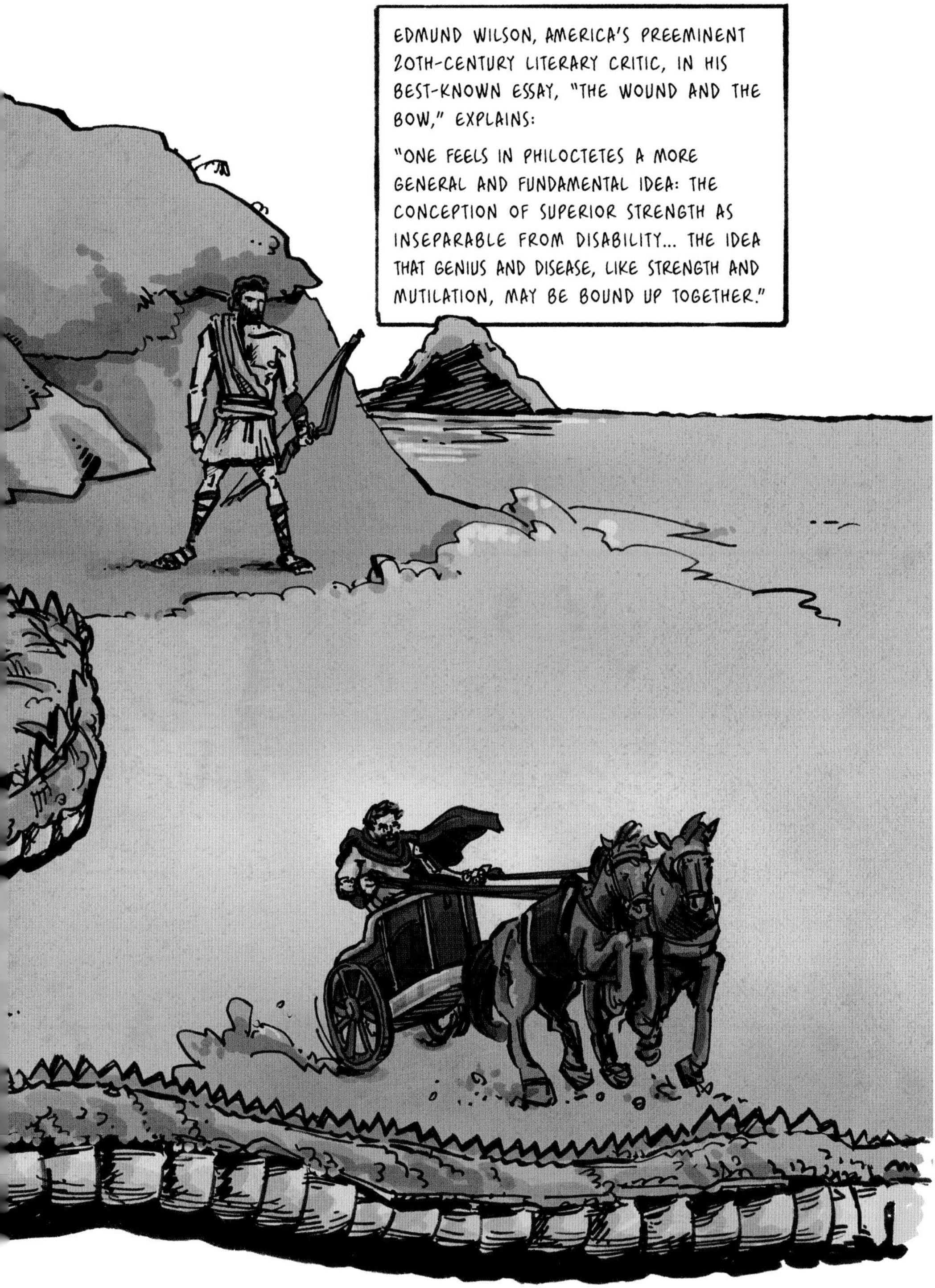
EDMUND WILSON, AMERICA'S PREEMINENT 20TH-CENTURY LITERARY CRITIC, IN HIS BEST-KNOWN ESSAY, "THE WOUND AND THE BOW," EXPLAINS:
"ONE FEELS IN PHILOCTETES A MORE GENERAL AND FUNDAMENTAL IDEA: THE CONCEPTION OF SUPERIOR STRENGTH AS INSEPARABLE FROM DISABILITY... THE IDEA THAT GENIUS AND DISEASE, LIKE STRENGTH AND MUTILATION, MAY BE BOUND UP TOGETHER."

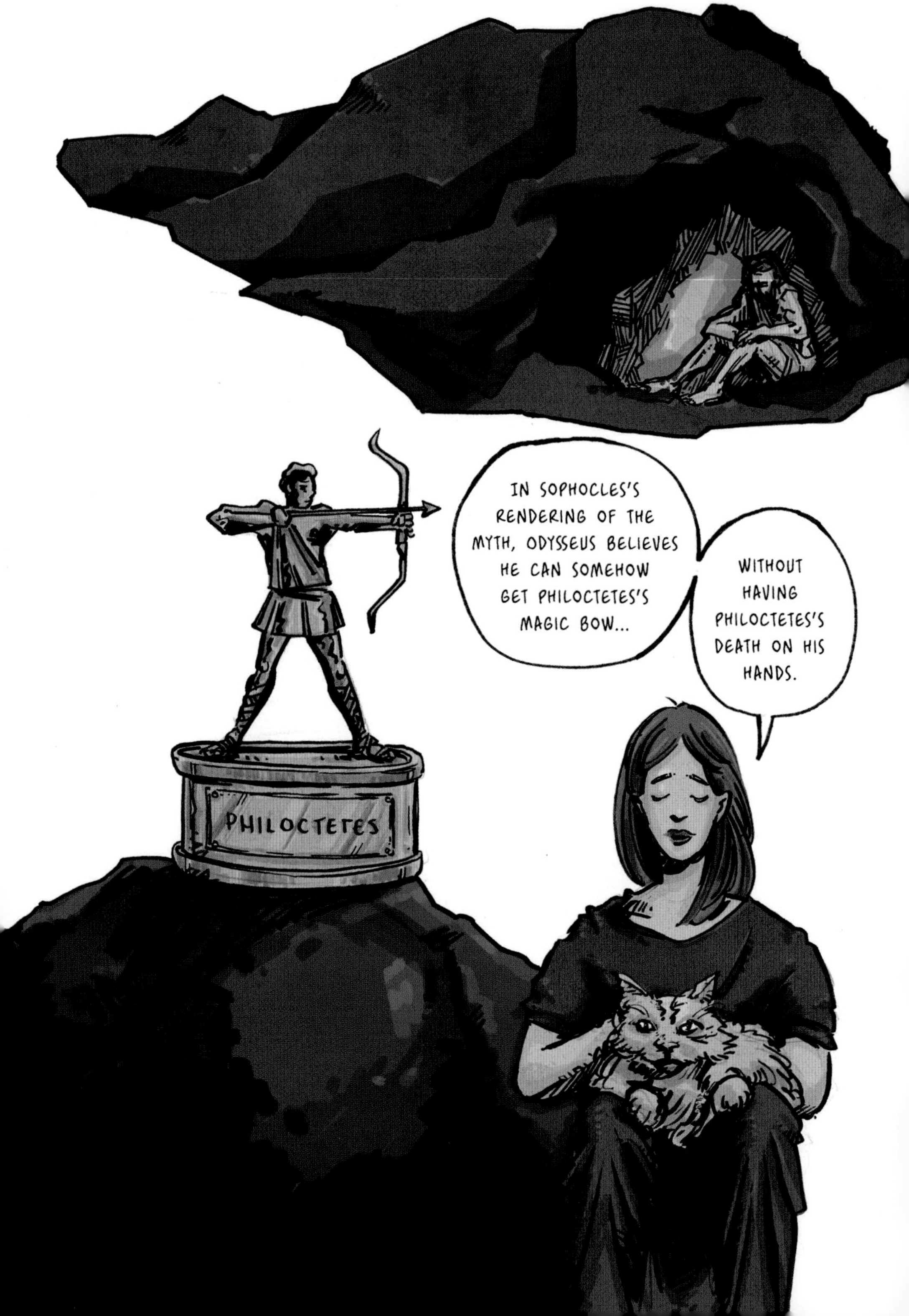
IN SOPHOCLES'S RENDERING OF THE MYTH, ODYSSEUS BELIEVES HE CAN SOMEHOW GET PHILOCTETES'S MAGIC BOW...
WITHOUT HAVING PHILOCTETES'S DEATH ON HIS HANDS.
PHILOCTETES

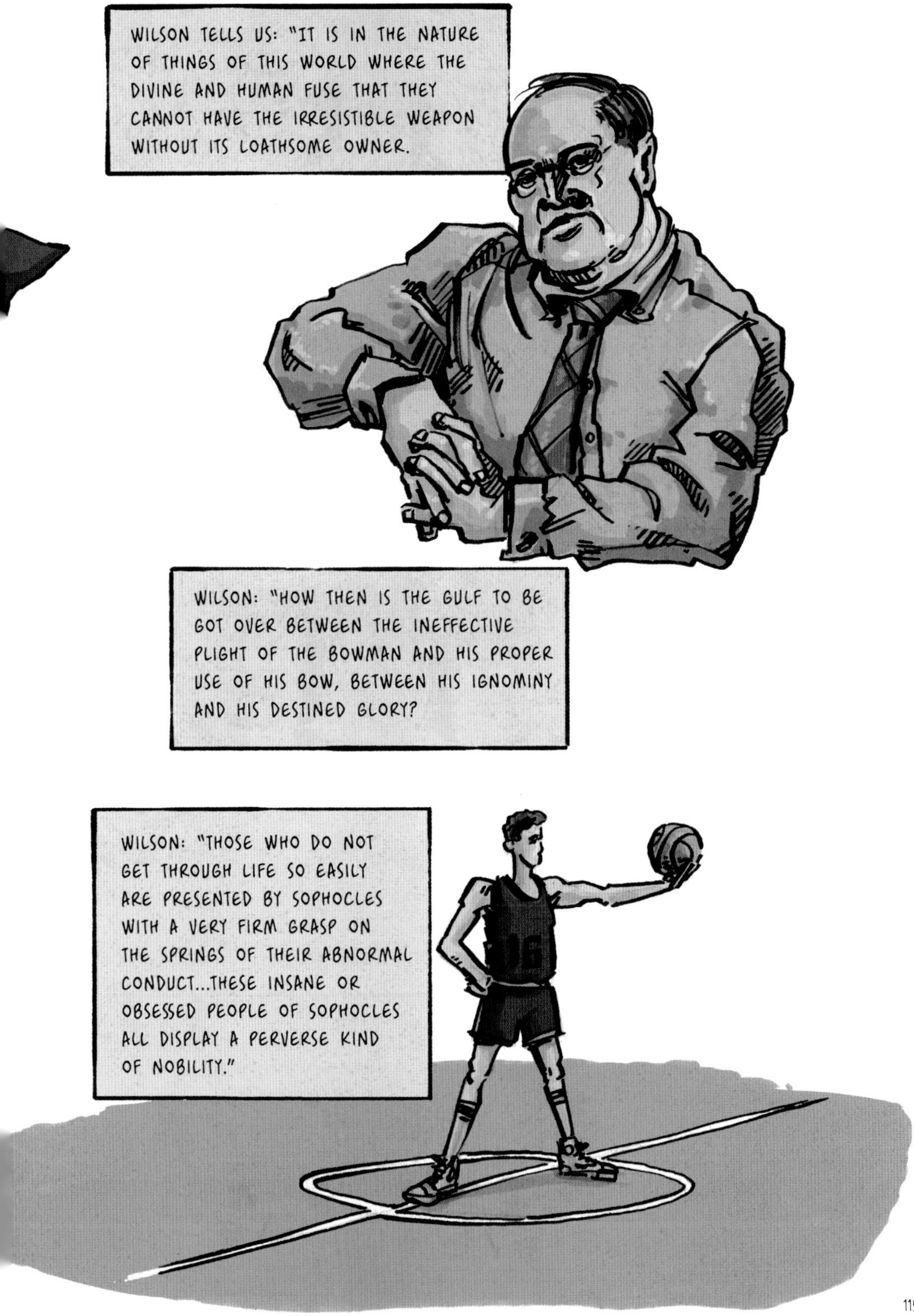
WILSON TELLS US: "IT IS IN THE NATURE OF THINGS OF THIS WORLD WHERE THE DIVINE AND HUMAN FUSE THAT THEY CANNOT HAVE THE IRRESISTIBLE WEAPON WITHOUT ITS LOATHSOME OWNER.
WILSON: "HOW THEN IS THE GULF TO BE GOT OVER BETWEEN THE INEFFECTIVE PLIGHT OF THE BOWMAN AND HIS PROPER USE OF HIS BOW, BETWEEN HIS IGNOMINY AND HIS DESTINED GLORY?
WILSON: "THOSE WHO DO NOT GET THROUGH LIFE SO EASILY ARE PRESENTED BY SOPHOCLES WITH A VERY FIRM GRASP ON THE SPRINGS OF THEIR ABNORMAL CONDUCT...THESE INSANE OR OBSESSED PEOPLE OF SOPHOCLES ALL DISPLAY A PERVERSE KIND OF NOBILITY."

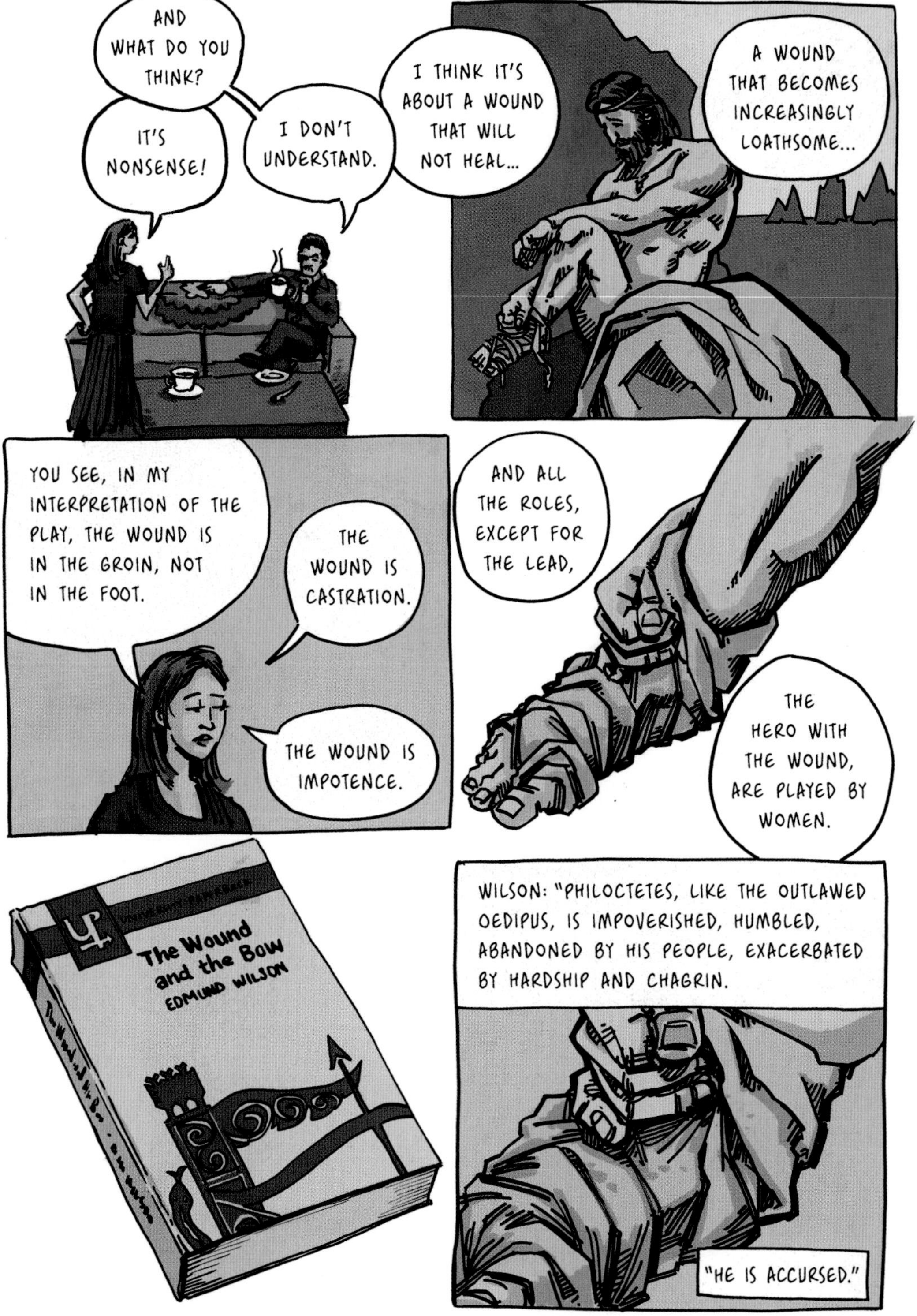
AND WHAT DO YOU THINK?
IT'S NONSENSE!
I DON'T UNDERSTAND.
I THINK IT'S ABOUT A WOUND THAT WILL NOT HEAL...
A WOUND THAT BECOMES INCREASINGLY LOATHSOME...
YOU SEE, IN MY INTERPRETATION OF THE PLAY, THE WOUND IS IN THE GROIN, NOT IN THE FOOT.
THE WOUND IS CASTRATION.
THE WOUND IS IMPOTENCE.
AND ALL THE ROLES, EXCEPT FOR THE LEAD,
THE HERO WITH THE WOUND, ARE PLAYED BY WOMEN.
The Wound and the Bow
EDMUND WILSON
WILSON: "PHILOCTETES, LIKE THE OUTLAWED OEDIPUS, IS IMPOVERISHED, HUMBLED, ABANDONED BY HIS PEOPLE, EXACERBATED BY HARDSHIP AND CHAGRIN.
"HE IS ACCURSED."

LATER THAT DAY...

TONY, I WANT TO READ YOU SOMETHING.

A PASSAGE FROM PHILOCTETES.

SURE, SWEETY, READ AWAY.

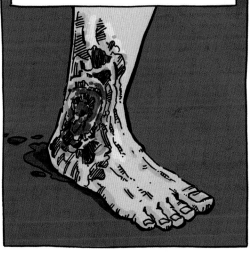

"THE CHORUS IS SPEAKING ABOUT OUR HERO. 'I MARVEL HOW HE KEPT HIS HOLD UPON A LIFE SO FULL OF WOE...

WITH NO LIVING SOUL IN THE LAND TO BE NEAR HIM WHILE HE SUFFERED...

"'NO COMPASSIONATE EAR INTO WHICH HE COULD POUR FORTH THE LAMENT, FOR THE PLAGUE THAT GNAWED THE FLESH AND DRAINED HIS BLOOD...NO ONE TO SOOTHE, WITH HEALING HERBS, THE BURNING PUS OOZING FROM HIS ULCERATED FOOT...

"'ALL HE CAN DO IS CREEP WITH PAINFUL STEPS—'"

ENOUGH, SWEETY, ENOUGH!

THE WOUND IS IN HIS HEART.

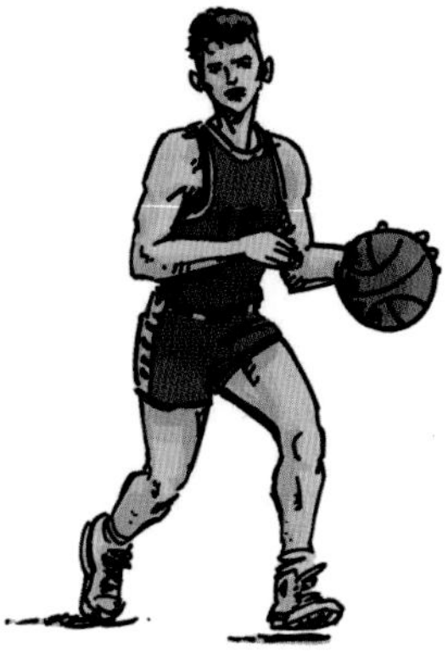

AS FRANK'S FAMILY BELIEVED, HIS PROWESS WITH A BASKETBALL, LIKE PHILOCTETES'S GIFT WITH HIS BOW, SEEMED A CURSE THAT BROUGHT ABOUT HIS DEATH AS A BASKETBALL PLAYER AND BECAME CENTRAL TO HIS SELF-WILLED ISOLATION—THE CAVE OF HIS ADULT YEARS, WHERE HE CUT HIMSELF OFF FROM THOSE WHO HAD BELIEVED IN THE EXCEPTIONAL TALENTS THAT HE HIMSELF NEVER VALUED.

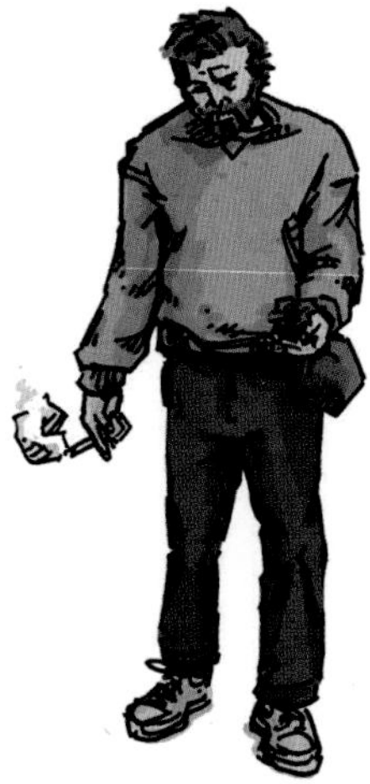

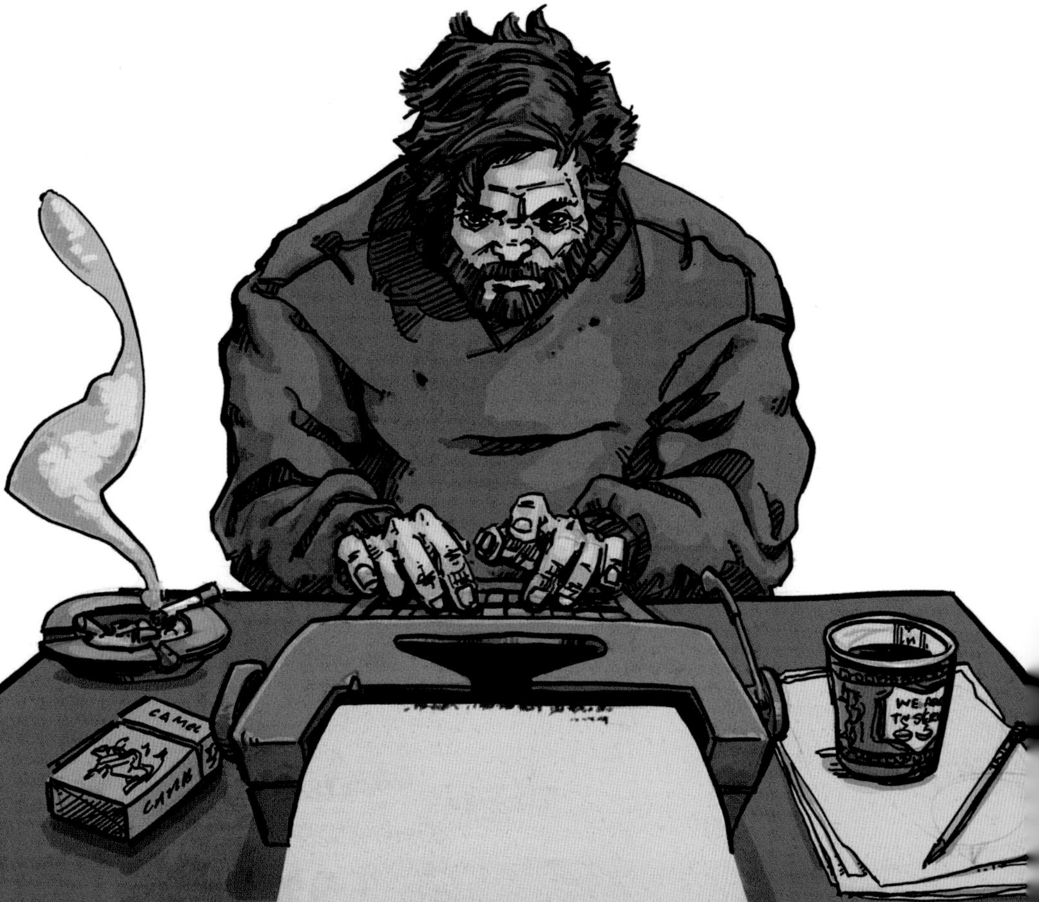

IN THE 60 YEARS THAT FOLLOWED AFTER
FRANK KING'S TIME IN FORT LEAVENWORTH,
WHICH INCLUDED 35 YEARS IN WHICH NONE
OF THE BOOKS HE WROTE WERE PUBLISHED,
HE CONTINUED TO WRITE EVERY DAY AND
TO CREATE A LARGE BODY OF WORK—DOZENS
OF BOOKS, PROPOSALS, POEMS, AND PLAYS
THAT REMAINED INVISIBLE, AS HE DID, TO
THOSE TO WHOM HE HAD ONCE ENDEARED
HIMSELF AS A HERO. AND THEN, IN A LIFE IN
WHICH, DESPITE NOT HAVING SEEN A DOCTOR
OR DENTIST DURING THESE 60 YEARS, HE
REMAINED REMARKABLY STRONG AND HEALTHY—
"I HAVE NO SKILLS," HE SAID TO CHARLOTTE
THE DAY BEFORE HE DIED, "BUT I'M STILL
STRONG AS A BULL"—HE WAS DONE IN BY AN
INFECTION IN HIS LOWER STOMACH THAT HE'D
REFUSED TO HAVE TREATED, AN INFECTION
THAT BECAME A GANGRENOUS AND INCURABLE
SUPPURATING WOUND.

end.

ACKNOWLEDGMENTS

For the rich hours in which they generously shared their memories of Frank King, Jay is particularly grateful to Frank's wife, Charlotte Carter, and to the King family: Frank's brothers, Steve and Jonathan, and his nephews, Seth, Richard, and Andrew. For the many conversations in which they shared their memories of Frank, and for their assistance in locating others who knew Frank and played ball with him, we owe special thanks to Billy Galantai, Ron Carner, and Rich Ratner. We are also indebted to the many individuals who gave freely of their time to talk with us at length about our book and about the Frankie King they knew and remembered. They include, among others: Mel Kessler, Steve Matell, Alex Mantel, Arthur Bobis, Charlie Hoffman, Stan Wasserman, Ed Krinsky, Paul Krinsky, Dick Kossoff, Sid Ganis, Henry Hochlerin, Ellen Edwards, Laraine Izzo, Richard Marek, Richard Parks, Sam Stoloff, Murray Weiss, Marcia Slatkin, Barry Goldsmith, Gene Roth, Susan Protter, Neal Singer, Arthur Brandon, Michaela Hamilton, Irv Alter, and Herb Bernstein.

Eli would like to thank his wife, Jennifer, and his boys Zack and Leo for their patience, support, and enthusiasm for this project. Thanks to Gideon Kendall for (re)starting this comics journey with me, for all the inspiration and support. Thanks to Sara Woolley for their support and for being so shiny. Thanks to Amy Lai-Pan for their work on the color flats. Thanks to our editor and publisher, Kendra Boileau, for believing in this project and helping us bring it to the world. Thanks to my Pop, Jay Neugeboren, for being a hero to me, and the easiest collaborator anyone could ask for.

Lastly, Eli would like to thank the borough of Brooklyn for all it has provided to the world.